SPELLING MATTERS TOO

TEACHER RESOURCE FILE

Jim Hildyard and Mark Morris

Heinemann

Heinemann is an imprint of Pearson Education Limited, a company incorporated in England and Wales, having its registered office at Edinburgh Gate, Harlow, Essex, CM20 2JE. Registered company number: 872828

www.heinemann.co.uk

Heinemann is a registered trademark of Pearson Education Limited

First published 2009

12 11 10 09

10 9 8 7 6 5 4 3 2

British Library Cataloguing in Publication Data is available from the British Library on request.

ISBN: 978 0 435 806 27 9

Designed and produced by Ken Vail Graphic Design

Illustrations by Phil Healey

Cover design by Ken Vail Graphic Design Limited

Printed and bound in the UK by Ashford Colour Press

Accompanying CD printed by Ashford Colour Press

Layout of Word files by Tag Publishing Services

Acknowledgments

Every effort has been made to contact copyright holders of material reproduced in this book. Any omissions will be rectified in subsequent printings if notice is given to the publishers.

Contents

Introduction

Spelling Matters Too comprises:

- Student Book
- Teacher's Resource File with CD-ROM (editable Word files of the TRF)
- Interactive CD-ROM containing front-of-class activities for use on an Interactive White Board.

This Teacher Resource File is designed to support the *Spelling Matters* Student Book in four ways:

- **Part A** offers guidance concerning the teacher's role in the tuition of spelling, based upon the best research carried out in the area of spelling. It also provides document models and guidance for the introduction of a whole school spelling policy.
- **Part B** offers a range of worksheet activities which reinforce the activities in the Student Book.
- **Part C** provides answers to the activities and self-tests in the Student Book. It also explains the rules for several spelling games which have all been used successfully in the classroom by experts in the tuition of spelling. The games provide an opportunity for students to use their skills in an entertaining educational context.
- **Part D** includes a student self-assessment table, along with extra self-tests.

Worksheets are available in this file, providing extra activities for students to carry out in class or at home. These reinforce the knowledge and skills the students have learned in the Student Book. They are designed for use by a wide ability range, providing reminders of spelling rules, a structured approach, and lots of consolidation and practice. The subject-specific crosswords and word searches on pages 65–69 contain the same words. Lower ability pupils will find the word search sheets more accessible.

When the original *Spelling Matters* first appeared, the National Literacy Strategy and Framework for the Teaching of English were relatively new concepts. As authors, and most importantly as teachers, we decided to focus the resource on the fundamental aspects of spelling with a solid grounding in rules and concepts. Technical accuracy in writing is always important, whatever the political climate. The approach found favour in the classroom and became a market leader.

This updated resource, in conjunction with *Spelling Matters Too* Student Book and *Spelling Matters Too* Interactive CD-ROM, provides that same methodology: a comprehensive coverage of Key Stage 3 spelling needs in an appropriately structured and refreshingly lively manner. Once more, we hope you enjoy using it.

Jim Hildyard and Mark Morris

Part A Teaching spelling

Practical advice for classroom teachers

Good spellers have often received good teaching. The advice that follows is derived from what is generally regarded as the best research carried out in the area of spelling.

Successful spelling tuition

Four myths about spelling should be dispelled from the beginning.

- *You can't teach spelling as English is so illogical and irregular.*

  English does contain some very peculiar anomalies, but approximately 85 per cent of it is regular, predictable and governed by rules. Learning these patterns and conventions will significantly increase the chances of spelling a word correctly.

- *The more they read, the better they'll spell.*

  Reading is a very different skill from spelling. Although there might be benefits for some students, a good reader is not necessarily a good speller. Good readers are hardly conscious of reading individual words and pay little attention to their structure as they are concentrating on meaning.

- *If you're not a good speller by Key Stage 3, you never will be.*

  Poor spellers of any age will benefit from structured spelling programmes and guidance from a teacher. Weak students, boys in particular, often feel comfortable in a 'rules'-based methodology.

- *Trendy teaching has meant spelling standards have declined.*

  Research shows that there has not been any significant deterioration in spelling standards during the past few decades.

Two important principles are worth noting because they underpin successful spelling tuition. The first is that students should be encouraged to develop an interest in words. A student who becomes intrigued by the structure of words, their origin and the families to which they belong is starting to win the battle.

The second principle is the integration of spelling tuition into normal classroom practice, rather than having special 'spelling lessons'. Students who spell well when they are fully focused on spelling often seem to forget everything they have apparently learned when they return to a 'normal' classroom environment. Even though it may be occasionally appropriate to teach a spelling lesson, research shows that the best results are gained when students can see a tangible learning outcome within the context of ongoing work.

Spotting the problems

Good spellers can:

- see an image of the word in their mind, and 'read' it as they spell
- break words into parts and spell them
- hear a new word and link the sounds with the correct letter patterns
- link a new word with others that are similar to it.

> Problems with spelling occur for two main reasons:
>
> **poor visual memory**
>
> or
>
> **poor auditory analysis.**

A weak speller with poor visual memory:

- is not always a weak reader
- cannot remember how words look and so has problems writing them down
- has a reasonable understanding of which letter patterns represent each sound.

A weak speller of this type will produce errors that are identifiable. They might write *cof* rather than *cough* or *sed* instead of *said.*

A weak speller with poor auditory analysis:

- cannot make the link between letter patterns and sounds
- cannot hear separate sounds within a word
- makes baffling, apparently random guesses
- struggles to see errors even when they are pointed out
- is likely to be a poor reader.

A weak speller of this type makes errors that are often difficult to interpret as the intended word.

It is important to decide what sort of speller each student is and with which sort of words they make their errors. The diagnostic tests on pages 18–23 and 103–111 of the Student Book will help you with this. Good spellers are obviously less of a cause for concern and require relatively little teaching. It is essential, however, that they should be taught to proof-read carefully. Thereafter the teacher need only keep a watchful eye.

Types of error

Most students make errors that conform to recognisable patterns. The ability to spot these enables teachers to be far more effective. The most common types are listed below.

Opening letters

Students over the age of 7 or 8 who make errors with the first letter of a word or an initial letter pattern such as **ch**, **sh** or **th**, need urgent support with reading and phonic recognition. Before children can be taught how to spell they need to be able to read.

Unstressed syllables

In words of more than one syllable, research indicates that most errors occur with the vowel of the unstressed syllables. Unfortunately, the vowel sounds of unstressed syllables often sound very similar in speech, while the actual spellings can vary greatly. Those students with a poor visual memory who rely on sound are prone to this particular error. For example:

matt<u>er</u> cult<u>ure</u> sug<u>ar</u> calculat<u>or</u>
gorill<u>a</u> behav<u>iour</u>

In normal speech the underlined endings all have very similar sounds.

Missing letters

Students miss out letters that are not clearly heard in pronunciation. The most obvious example of this is with silent letters. For example:

nee instead of *<u>k</u>nee* *case* instead of *cas<u>t</u>le*
thum instead of *thum<u>b</u>*.

This problem can also occur with letters not usually considered to be silent, and as a result of accent. For example:

happend instead of *happen<u>e</u>d*

offen instead of *of<u>t</u>en*.

Phonic substitutes

The student chooses an incorrect letter pattern that actually makes the sound they require, and would be right in different contexts. For example:

<u>fase</u> instead of *face*, a correct sound/letter match for the word *<u>case</u>*

<u>plow</u> instead of *plough*, a correct sound/letter match for the word *<u>cow</u>*

gra<u>ff</u> instead of *graph*, a correct sound/letter match for the word *st<u>aff</u>*.

A variation of this mistake occurs when the student uses a letter pattern that is not a normal English spelling pattern. For example:

<u>kw</u>ality instead of *quality* – *kw* is not an English letter pattern

sip<u>pd</u> instead of *sipped* – *pd* is not an English letter pattern.

These errors are normally a result of a poor visual memory. The second variation, however, is somewhat more serious than the first.

Single or double?

This error revolves around misunderstanding the effect on vowels of single/double letter combinations. Problems with the letter **e** at the end of words can also contribute to this error. For example:

su<u>p</u>er instead of *supper* *wi<u>n</u>ing* instead of *wi<u>nn</u>ing*

pilow instead of *pillow* *writter* instead of *writer*
hiden instead of *hidden* *rober* instead of *robber*

Prefixes and suffixes

Problems with prefixes tend to be concerned with effect and meaning. Problems with suffixes are more common, particularly with words ending in a vowel or the letter **l**. For example:

echod instead of *echoed* *skillful* instead of *skilful*
hateing instead of *hating*.

Students often struggle with the difference between **-able** and **-ible**, **-ance** and **-ence** or **-ate** and **-ite**, for example, as there is very little difference between the sound of these suffixes.

This list does not cover all the errors that students make, but the majority of mistakes fall into one or more of these categories. However, there is one more category that should be considered.

'Careless' errors

The term 'careless' does not necessarily mean ignorance or apathy. Mistakes of this sort are inevitable in the writing process. They may occur because the student is in a rush to get all their ideas down or concentrating on a different aspect of their writing. Mistakes such as these can be missed in the proof-reading stage. The students read what they think they have written, rather than what is actually in front of them. A different reader will notice these errors quickly, which is why publishers employ proof-readers. It is very important that a teacher is sure whether an error is the result of a lack of understanding or merely a slip of the pen.

Correcting work

It is not a teacher's job simply to correct mistakes a student has already made, but to help that student avoid making that mistake again. A piece of work with every single error covered in red pen is of little benefit, and is actually likely to have a negative effect.

There is not a single, universal, marking strategy that is suitable for all students. The teacher needs to do what is appropriate for a particular student at a particular time. In short, there is no substitute for knowing your students.

- Do not mark every single mistake. Prioritise the errors in order of difficulty, type and importance. There is little point in focusing on an error with the word *diaphragm* if the student is misspelling *house*.
- The most effective marking is done with the student present. Of course, this is often not practical, but whenever possible this is the method that should be employed.
- Red pen can be demoralising as it signifies reproach rather than support, but using pencil, black or blue does not draw attention to errors as effectively. Flexibility and discretion are the solution: avoid red pen with those easily disheartened and perhaps try green.
- Asking a student to read their work aloud will help some, particularly those who are competent readers, to spot their errors.
- Recording words that cause problems is helpful. Students could also be encouraged to underline those parts of words that cause them the most difficulty. It is important that words should be recorded somewhere other than in the place where their writing is done.
- Give help with the proof-reading process. Rather than just telling the student to correct their mistakes, tell them how many they are looking for, what sorts of errors have to be found, or narrow down the area of text that has to be re-read.

Drafting

The drafting process should not be seen as simply copying work again. Research suggests that students *can actually make more errors* when they regard drafting in this manner. The whole process must be seen as constructive, not as a pointless chore.

- Students should be encouraged to mark work belonging to peers and as such, *Spelling Matters Too* Student Book contains a number of peer evaluation activities. This sharpens skills regarding error identification and provides a real context for their activities.

Giving out special 'teacher pens' (which are all the same colour) is a successful method of focusing the student while also providing a little classroom theatre.

- In a first draft, ask students to 'help' the teacher by underlining any words they are uncertain about. This helps to formalise the checking procedure for the students.
- Try and remain positive at all times. Students can become disheartened easily about spelling. Remarks like: *That's a good attempt. You've got all the right sounds in there but we actually spell this sound like this...* are more likely than admonishment to keep students enthusiastic.

Marking

The marks a teacher puts on the page are very important. It is important to modify them depending on the ability of the student. Departmental marking policy is essential. This is especially important if a class has more than one teacher. It is a waste of valuable time to mark work if the result is not crystal clear to the student, which is unlikely if teachers mark idiosyncratically.

- Simply putting *sp* (or some other symbol) in the margin is usually unproductive. Students feel they have been told off and are not given help to improve. This method should only be used with strong spellers, those who are extremely confident or who would enjoy the challenge of actually finding the word.
- Research indicates that inserting letters into misspelled words can cause confusion. It is better to write the word out again, either above the error or in the margin.
- If the incorrect word itself is indicated, help should be given depending on the student's ability. The incorrect part of the word can be indicated, or the first few letters of the correct version written in the margin to encourage students to refer to a dictionary. Under normal circumstances writing the correct word in its entirety is only appropriate for weaker spellers.
- There are a wide range of stickers and stamps available commercially. Students enjoy receiving them and are more likely to respond to any advice.

> It should always be remembered that spelling, although important, is ultimately less significant than the content of a student's work. Paying too much attention to spelling can easily distract the student from what they are actually trying to say. Spelling is only one part of the writing and communication process and should always be seen as a means to an end, not an end in itself.

Dyslexia

Dyslexia is a subject that provokes strong and vigorously defended opinions and considerable disagreement. Since the Education Act of 1993 and the 1994 Code of Practice, teachers have been paying more attention to the concept of dyslexia. The following publications and addresses will prove useful for those wishing to find out more about dyslexia.

Publications

Thompson, M.E. (2004) *Developmental Dyslexia* London: Whurr Publishers Ltd

Miles, E. (1998) *The Bangor Dyslexia Teaching System* London: Whurr Publishers Ltd

Thompson, M.E., Watkins, E.J. (1998) *Dyslexia: A Teaching Handbook* London: Whurr Publishers Ltd

Ott, P. (1997) *How To Detect And Manage Dyslexia* Oxford: Heinemann Educational

Bramley, W. (1996) *Units of Sound* Staines: The Dyslexia Institute

Hornsby, B. (1996) *Overcoming Dyslexia* London: Vermilion

Organisations

The British Dyslexia Association

Unit 8, Bracknell Beeches

Old Bracknell Lane

Bracknell

RG12 7BW

Helpline: 0845 251 9002

Office: 0845 251 9003

Fax: 0845 251 9005

Helen Arkell Dyslexia Centre
Frensham
Farnham
Surrey GU10 3BW
Tel: 01252 792400
Fax: 01252 795669

Websites

www.bdadyslexia.org.uk/
www.dyslexia.eu.com/
www.wdnf.info/index.html
www.dyslexia-advice.com
www.interdys.org/
www.dyslexic.com
www.dyslexic.org.uk/
www.dyslexiaaction.org.uk/

Towards a whole school spelling policy

Any school policy has two distinct parts: the piece of paper and the actual practice. The following pages provide both the structure for a document and advice that will enable the policy to be implemented in the classroom.

The aim of any school spelling policy should be to establish a whole school approach to the tuition and correction of spelling. Even though it is only one of a number of technical skills that should be acquired by students, it has a particular importance in the development both of effective communication and of confidence. It should be recognised as an area that causes great concern for students and parents alike.

English specialists accept that basic instruction in the tuition of such skills is an integral part of the English curriculum, but these skills must be fostered and reinforced in all subject areas. Spelling penalties for technical inaccuracy exist in all subjects; every subject has their own specific vocabulary.

> Research indicates that consistency across subjects and teachers is the single most important factor that contributes to an improvement in spelling.

Achieving this consistency is a much more difficult task than producing a policy document.

Implementation

Many teachers and departments tend to operate within their own subject worlds. The mention of a cross-curricular approach to spelling and literacy in general is usually greeted by mutterings of 'Isn't that the English Department's job?' It is often claimed that every teacher is a teacher of English but a more accurate statement would be that every teacher is a teacher of language. Everyone is a teacher of their own subject-specific language, thereby rendering everyone, to a degree, a teacher of the English language. In any case, no one will be asking science or maths teachers to deliver the concept of doubling letters and long vowel sounds. They would be expected, however, to support procedures and principles that will enable students to grasp concepts with more clarity.

While every school is different, the following notions have been present in schools with successful cross-curricular spelling policies.

- **Status** – the driving force for any policy must come from senior management. Without explicit support from the top, any policy faces the danger of being perceived as a minority interest. The National Literacy Strategy helped to enhance the status of spelling; the distinct examination of Functional Skills should increase even further the chances of any initiative being regarded as a priority. A spelling policy should be identified within a school development plan and reviewed annually. The allocation of responsibility points, possibly as part of the wider role of literacy coordination, is a highly effective way to raise status. INSET time should be made available to ensure all teachers are familiar with the content of the policy.
- **Coordination** – a working party, management committee or steering group should be formed to plan, implement and monitor the effectiveness of a policy. Representation from every curriculum area is essential. It is also recommended that the chair of such a group should not be the Head of English or an English specialist, as this detracts from a cross-curricular perception of the policy. Baseline testing in year 7 should incorporate the basis of any monitoring process. As school literacy coordinators are increasingly common, they would obviously take a lead role in any such group. Again, automatically assuming that the Head of English should assume this role will decrease cross-curricular impact.
- **Launch** – any new initiative must be introduced with the greatest possible fuss and noise! Assemblies, specially called whole school meetings, newsletters, senior management involvement, addresses at parents' evenings, and even 'celebrity' guests could all play a part.
- **Reinforcement** – after an initial burst of energy, it is important to maintain momentum. Competitions, prizes and 'spot-checks' achieve this end. Tutor sessions and registration periods are timetable spaces that can be usefully employed. Concentrating on subject specific spelling for short periods is another way to sustain interest (this week is 'Science spellings week!). Rewards and prizes are also successful in this respect. At this point in the process it should be the steering group's main concern to devise ways of keeping the profile of spelling on the agenda. It goes without saying that whatever schemes are planned, they should be carried out with the highest possible profile.
- **Primary liaison** – the smooth transition of all students from Key Stage 2 to Key Stage 3 is very important. The more familiar that new students are with procedure, the more likely they are to settle in quickly. Most schools now have strong primary links and the spelling policy should form a part of prospective parents' evenings, taster visits and transition courses. Opportunities should be made to discuss with primary colleagues what experiences students have already had of spelling tuition. In ideal circumstances, feeder primary schools should be encouraged to adopt as many elements of the policy as is appropriate to ensure progression and continuity. The results of Key Stage 2 assessments should be used to target support as soon as possible. If a school runs any form of literacy summer school, the spelling policy should take a central role.

The following pages are intended to be used as a basic model for a school's own spelling policy. It is not intended to be used wholesale, as every school has its own idiosyncrasies and methodologies. It should be amended and developed as necessary.

Whole School Spelling Policy

The School recognises that spelling is an important part of effective communication and the learning process in general. We are committed to promoting and monitoring positive attitudes and raising standards in spelling.

The spelling policy and future significant developments are identified in the School Development Plan, which identifies the School's framework for teaching and learning. All employees, students, parents and governors will be made aware of the provisions of this policy and all employees are required to ensure the policy is effectively implemented. An annual review of the policy will take place through the School Development Plan.

Principles informing the policy

- All pupils should be familiar with a range of strategies to work out spellings they do not know.
- The responsibility for any whole class tuition of spelling-related matters should be coordinated and monitored across departments. This ensures effective coverage and unnecessary repetition.
- Accurate spelling is the responsibility of all departments and all staff. The approach must be consistent across departments.
- The spelling policy should be introduced early in year 7 to establish practices and attitudes that can be built upon in later years.
- Parents and feeder primary schools should be kept informed about approach and progress.
- Weaker spellers are entitled to support and specialist help. All students should receive a baseline assessment in Year 7.
- Target setting is acknowledged to be an effective way of improving standards and motivating students.

Curriculum content

The following spelling aspects will be introduced, reinforced and monitored (see footnote 1).

- Use of dictionary and thesaurus will be encouraged.
- The following strategies for learning spellings will be taught:
  - look, say, cover, write, check
  - spelling checkers
  - mnemonics
  - breaking words into parts
  - speaking syllables and speaking silent letters
  - drafting and proof-reading
  - history of words.
- Spelling rules and letter pattern recognition techniques will be an integral part of the English and Learning Support Schemes of Work.
- Use of the spelling book (see footnote 2).

Departments and subject teachers

All teachers will:

- mark spellings in a manner consistent with a whole school approach
- give positive feedback to pupils who make effort and progress in spelling-related matters
- apply consistent use of rewards, incentives, the spelling book and the correction procedure for students
- display in classrooms key subject specific terms, the most commonly misspelled words and explanations of marking policy
- have dictionaries available in every lesson and encourage their use
- present spelling as an integral part of their subject and encourage accuracy at all times
- pass any concerns regarding general trends or areas of weakness to the English and Learning Support departments.

Parents

All parents will be:

- informed about school policy when students first enter the School and be encouraged to play an active part in the monitoring process
- encouraged to have a dictionary at home and support its use when students are completing homework
- encouraged to inform the school about any spelling-related concerns
- given the opportunity to attend specially arranged sessions to support the work of the school.

Spelling and the marking process

The classroom teacher will:

- discuss individual spelling problems with students. The school recognises that the most effective tuition is carried out during drafting, and will strive to ensure this happens whenever possible
- ensure that students employ a range of learning and correction strategies rather than just writing down the correct spelling for them
- ensure that, where appropriate, correction involves reference to rules, roots or other significant features of the misspelled word
- set short-term, achievable spelling targets and monitor progress in achieving them
- make sure that corrections are recorded in the students' spelling books.

Footnotes

1 *After negotiation and discussion, the policy should identify which subject is responsible for each aspect of the policy. Where appropriate, individuals with responsibility should also be named.*

2 *Most schools have some sort of book where students can record misspelled words. This takes the form of a planner, homework diary or some other form of organiser. If a school does not operate such a system it is highly recommended that they should do so immediately. It is not recommended that a spelling book should be part of the English Department's responsibilities, and certainly not 'at the back of their English book'. It is important that a completely separate, non-subject specific means is used, which can be taken to all lessons and remain with students at all times.*

SB page 8

Part B Worksheets

Unit 1 SPELLING STRATEGIES

1 Alphabetical order

REMEMBER

Words in dictionaries are grouped in alphabetical order.

- First look at the letter that the word starts with.
- Next look at the second letter, then the third, and so on. For example, dreamy; dreary; dress.

Activity 1

Word challenge!

Work with a partner on the next four challenges. Race against each other to see who is the quickest at putting the following lists of words into alphabetical order.

Challenge list 1: Easy

zebra ________________
apple ________________
banana ________________
school ________________
table ________________
iPod ________________
breakfast ________________

Challenge list 2: Tricky

greedy ________________
guitar ________________
sugar ________________
house ________________
hatred ________________
peel ________________
paper ________________

Challenge list 3: Difficult

chisel ________________
China ________________
chilli ________________
choir ________________
chin ________________
chivalry ________________
chimpanzee ________________

Challenge list 4: Nearly impossible

bullfrog ________________
bungalow ________________
bunion ________________
bully ________________
bundle ________________
bump ________________
bird ________________
bill ________________

Activity 2

How many words can you think of that come between the words *treat* and *trick* in the dictionary?

________________ ________________ ________________ ________________
________________ ________________ ________________ ________________
________________ ________________

SB page 10

2 Mnemonics

REMEMBER

A mnemonic is a rhyme or saying that sticks easily in the mind.
Use mnemonics to help you to remember how to spell a word.

Activity 1

The mnemonic below helps you spell the word *necessary*.

never
eat
cake
eat
salad
sandwiches
and
remain
young

Make three mnemonics to help you spell these three difficult words: *skiing, vehicle, knowledge*.

s ______
k ______
i ______
i ______
n ______
g ______

v ______
e ______
h ______
i ______
c ______
l ______
e ______

k ______
n ______
o ______
w ______
l ______
e ______
d ______
g ______
e ______

Activity 2

Which word does this mnemonic help you to spell?

George eats old grey rats and paints houses yellow

Activity 3

Mnemonics can also be useful to remember other facts and figures like the colours of the rainbow. Collect as many mnemonics as you can by asking friends, family or your teacher. Write them in the space below.

SB page 11

3 Saying words as they are spelled

REMEMBER

It can help you spell some words if you say them to yourself as they are spelled. In Old English, the **k** of words like *knuckle* was spoken. It would have sounded like *'ke'-nuckle*. People wouldn't forget to spell it with the **k**.

Activity 1

The answers to these quiz questions all contain silent letters. When you have solved the clues, say the words to yourself as they are spelled.

1	Land surrounded by sea	i _ _ _ _ _
2	The opposite of innocent	_ _ _ _ _ y
3	Give up your job	_ e _ _ _ n
4	A newborn sheep	_ _ m _
5	Day in the middle of the week	_ e _ _ _ _ _ _ y
6	The season when leaves fall	a _ _ _ _ _
7	60 minutes make an...	_ o _ _
8	At the end of your arm before your hand	_ r _ _ t
9	A defensive building with thick walls and turrets	c _ _ _ _ e
10	Wrist mounted time machine	_ _ t _ _

Activity 2

There are 11 words hidden in this grid. Each contains silent letters. When you have found the words, write them out below.

E	H	I	K	W	Q	C	G	N	C
W	J	C	D	N	R	A	H	O	H
I	D	A	J	B	O	S	A	T	L
K	B	L	H	V	A	T	S	P	X
N	I	M	I	Z	U	L	T	G	S
A	W	H	T	S	W	E	L	E	Z
C	G	H	O	S	T	H	Y	E	D
K	N	O	C	K	B	E	A	Q	T
E	J	A	U	T	U	M	N	T	Q
R	C	A	I	B	W	V	O	N	U

____

____

____

____

____

____

____

____

____

____

____

SB page 12

4 Breaking words into parts (1)

REMEMBER

Sometimes a word can be broken down into stem words that have been joined together. This is called a **compound word**. For example:

moon + light = moonlight

The words in the boxes below form four compound words: *daylight, lighthouse, houseboat, boatyard.*

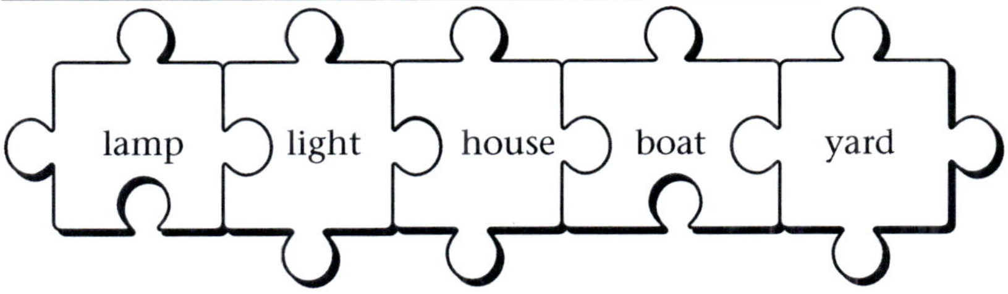

Activity 1

Identify and underline the compound words in these sentences.

1. The airman kept having flashbacks about the crash.
2. I used a flashlight when we had a power cut.
3. Guy Fawkes wanted to use gunpowder to blow up parliament.
4. The hairdresser gave me a great haircut.
5. The handbook was missing from that second hand motorcar I bought.
6. 'Hollywood is my homeland,' said the actor.
7. After our fantastic honeymoon we are going homeward bound.
8. My school is a madhouse. The behaviour is terrible.
9. The outspoken tennis player gave an outstanding performance.
10. The benefits outweigh the drawbacks.

Activity 2

Look at the following examples of compound word strips.

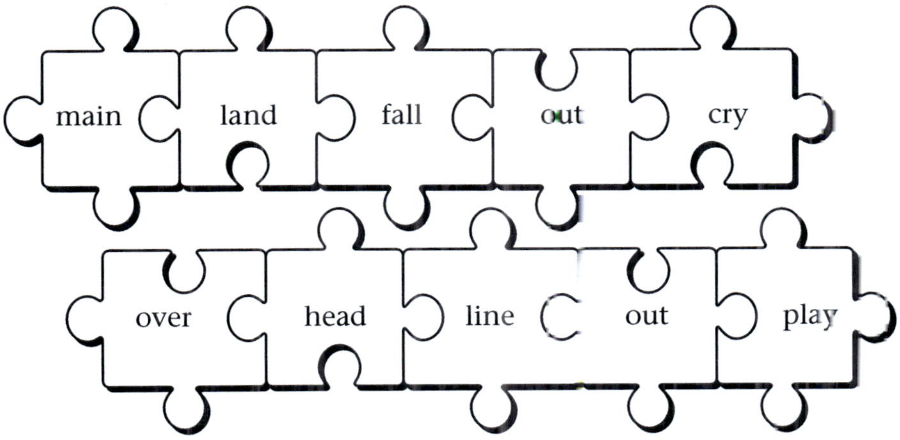

Write out all the compound words in the spaces below:

______________ ______________ ______________ ______________

______________ ______________ ______________ ______________

SB page 12

5 Breaking words into parts (2)

Activity 1

Now it's time to design your own compound word strips. Read the rules below carefully before you begin.

- Use a pencil.
- Write a stem in the first box. The word must make sense on its own.
- In the next box, write a word which can be joined to the first to make a compound word. Use a dictionary to help.
- Look at the second word. What word can you add to it to make another compound word?

Activity 2

Word wizard challenge

What is the longest chain of compound words you can make? Work with a partner to become a word wizard.

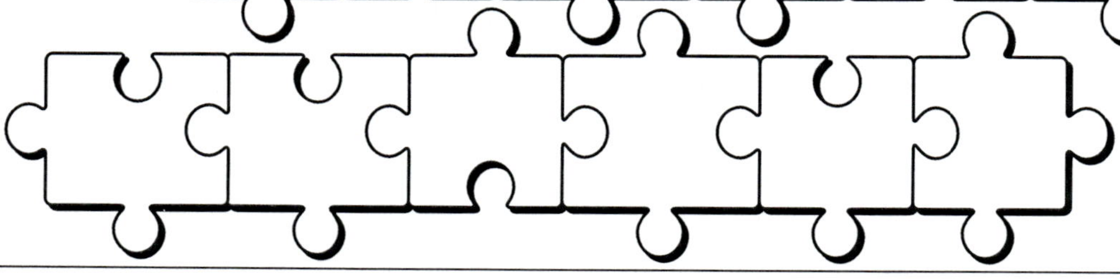

SB page 14

6 Proof-reading

REMEMBER

Always check your work for spelling mistakes. If you need to check how a word is spelled, use the LOOK, SAY, COVER, WRITE, CHECK steps to learn it.

With any piece of writing:

- read your work carefully and underline any mistakes
- check any word you are unsure how to spell using a dictionary
- swap work with a partner and look for each other's mistakes
- use a spell checker if you are working on a computer.

Activity 1

Find the spelling mistakes in this advertisement.

Underline each one and write the correct spelling in the margin.

The New Land Rover LRT

With its 5 litre enjine and 450bhp power the Land Rover LRT is a vehicle for the adventurous and free spirited driver. This car has all the puling power of a traktor yet looks as sleak and bootiful as a sports car. It has a full lether intereor, a 17 speaker stereo sistem and a host of gagets that will make your eyes pop out.

In the frunt there's electric seets, a satellite navigation system, wirless telephone system and an MP3 player that will blow your brains out. In the back there are enough seats for the whole family and automatic clymate control ensures the comfert of all your passangers.

The real deal comes with the off-road potential We have tested this vehicle in mountain regons at tempratures of minus 15 degrees. It didn't break sweat. We have forced it up incredable inclines and pulled it through tons of mud! And it kept asking for more.

If you need something really special parked in your driveway and you want to impress your neighbours with a truly impressive beast of a motor, then your search is over.

The Land Rover LRT: the closest thing to purfect you'll ever drive.

Activity 2

Work with a partner. Each create a car advertisement which includes 15 deliberate mistakes. Swap your work and correct the mistakes.

SB page 24

Unit 2 VOWELS AND CONSONANTS

7 Vowels and consonants

REMEMBER

The five vowels are: **a e i o u**

The rest of the letters in the English alphabet are consonants, but **y** can be used as a vowel *and* as a consonant.

- The letter **y** becomes a **vowel** when it sounds like:
  – long **i** in *why, shy,* short **i** in *myth, crypt* and **e** in *berry, ferry*.
- The letter **y** is a **consonant** when it sounds like:
  – **y** in *year* or *yesterday*.

Activity 1

Many vowels are missing from this passage.

Write it out again adding the correct vowels.

Fr_nk_nst_ _n

Th_ n_v_l Fr_nk_nst_ _n w_s wr_tt_n by M_ry Sh_ll_y. Sh_ w_s _nly eight_ _n wh_n sh_ wr_t_ _t. _t has b_c_m_ on_ of the most p_pul_r h_rr_r st_ries of _ll t_m_.

Activity 2

Can you work out these words? They all have missing vowels. Write them out in the space provided.

1 d_l_ghtf_l ____________
2 _nn_c_ss_ry ____________
3 r_m_rk_bl_ ____________
4 _mp_ss_bl_ ____________
5 ch_ll_ng_ng ____________
6 p_w_rf_l ____________
7 bl_ _k ____________
8 _m_z_ng ____________
9 W_mbl_y St_d_ _m ____________
10 r_d_ ____________

Activity 3

Can you work out these words? They all have missing consonants. Write them out in the space provided.

1 _ea ____________
2 _ea_ ____________
3 i_e ____________
4 ea_ ____________

SB page 25

8 Short vowels

REMEMBER

When you hear a short vowel sound in a short word, it is usually spelled with only one vowel:

*t**a**p, t**e**n, t**i**n, t**o**p, t**u**b.*

Sometimes a short vowel sound is made from more than one vowel, for example, **e** as in *tr**ea**d*, **u** as in *en**ou**gh*.

Activity

Word challenge!

Play this game in pairs. How many words can you make from these letter wheels?

Scoring chart

5 words = try harder

10 words = pretty special

15 words = word wizard

20 words = total genius

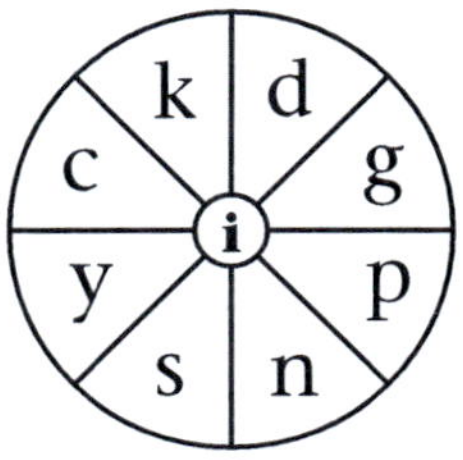

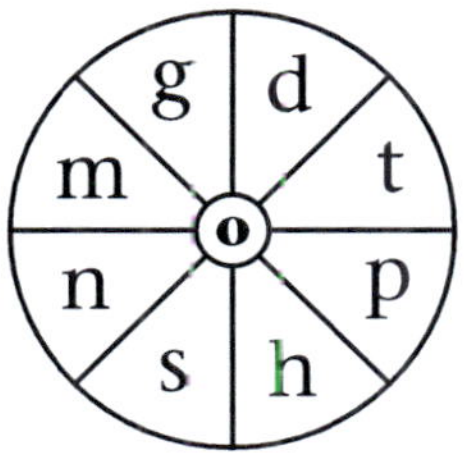

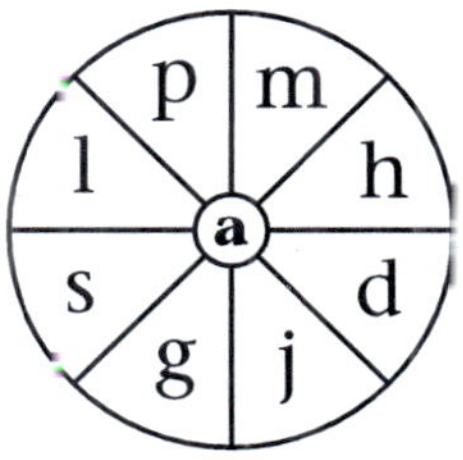

SB page 26

9 Long vowel sound 'a'

REMEMBER

A long vowel sound can be made by a vowel on its own or by using a few common letter patterns. For example:

- the long vowel sound **a** can be spelled *st**ay**, st**ea**k* and *st**a**l**e***.

Activity

These words all contain the long vowel sound **a**. They need guiding to the correct truck below.

survey prey frail disobey break stain made afraid grey weight table cave sail staying pray games reign they playing raider steak great day eight make gave grain obey pain convey crayon relay freight

SB page 27

10 Long vowel sounds 'e' and 'i'

REMEMBER

Long vowel sounds can be made using a few common letter patterns. For example:

- long vowel sound **e** as in: *these, sl**ea**ze, kn**ee***
- long vowel sound **i** as in: ***ey**e, m**i**ne, d**ie***

Activity 1

Underline the long vowel sound in these words.

team	dream	feet	these	seem	be	even
ravine	magazine	chief	agreed	he	achieve	being
we	feel	screaming	ceiling	machine	three	bean

Activity 2

Write a short paragraph using some of the words above. Try to include as many words as you can which contain the long vowel sound **e**.

Activity 3

Complete this table by adding your own examples of words which contain long vowel **i** letter patterns.

Long vowel i	i (common)	y (common)	ie (uncommon)	uy (uncommon)
Example word	m**i**ne	t**y**pe	d**ie**	b**uy**
Your example				
Your example				
Your example				
Your example				
Your example				

Activity 4

Find all the long vowel **i** words in this article. Underline the letter pattern which makes the sound.

Last night I went to the big fight. It was Bill 'The Machine' Green against Chris 'The Fist' McLain. What a delight! I thought I'd buy tickets for ringside. They cost me a fortune. The contest was judged a draw, after the big guys knocked each other out!

SB page 28

11 Long vowel sounds 'o' and 'u'

REMEMBER

Long vowel sounds 'o' and 'u' can be made using a few common letter patterns. For example:

- long vowel sound **o** as in: *g**o**, t**oa**d, thr**ow***
- long vowel sound **u** as in: *t**u**n**e**, z**oo**m, d**o***
- long vowel sound **u** as in: *t**u**b**e**, T**ue**sday, f**ew***

Activity 1

Complete the answers to this quiz. All the answers contain the long vowel sound **o**.

1	Chuck an object	_ _ _ _ _
2	A theatre production	_ _ _ _
3	Garment a person wears to keep warm	_ _ _ _
4	Drive a car on the	_ _ _ _
5	Mend with a needle and cotton	_ _ _
6	Bees are black and...	_ _ _ _ _ _
7	At the green light	_ _
8	Falls in very cold weather	_ _ _ _
9	Opposite of above	_ _ _ _ _
10	Vessel for travelling on water	_ _ _ _

Activity 2

Find the words in this passage which contain letter patterns that make the long vowel sound **u**. Write each word in the correct place in the table.

> The blue crew in the boat race set off yesterday afternoon for a training session. They wanted to win the loot for first prize and had improved their times since the previous year. The red team were gloomy and a few men were too unfit to do their best. None of them wanted to win the wooden spoon for coming last.

oo	o	ue	ew

SB page 30

Unit 3 PLURALS

12 When to add 's' or 'es'

REMEMBER

- The most common way to make a word plural is to add **-s**, for example: *cars*.
- If a word ends in **s**, **sh**, **ch**, **x** or **z**, add **-es** to make a plural, for example: *church**es**, fox**es**, wish**es***.

Activity 1

Add **-s** or **-es** in the spaces to make plurals of the words in this advertisement

Some product__ simply promise miracle__. This one really delivers. Jus-Like-New is an amazing multi purpose cleaner that makes thing__ around the home as good as new.

Got a problem with wood? Two quick coat__ and the result__ are astonishing. No need for expensive polish__ or messy varnish__.

Glass__ suffering from stain__ or scratch__? Soak for ten minute__ and the sparkle returns.

Clothes looking tired? Do away with fabric conditioner__ and your dress__ will dazzle and your shirt__ will look stunning. Guaranteed to remove even the tiniest blemish__.

All your household dream__ come true with Jus-Like-New. Stocked by all the top store__ and available from a range of Internet supplier__ and business__.

Activity 2

Add **-s** or **-es** to these words to make them plural.

radish__	hoax__	staple__	block__	traitor__
witness__	finger__	princess__	couch__	bowl__
splash__	peach__	abscess__	cabbage__	phoenix__
stitch__	compass__	fountain__	mirror__	weakness__
crutch__	relish__	beach__	magnet__	season__
ostrich__	guess__	frame__	moment__	sandwich__

SB pages 30–31

13 Apostrophe problems

REMEMBER

Simple plurals DO NOT require apostrophes.

Activity

Read the magazine article below. Some apostrophes are in the right place but others are missing or not needed. On your sheet, mark all the mistakes made by the student.

Chef's Amazing Burger Binge

Denny's Beer Barrel Bar in Clearfield, Pennsylvania has been the home of one of the strangest food challenge's of recent year's. The Beer Barrel Belly Bruiser is a gigantic burger that weigh's in at just over 9 kilo's. The burger itself contain's 6.8 kilo's of prime beef and there are also 2.3 kilo's of topping's to wrestle with. Unsurprisingly, no one's ever finished one.

That was until Brad Sciullo, an Italian restaurant chef, walked into the building. Four hour's and thirty-nine minute's later, Mr Scuillo raised his arm's in triumph – the Belly Bruiser had met it's match!

Chef's are well known for their love of food, but this adventurer's action's seemed rather extreme. Asked why he'd taken on the ultimate burger battle, Mr Scuillo replied simply, 'I wanted to see if I could.' The chef's trousers did look a little tighter around the middle when he stood up to leave and he said he didn't intend to stop for a MacDonald's on the way home.

The Beer Barrel Belly Bruiser includes a specially baked bun, tomatoe's, cheese, onion's, pepper's and lettuce. The dressing consist's of mayonnaise, relish, ketchup and two different mustard's. In total, there's over half a litre of it!

SB pages 30–31

14 More apostrophe problems

REMEMBER

Simple plurals DO NOT require apostrophes.

Activity

This student is having trouble with apostrophes. Some are in the right place but others are missing or not needed. On your sheet, mark all the mistakes made by the student.

Dear diary
I wonder why lot's of kid's think I'm strange and a little
unusual? I haven't got two head's or several nose's. I've no strange
look's at all. I talk quite normally and do all the sort's of things
that normal 13 year old's do. Apart from one... I really love doing
homework. Now you wouldn't think that this was a big deal –
you try telling that to the girls' and boys' at my school! You'd
think I was a serial killer or something. I suppose I'm just curious
and nosy – I want to know everything about all the subject's.
That's why I like all the homework's because it all help's me to
learn more and find out lot's about ton's more thing's. Lot's of the
lad's in my school think it's cool to do no work and to be stupid.
Even the bright one's sometime's pretend that they're thick!
What's cool about being dim? I just don't understand.
Sometime's I even see strange expression's on the teachers' faces'.
It's normally when I ask for extra things' to do at home. My
math's teacher was the funniest. I only asked for a few extra
sum's to do. Another two hundred long divisions' isn't really
that many is it? Then there were the gasp's of shock from Mrs
Pemberton when I wanted more spelling's to learn. Perhap's all the
word's beginning with T were a few too many for her to mark?
Never mind, tomorrow's another day.

SB page 33

15 Plurals: words ending in 'y'

REMEMBER

- If there is a vowel before the **y**, add **-s**:
  *donk**ey** → donkey**s***.
- If there is a consonant before the **y**, change the **y** to **i** then add **-es**:
  *bul**ly** → bull**ies***

Activity 1

Change the words in italics into plurals. Write them in the spaces provided.

Kangaroos in Staffordshire?

Well, not quite. You won't see any Kangaroos, but you might spot a few *wallaby* __________.

Escaping from a private zoo in the 1930s, these bouncing *beauty* __________ bred in an area known as The Roaches, to the north-west of Leek. Several *colony* __________ exist although *survey* __________ have had difficulty estimating the population. Severe winters and speeding *lorry* __________ have claimed a few *casualty* __________ over the years, but the *wallaby* __________ have survived, becoming local *celebrity* __________ in the process.

Can there be a finer sight than these wonderful beasts hopping along, their *baby* __________ tucked into their *belly* __________? And you haven't lost all your *faculty* __________ if you spot them in the North Midlands!

Activity 2

Write down the plural of each of the following words. Make up a sentence using the word and write it in the space provided.

1. burglary 2. decoy 3. identity 4. laboratory 5. charity
6. atrocity 7. lullaby 8. category 9. stairway 10. penny

	Plural	Sentence
1	__________	______________________________
2	__________	______________________________
3	__________	______________________________
4	__________	______________________________
5	__________	______________________________
6	__________	______________________________
7	__________	______________________________
8	__________	______________________________
9	__________	______________________________
10	__________	______________________________

SB pages 32, 35

16 Plurals: 'f', 'ff', 'fe' endings and words ending in 'o'

REMEMBER

- Any words that end in **ff** need an **-s** to make them plural, for example:
  *sheri**ff** → sheriff**s**, cu**ff** → cuff**s***
- Words that end in **f** or **fe** are more tricky. Some form their plurals by adding **-s**, for example:
  *proo**f** → proof**s**, chie**f** → chief**s***
- Other words ending in **f** or **fe** change the **f** to **v** and add **-es**, for example:
  *wi**fe** → wi**ves**, hal**f** → hal**ves***
- Remember to say the plural of these words aloud. If you can hear a **v** sound, it usually means the plural ends in **-ves**.

Activity 1

Write the following words as plurals. Use a dictionary to look up the meaning of any words you do not know. Then invent a sentence that has each word in it.

1 chef 2 midwife 3 giraffe 4 waif 5 motif 6 whiff 7 aperitif 8 gaffe 9 neckerchief 10 sheaf

	Plural	Sentence
1	______	______
2	______	______
3	______	______
4	______	______
5	______	______
6	______	______
7	______	______
8	______	______
9	______	______
10	______	______

REMEMBER

- If a word ends in **o**, it usually needs **-s** to make it plural: *disco**s**, shampoo**s***.
- A few words ending in **o** need **-es**: *potato**es**, mosquito**es***.
- There is no clear rule, so always check in a dictionary if you are unsure.

Activity 2

Complete the sentences below by adding the correct **-s** or **-es** to the words ending in **o**.

1 The zoo contained many beautiful flamingo__ and cockatoo__.
2 The commando__ took cover from the salvo__ of shells flying overhead.
3 The orchestra contained five cello__ and three piccolo__.
4 He took many photo__ of the torpedo__ hitting the ship.
5 Several memo__ were sent warning that the volcano__ were going to erupt.

SB pages 37–40

Unit 4 PREFIXES AND SUFFIXES

17 Prefixes and suffixes

REMEMBER

In most cases neither the stem word nor the prefix changes its spelling when they are fixed together: ***dis*** + *allow* = ***dis****allow*.

Activity 1

Match each prefix to the correct stem. Write out the new word you have made.

under	unite	1 ____________	*im*	select	6 ____________
im	belief	2 ____________	*over*	polite	7 ____________
re	equal	3 ____________	*mis*	change	8 ____________
un	ground	4 ____________	*ex*	spell	9 ____________
dis	possible	5 ____________	*pre*	react	10 ____________

Activity 2

This passage contains a number of words with missing prefixes or suffixes. Choose the correct prefix from the box to fill each one. Don't worry if the last letter of the prefix 'doubles up' with the first letter of the root when you follow the rule, for example: *un* + *necessary* = ***un****necessary*.

pre-	dis-	un-	re-	under-	over-	im-	mis-	in-	-ment	-ful

The Globe Theatre – an _ _authorised guide

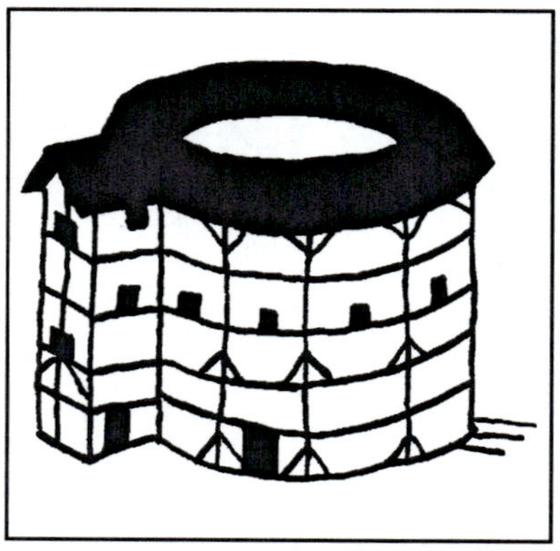

Four hundred years ago a wooden theatre stood on the edge of the Thames River in London. It was the _ _markable location where many of William Shakespeare's plays were performed. The original Globe Theatre was an _ _ _ _crowded place which could fit up to 4000 people _ _side. It must have been pretty dread_ _ _ and _ _pleasant with the crush and the lack of toilets! _ _surprisingly the audience would like to see action and excite_ _ _ _. The plays often began with violent fights or mysterious ghost scenes to provide interest immediately. Shakespeare would sit in the Writer's Room making changes to certain scenes if they were _ _success_ _ _. When a play was about to start, a red flag was hoisted above the theatre.

Write out each word you have made.

____________ ____________ ____________ ____________

____________ ____________ ____________ ____________

____________ ____________

SB page 41

18 Suffixes: adding -ful to stems

REMEMBER

When the suffix **-ful** is added to a stem word, it only needs one **l**.
For example: *care* + *full* = *careful*.
Remember this by thinking: when adding **full** to a stem, be care**ful**!

Activity 1

These words ending in **-ful** are all negative. Choose a selection of them and write a short letter of complaint. You could complain about a holiday, a terrible product or an unsuccessful event, or you could invent your own topic.

woeful	fateful	fearful	harmful
hateful	painful	pitiful	tearful
doubtful	dreadful	awful	boastful
disgraceful	disrespectful	distasteful	
forgetful	frightful	deceitful	
mistrustful	shameful	spiteful	
stressful	ungrateful	unsuccessful	
untruthful	wasteful	wrongful	

Dear …

Activity 2

These words ending in **-ful** are all positive. Use some of them to write a postcard. Explain the best things about the holiday using as many positive **-ful** words as you can.

beautiful	cheerful	
colourful	delightful	
graceful	grateful	
helpful	hopeful	joyful
lawful	peaceful	
plentiful	powerful	
playful	restful	rightful
successful	tasteful	
thankful	thoughtful	
truthful	useful	
wonderful	eventful	
blissful	skillful	

Dear …

SB pages 42–43

19 Adding suffixes to stems: when to keep the 'e'

REMEMBER

When you add a suffix starting with a **consonant** (-**f**ul, -**m**ent) to a stem ending in **e** you usually keep the **e** then add the suffix. For example:

stem	**consonant suffix**		**new word**
force	+ ***f**ul*	=	*forc**e**ful*
care	+ ***l**ess*	=	*car**e**less*
state	+ ***m**ent*	=	*stat**e**ment*
excite	+ ***m**ent*	=	*excit**e**ment*

DANGER

The one exception to this rule is *argue* + *ment* which loses the **e** to become *argument*.

Activity 1

Join these root words to their suffixes correctly.

1	describe	+	ing = ________	**7**	amuse	+	ing = ________
2	amuse	+	ment = ________	**8**	price	+	less = ________
3	rate	+	ed = ________	**9**	grace	+	ful = ________
4	save	+	er = ________	**10**	excite	+	ing = ________
5	hope	+	ful = ________	**11**	force	+	ed = ________
6	excite	+	ment = ________	**12**	force	+	ful = ________

Activity 2

Fill in the gaps in this passage with words from the box. Use the rules you have learned to help you decide whether to keep the **e** in each one.

courage	practise	balance	enjoy	live

I think that skydivers are very ________ous. They have to wait in the aircraft as it flies upwards, ________ing on the edge of the opening ready to jump! Although their lives are full of ________ment, they need to do an awful lot of ________ing on the ground before they are allowed in the sky. There are many dangers because these men are ________ing on the edge all the time.

SB pages 44–45

20 Suffixes and stems: doubling

REMEMBER

When you add a suffix that starts with a **vowel** (-**e**d, -**e**r, -**i**ng) to a stem that ends in a **consonant**, you usually need to double the last letter of the stem. For example:

*slip + ed = sli**pp**ed* *slip + ing = sli**pp**ing*

*slip + er = sli**pp**er* *slip + y = sli**pp**y* (**y** as a vowel sound **e**).

This rule only applies to words that have:

- ONE syllable: ***slip***
- ONE short vowel: *sl**i**p*
- ONE consonant as the final letter: *sli**p***

This is known as the ONE, ONE, ONE rule.

Activity 1

Take the following stem words and add either **-ed** or **-er** or **-ing**. How many real words can you make in total? The first one has been done for you.

Stem word

bat	batted, batter, batting
slip	__________
clap	__________
ship	__________
beg	__________
clip	__________
fat	__________
quit	__________
hit	__________
sad	__________
squat	__________
trek	__________

Activity 2

Read the piece to the right. The bold words are missing a **vowel suffix**. Fill in the suffix and don't forget to double the last letter of the stem.

I remember my school sports days very fondly. My favourite event was the **skip** __________ race which I always won. I remember my mum and dad **clap** __________ with delight as I crossed the finish line. I also remember **hop** __________ about for the sack race, but I **slip** __________ over and made a fool of myself. I remember **sit** __________ on my bum feeling really embarrassed! I wasn't a bad **run** __________ either.

SB page 46

21 Suffixes and stems: the 'l' rule

REMEMBER

If you add a suffix that starts with a **vowel** (-**e**d, -**i**ng) to a stem that ends with an **l**, double the **l**:
*marve**l** = marve**ll**ous, trave**l** = trave**ll**ing.*

DANGER

However, there are exceptions!
If the **l** follows a pair of vowels, it is never doubled. For example:
*app**eal** = appea**l**ing, conc**eal** = concea**l**ing*

Activity 1

Underline all of the words in this report that contain double **l**.

Marvellous Modelling Material

When the curriculum was boring, many students were expelled for poor behaviour. But now one school is coming up with a very exciting new approach.

Students at Middle Earth High School are enjoying a new GCSE qualification, in animation. Students fulfilled their dreams after other boring qualifications were cancelled. They chiselled models, made plasticine creatures, found themselves quarrelling over camera angles and propelled lifeless lumps of stuff into living beings on screen. A visiting expert travelled from America to give a series of lectures and he labelled the new students on the course as geniuses. He signalled that many of them might one day be revelling in celebration at getting a job with his company. Only one boy was appalled. The visiting professor sat on one of his models and squashed it.

Activity 2

Write out the words you have found below. For each word underline the double **l** in the middle.

__________ __________ __________ __________

__________ __________ __________ __________

__________ __________ __________ __________

____

SB page 47

22 Suffixes and stems: changing 'y' to 'i'

REMEMBER

When adding a suffix to words that end in **y**:

- if there is a **vowel** before the **y**, just add the suffix. For example:
  delay = delayed, destroy = destroying, joy = joyful
- if there is a **consonant** before the **y**, change **y** to **i**, then add the suffix. For example:
  vary = varied, occupy = occupied, city = cities.

DANGER

Exception! If you add the suffix **-ing** to a word ending in **y**, whether it has a vowel or a consonant before the **y**, always just add **-ing**: *carry = carrying, buy = buying.*

Activity 1

Underline the words which require **y** to change to **i** when a suffix is added.

relay portray injury heavy delay lady uneasy fancy carry skinny happy

Activity 2

How many words can you make by joining these stems to suffixes? The first one has been done for you.

Stems	Suffixes
enjoy	-ing
pray	-ment
play	-ful
copy	-ed
reply	-es
injury	-est
happy	-ness

enjoying, enjoyment, enjoyed

____

____

____

____

____

____

Activity 3

Choose a suitable suffix to add to each bold word in this passage. Write the new words out in full below:

During my maths exam I **copy** the person next to me. You might think I'm the **crazy** kid around but I hate maths. I wanted to be **victory** in the exam. I've never **enjoy** the subject. I prefer **play** football to be honest.

______________ ______________ ______________

______________ ______________

SB pages 50–52

Unit 5 COMMON LETTER PATTERNS

23 Common letter patterns: hard and soft 'c'

REMEMBER

- **c** usually makes a soft sound when followed by **e**, **i** or **y**: *cereal, suicide, juicy*.
- **c** usually makes a hard sound when followed by **a**, **o**, **u** or a consonant: *camera, apricot, curl, clap*.

Activity 1

Use a dictionary to find 36 words with a soft **c** sound.

- Twelve words must have the **ce** pattern (for example, ***ce**ment*).
- Twelve words must have the **ci** pattern (for example, ***ci**nema*).
- Twelve words must have the **cy** pattern (for example, ***cy**gnet*).

The letter pattern does not have to appear at the start of the word (for example, *fan**cy***).

Write your answers in the table opposite. An example has been completed for you.

Soft c words			
ce			
1 cell	2 dunce	3	4
5	6	7	8
9	10	11	12
ci			
1	2	3	4
5	6	7	8
9	10	11	12
cy			
1	2	3	4
5	6	7	8
9	10	11	12

Activity 2

Use a dictionary to find 48 words with a hard **c** sound.

- Twelve words must have the **ca** pattern (for example, ***ca**t*).
- Twelve words must have the **co** pattern (for example, ***co**tton*).
- Twelve words must have the **cu** pattern (for example, ***cu**pboard*).
- Twelve words should have the **c-consonant** pattern (for example, ***cr**ash*).

The letter pattern does not have to appear at the start of the word (for example, *ex**cu**se*).

Write your answers in the table opposite. An example has been completed for you.

Hard c words			
ca			
1 candle	2 scar	3	4
5	6	7	8
9	10	11	12
co			
1	2	3	4
5	6	7	8
9	10	11	12
cu			
1	2	3	4
5	6	7	8
9	10	11	12
c-consonant			
1	2	3	4
5	6	7	8
9	10	11	12

SB pages 51–52

24 Common letter patterns: soft 'c' spellings

REMEMBER

- The letter **c** usually makes a soft sound when followed by **e**, **i** or **y**: *c**e**real, suic**i**de, juic**y**.*
- The letter **c** usually makes a hard sound when followed by **a**, **o**, **u** or a consonant: *c**a**mera, apric**o**t, c**u**rl, c**l**ap.*

Activity 1

Read the following invitation. Mistakes have been made with soft **c** spellings. Find the eight errors and write them out correctly.

1 ________
2 ________
3 ________
4 ________
5 ________
6 ________
7 ________
8 ________

> *The Pasific Islands Veterans' Sosiety*
> *Formally invites you to a selebration danse*
> *Commemorating the legasy of half a century of pease*
>
> TICKET PRISE $75.00 R.S.V.P.
> Strict dress polisy applies

Activity 2

Check this spelling test. The student got half of the words wrong. Use a dictionary to help you find the mistakes. Write the words correctly in the spaces.

1 ________
2 ________
3 ________
4 ________
5 ________
6 ________
7 ________
8 ________
9 ________
10 ________

1. sivilian	2. cease
3. secure	4. resipe
5. singular	6. sigarette
7. jaundise	8. several
9. cellar	10. centimetre
11. sivic	12. novise
13. cellophane	14. privasy
15. sylinder	16. secresy
17. finanse	18. sequin
19. precise	20. cyclist

SB page 53

25 Common letter patterns: hard and soft 'g'

REMEMBER

- The letter **g** usually makes a soft sound (like **j**) when followed by **e**, **i** or **y**: *gentle, ginger, edgy.*
- The letter **g** usually makes a hard sound when followed by **a**, **o**, **u** or a consonant: *gate, goal, gum, green.*

Activity 1

Use a dictionary to find 42 words with a soft **g** sound.

- Twelve words must have the **ge** pattern (for example, ***ge**neral*).
- Twelve must have the **gi** pattern (for example, ***gi**nger*).
- Eight must have the **gy** pattern (for example, *squid**gy***).

The letter pattern does not have to appear at the start of the word (for example, *stran**ge**r*).

Write your answers in the table below. An example has been completed for you.

Soft g words			
ge			
1 **ge**nder	**2** nud**ge**	**3**	**4**
5	**6**	**7**	**8**
9	**10**	**11**	**12**
gi			
1	**2**	**3**	**4**
5	**6**	**7**	**8**
9	**10**	**11**	**12**
gy			
1	**2**	**3**	**4**
5	**6**	**7**	**8**

Activity 2

Use a dictionary to find 48 words with a hard **g** sound.

- Twelve words must have the **ga** pattern (for example, ***ga**p*).
- Twelve must have the **go** pattern (for example, ***go**ing*).
- Twelve must have the **gu** pattern (for example, ***gu**nge*).
- Twelve should have the **g-** consonant pattern (for example, ***gl**ass*).

The letter pattern does not have to appear at the start of the word (for example, *re**gu**lar*).

Write your answers in the table below. An example has been completed for you.

Hard g words			
ga			
1 **ga**te	**2** a**ga**in	**3**	**4**
5	**6**	**7**	**8**
9	**10**	**11**	**12**
go			
1	**2**	**3**	**4**
5	**6**	**7**	**8**
9	**10**	**11**	**12**
gu			
1	**2**	**3**	**4**
5	**6**	**7**	**8**
9	**10**	**11**	**12**
g-consonant			
1	**2**	**3**	**4**
5	**6**	**7**	**8**
9	**10**	**11**	**12**

SB page 54

26 Common letter patterns: '-ge' and '-dge' endings

REMEMBER

For English words that end with a soft **g** sound, use **-ge** or **-dge**.

- When there is a **consonant** before the soft **g** sound, use **-ge**: *orange, diverge.*
- When there is a **vowel** before the soft **g** sound:
  - if the word is one syllable and the vowel sound is short, usually use **-dge**: *smudge, dredge.*
  - otherwise use **-ge**: *garbage, lozenge.*

Activity 1

Complete each word below with **-ge** or **-dge**. Then write a sentence for each word to show you understand its meaning. Use a dictionary if you need help.

1. begru____ ____________________
2. lun____ ____________________
3. privile____ ____________________
4. refu____ ____________________
5. dislo____ ____________________
6. ju____ ____________________
7. camoufla____ ____________________
8. discoura____ ____________________
9. loun____ ____________________
10. divul____ ____________________

Activity 2

Complete each headline with -ge or -dge.

Chelsea ple____ to aven____ defeat

Players' wa____s soar out of control

Everton go on goal rampa____

Spurs lo____ complaint over sending-off

Villa do____ disappointment with late equaliser

Advanta____ United in close title race

SB page 55

27 Common letter patterns: 'ph' words

REMEMBER

Sometimes the **f** sound in a word is spelled **ph**, for example: *autogra**ph**, ele**ph**ant.*

These words are usually based on Ancient Greek words.

Activity 1

The incomplete words below all contain the **f** sound. Some are spelled with **ph** and some with **f**. Complete each word, then write it out in full.

1 A _____easant is a wild bird found in Britain. ____________________
2 A_____ids are insects that are not popular with gardeners. ____________________
3 The chemical _____ormula of salt is NaCl. ____________________
4 An am_____ibian can live both on land and in water. ____________________
5 Ty_____oid fever is a deadly disease. ____________________
6 Ice cream is sometimes served with wa_____ers. ____________________
7 Dol_____ins are considered to be very intelligent. ____________________
8 A drastic food shortage is called a _____amine. ____________________
9 An or_____an is a child whose parents have died. ____________________
10 _____ysical exercise is necessary to stay fit. ____________________

Activity 2

Draw a circle around the correct spelling.

1 symphony or symfony?
2 emphasise or emfasise?
3 rephund or refund?
4 blaspheme or blasfeme?
5 decipher or decifer?
6 atmosphere or atmosfere?
7 pheature or feature?
8 euphoria or euforia?
9 emphatic or emfatic?
10 phallacy or fallacy?

Activity 3

Use the correct spellings from activity 2. Write a sentence for each word that shows you understand its meaning. Use a dictionary to help you.

1 ____
2 ____
3 ____
4 ____
5 ____
6 ____
7 ____
8 ____
9 ____
10 ____

SB page 56

28 Common letter patterns: 'ei' or 'ie'?

REMEMBER

- **i** before **e** except after **c** but only when the **ie** sound rhymes with **me**.
- When **cie** sounds like **sh**, the **i** comes before the **e**.
- Hear two separate sounds? Ignore other rules and spell as you hear it.

Activity 1

Choose **ei** or **ie** to complete the words below. Write each complete word in the table below under the rule you used to get the correct answer.

1	airf____ld	**6**	sold____r	**11**	unw____ldy	**16**	bel____f
2	barr____r	**7**	repr____ve	**12**	h____ght	**17**	p____rcing
3	ach____ve	**8**	th____r	**13**	grad____nt	**18**	aggr____ved
4	perc____ve	**9**	qu____t	**14**	defic____nt	**19**	al____n
5	effic____nt	**10**	rel____ve	**15**	dec____t	**20**	w____ght

ie rhymes with 'me'	except after c	two separate sounds	cie makes sh sound	ie doesn't rhyme with 'me'

Activity 2

The words below are all spelled correctly. Use as many of them as you can in a message to a friend, but deliberately reverse the ie/ie pattern. Then swap letters with a partner and see if you can spot all the mistakes. (Here's a tip: don't reverse every letter pattern – leave some correct. This way your partner cannot simply reverse every ie/ei pattern they see!)

friend	believe	shield	diet	audience	receive
their	ancient	field	relief	brief	experience

You may use other ie/ei words if you wish.

SB pages 58–59

29 Common letter patterns: 'ch' or 'tch' and 'ch' or 'k'?

REMEMBER

- As a rough guide, words are usually spelled with **-tch** if the **ch** sound follows a short vowel sound: *sti**t**ch, s**a**tchel, wi**t**ch.*
- Exceptions include *su**ch**, whi**ch**, mu**ch**, ri**ch**.*

Activity 1

Complete the words in the speech bubble with **-tch** or **-ch**.

Ain't she a pea______ then? You won't find one to ma______ this little beauty. Not a scra______ on her… well… apart from that one there, and that little pa______ on the rear. But they've been tou______ed up beautifully. You won't see any bo______ jobs at Honest Al's. I promise you this will be your best pur______ase of the year. Five hundred is my best price though… I'm not flin______ing, not an in______. Oh, go on then…three hundred.

Activity 2

Underline the correct spelling. Use a dictionary to help you.

echo/eko	charisma/karisma	chiosk/kiosk	chaos/kaos
stomach/stomack	schull/skull	scheme/skeme	scholar/skolar
archive/arkive	asterisch/asterisk	limerich/limerick	mechanic/meckanic

SB pages 60–61

30 Common letter patterns: 'ou' and 'ow' and short sound 'ou'

REMEMBER

If a word has an **ou/ow** sound:

- use **ow** before **n** or **l** when it is the last letter of a root word: *bro**wn**, gro**wl***
- use **ow** at the end of a word or the end of a syllable: *c**ow**, fl**ow**er*
- use **ou** for most other words: *s**ou**nd, m**ou**th*.

Exceptions include: *crowd, foul, noun*.

Activity 1

Complete the words below with **ow** or **ou**. Write a sentence including *both* words to show you understand their meaning.

1	fl____t	p____er	____________________
2	sh____er	sp____t	____________________
3	d____bt	acc____nt	____________________
4	g____n	shr____d	____________________
5	spr____t	disc____nt	____________________
6	c____nt	conf____nded	____________________
7	cl____d	f____ndry	____________________
8	r____nd	b____ncer	____________________
9	r____t	param____nt	____________________
10	t____n	b____ndary	____________________

REMEMBER

- The short vowel sound **ou** can be spelled using **u** as in *m**u**g*. It can also be spelled **ou** as in *t**ou**ch*.
- There are no clear rules to follow. Use a dictionary.

Activity 2

Complete the following words with **ou** or **u**.

1 Be cauti____s walking past that enorm____s pile of building r____bble.

2 You'll need c____rage, but learning self-defence sh____ld t____ghen you up.

3 No need to be so gener____s: that's more than en____gh.

4 That was a c____nning and ingeni____s way of solving a t____gh problem.

5 There were h____ndreds of gorge____s hats but I was anxi____s none w____ld fit me.

SB pages 60–61

31 Common letter patterns: adding 'r' to 'ou'

REMEMBER

When **r** is added to the **ou** pattern the following sounds can be made:

- **or** (rhyming with floor: t***our***)
- **our** (rhyming with power: h***our***)
- **er** (rhyming with her: hum***our***).

Activity 1

The missing sound from the following words is **er**. Fill in the correct spelling of this sound.

Celebrity Mystery

There is a strong rum____ that a famous celebrity will hon____ the opening of the new harb____ this week. It is thought the celebrity is a form____ resident of the town and possibly even a don____ to the project. It seems likely they will already own a large mot____ boat. After all the err____s during construction, it is hoped a little glam____ will ensure a bump____ crowd this weekend. A local j____rnalist discovered that a lim____sine has been booked for the occasion, but no one would reveal who the passenger would be.

Activity 2

Complete the following quiz answers with **or** or **our**.

1. Where might you find a judge, jury and witnesses? c______t
2. The starting point of a river is known as its...? s______ce
3. A word for lying asleep or not moving. d______mant
4. Someone on holiday is a...? t______ist
5. A musical instrument. tamb______ine

Activity 3

Complete the following words with **our** or **ower**.

1. The milk smells awful: it must have gone s______.
2. The striker hit a really p______ful volley into the top corner of the net.
3. I had to sc______ the Internet for that bargain.
4. He was so hungry he dev______ed a meal meant for two.
5. You could tell he felt gloomy by his d______ expression.

SB page 63

32 Common letter patterns: 'q' letter patterns

REMEMBER

In English, the letter **q** is always followed by the letter **u**. These two letters are then followed by another vowel: *squirrel, quarter*.

Activity 1

The following words are completed with either **que** or **k**. Underline the correct spelling.

1 picturesque/picturesk
2 pranque/prank
3 oblique/oblik
4 cheque/chek
5 opaque/opak

Activity 2

Complete each word in the sentences below.

1 That duck is really noisy. Have you heard how loud it q _ _ _ ks?
2 He must use the gym fr _ q _ _ _ _ _ y as I see him there each time I go.
3 If the rules are broken you will be d _ _ q _ _ _ _ _ _ _ d.
4 The football pitch was so muddy it had turned into a q _ _ gm _ _ e.
5 Let's not fall out, there's no need to q _ _ _ _ ll.
6 It was a huge aq _ _ _ _ _ m containing hundreds of fish.
7 Did you feel the ground shake during the e _ r _ _ q _ _ _ e?
8 I hope we q _ _ _ _ fy for the next stage of the competition.
9 The _ q _ _ t _ r is an imaginary line running around the world.
10 Ask me another q _ _ _ _ _ _ n, I'm feeling brainy today!

Activity 3

The following words need **q** and **a vowel** to complete them. Match the correct word with its meaning below. Use a dictionary to help you.

ex____isite	van____ish	in____est	____aint	____intuplets
ac____aintance	ade____ate	brus____e	li____id	____alm

1 ________________ Five children born at one birth.
2 ________________ Not a solid or a gas.
3 ________________ Barely satisfactory or sufficient.
4 ________________ Of great beauty or excellence.
5 ________________ An uneasy feeling.
6 ________________ An inquiry, especially into the cause of death.
7 ________________ Abrupt manners or rudeness.
8 ________________ Charmingly odd, especially in an old-fashioned way.
9 ________________ A person you know.
10 ________________ To defeat in a contest or battle.

SB page 66

Unit 6 COMMON ENDINGS

33 Common endings: '-ough', '-ought', '-aught'

REMEMBER

The letter patterns **-ough**, **-ought** and **-aught** have many different sounds. Look at the example words in the box below.

Activity

Write these words in the correct circle according to how they sound.

dough	tough	although	borough	taught	enough
fought	naughty	rough	nought	laughter	trough
bought	daughter	draught	bough	ought	thought
though	cough	plough	thorough	brought	caught

Rhymes with:

cuff

tough

toe

off

cow

terror

sport (ought)

sport (aught)

craft

SB page 67

34 Common endings: '-ous'

REMEMBER

The ending **-ous** is the most common letter pattern at the end of an adjective or describing word:

noun	→	**adjective**
mountain	→	*mountain**ous***
poison	→	*poison**ous***

Activity

Complete this article by writing the correct **-ous** words in the spaces provided. Choose your words from the list below the article.

In the m_ _ _ _ _ _ _ous regions of Peru, certain tribes exist who have never been contacted by the outside world. Some of these _ _ _nymous peoples are believed to be extremely _ _ _ _ _ _ous. Rumours state that they use _ _rr_ _ _ous and t_ _ _ _ _ _ous techniques to hunt other humans and it is believed they use _ _ _ _ _ _ _ous darts to _ _ _derous effect. In 2008 an i_ _ _ _ous photograph taken from a helicopter showed _ _ _ _ous tribesmen painted bright red, firing arrows upwards, seemingly trying to attack the aircraft.

In Peru, many _ _ _ _ _llous and e_ _ _ _ous forested areas are unexplored. _d_ _ _ _ _rous explorers face per_ _ous journeys. There are no roads and the jungle can be _ _eac_erous. It is hard to believe that such vast areas of the planet have never been touched by civilisation. If you think exploration is _ _am_ _ous, think again. Peru's untouched wilderness could be one of the most terrifying spots around.

perilous	anonymous	torturous	treacherous	mountainous
enormous	infamous	horrendous	poisonous	adventurous
nervous	dangerous	glamorous	marvellous	murderous

SB page 68

35 Common endings: '-ious'

REMEMBER

The ending **-ious** is mainly used in two cases:

1 When you hear the sound **shus** at the end of a word, following the letters **t**, **c** or **x**: *cau**t**ious, vi**c**ious, an**x**ious.*

2 When you can hear the **i** as a syllable on its own:

*hilar**i**ous* *ser**i**ous* *ingen**i**ous*

hilar / **i** / ous ser / **i** / ous ingen / **i** / ous.

Activity 1

These **-ious** words all make the **shus** sound at the end of the word:

atrocious	ferocious	gracious	precious	spacious	suspicious
cautious	vicious	anxious	noxious	luscious	ambitious
delicious	obnoxious	vivacious	ungracious	conscientious	conscious

Complete these clues using words from the list above:

1 very careful ____________________
2 aggressive and fierce ____________________
3 valuable and rare ____________________
4 keen to get on in a career ____________________
5 tasty and desirable ____________________
6 hard working ____________________
7 worried and concerned ____________________

Activity 2

In these **-ious** words the **i** can be heard as a syllable on its own:

curious	delirious	hilarious	notorious	previous
dubious	envious	furious	obvious	tedious
serious	various	glorious	amphibious	odious

Complete these clues using words from the list above:

1 extremely funny ____________________
2 jealous of another ____________________
3 very angry ____________________
4 boring and repetitive ____________________
5 underwater creature or vehicle ____________________
6 wonderful and celebrated ____________________
7 keen to know more ____________________

SB page 68

36 Common endings: '-eous'

REMEMBER

Use the **-eous** ending when:

- a stem ends in soft **-ge:**
  outrage → *outra**geous***
- you can hear an **e** in a word as a syllable on its own:
  *hid**e**ous*.

Activity

Can you find where the words below fit into this word grid? When you have completed the puzzle, a hidden word will be revealed on the winning line. One letter of the word has already been given to you.

hideous piteous beauteous bounteous gorgeous plenteous
spontaneous outrageous simultaneous miscellaneous nauseous

Winning line!

SB page 69

37 Common endings: '-tion'

REMEMBER

- Use the ending **-tion** if you can hear a long vowel before the **shun** sound: *n**a**tion, excr**e**tion, em**o**tion, evol**u**tion.*
- Use the ending **-tion** if there is a consonant before the **shun** sound: *se**c**tion, addi**c**tion.*
- Use the ending **-tion** after a short vowel **i** sound when the word doesn't end in **-mission**: *trad**i**tion, compet**i**tion.*

Activity

Address | Go | Links | Web assistant | Norton AntiVirus

Channel 6: TOTAL FUN TOTAL ENTERTAINMENT
HIGHLIGHTS THIS WEEK
Alien Civilisation Has Been Visiting Earth For Years! Yeah Right!

Did you know that one in three Americans claim to have been abducted by aliens? Yes that's right. One in three people in that crazy nation has the perception that they have been picked up by a spaceship, used for experimentation and then dropped back down on earth again in a more or less normal condition. These dudes sometimes say they have been given inoculations and vaccinations, have been subject to electrification, brain implants and other such trifles. But is it their imagination? Or are they really madder than a box of frogs?

In our new series on Channel 6, a team of top scientists examine these alien communications and get to grips with a small fraction of these freaks. Some claim they went through a total transformation after the abduction, and had to change their occupation. Others have found the transition back to normal life impossible. We meet one woman who claims to have also had a head transplantation! Weird man!

Channel 6: Wednesday 7:15–8:15

Done | Internet

Write the words you have found in the table below according to which part of the rule they follow:

Long vowel before shun sound	Consonant before the shun sound	Short i or e before the shun sound where the word doesn't end in - mission

SB page 70

38 Common endings: '-ssion'

REMEMBER

- Use the ending **-ssion** if you can hear the short vowel sounds **a**, **e** or **u**, before the **shun** sound:
  *p**a**ssion, aggr**e**ssion, disc**u**ssion.*
- Use the ending **-ssion** after the short vowel **i** when the word ends with **-mission**. Otherwise use **-ition**:

Short i ending -mission	**Short i not ending** -mission
permission	*tradition*
admission	*audition*

Activity

Circle the words ending **-ssion** in this article. Fit them into the word strips below.

DEPRESSION AS RECESSION LOOMS

Banks have finally made a confession that the recent banking crisis is their fault! The admission came after studies showed their obsession with multi-million pound bonuses has created a procession of bank collapses. Savers have reacted with aggression.

'We intend to commission an enquiry. The banks have grabbed all our cash. They show no compassion,' a spokesman said. 'We want the government's permission to stop these bankers pinching our pounds.'

1		E		R		S	S	I	O	N
2	■		D		I	S	S	I	O	N
3	■	O			E	S	S	I	O	N
4	P		O			S	S	I	O	N
5	P		R			S	S	I	O	N
6			G			S	S	I	O	N
7				M		S	S	I	O	N
8						S	S	I	O	N
9	■			C	E	S	S	I	O	N
10		O		F	E	S	S	I	O	N

SB page 71

39 Common endings: '-cian'

REMEMBER

The ending **-cian** is used when a word refers to a person's job or occupation: *magi**cian**, opti**cian**, mathemati**cian**, beauti**cian**.*

Activity

Fill in the correct words on these vans. They all belong to people with a particular profession and they all end with **-cian**.

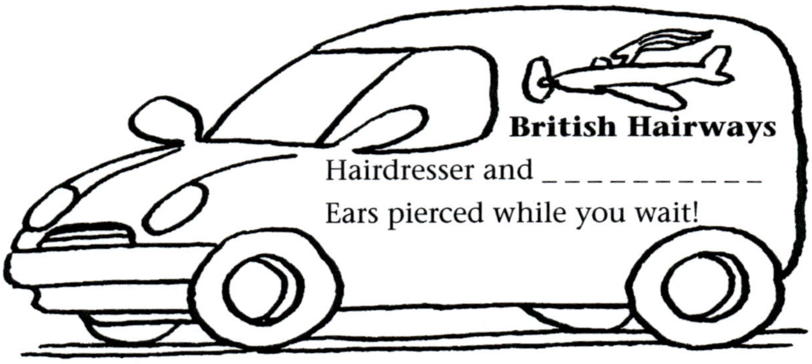

Create your own van designs for two of the following professions:

magician technician politician physician mathematician musician

SB page 71

40 Common endings: '-sion'

REMEMBER

You can usually hear words that end with **-sion** as they have a slightly different sound: **zhun** as in *revi**sion*** instead of **shun** as in *permis**sion***.

Activity

Find the words ending in **-sion** in this brochure for a holiday retreat.

GLEN LYONS MANSION HOUSE RETREAT - A FUSION OF OLD CHARM AND NEW TECHNOLOGY

Why not visit our Scottish estate and find peace and tranquility again? Fancy letting our hospitable staff take care of all your troubles?

Is your life one long collision of different stresses and responsibilities? Do you find balancing life and work a constant confusion? Do you need to relieve your tension with a get-away-from-it-all-break?

If you have a passion for quality and a love of luxury then this experience will be the perfect diversion from your stressful life. All our rooms have television, whirlpool baths, saunas and fully trained staff to cater for your every need.

- Ease away the tension with a session in our spa.
- Why not take advantage of our optional excursions?
- Drink a herbal infusion or relax with our healthy fruit smoothies.

Place the words you have found in this table according to whether the ending sounds like **zhun** as in *revision* or **shun** as in *permission*.

zhun as in revision	shun as in permission

SB page 72

41 Common endings: '-le'

REMEMBER

Most words ending in the **ul** sound are spelled with **-le**: such as *batt**le***.
There are no clear rules, but the activities below will help you.

Activity 1

Circle the words ending with **-le** in these headlines.

Grandma's Humble Bramble Crumble Wins Prize Double

FUEL NOZZLE MUDDLE CAUSES FIRE IN F1 VEHICLE

Swindle Riddle As Robber Leaves No Clues

VALUABLE LITTLE POODLE UNBEATABLE AT CRUFTS

Horrible Gargoyle of the Deep Found! With 30 Foot Tentacle

Impossible Motorcycle Stunt Goes Wrong

POSSIBLE NEW PARTICLE FOUND BY HADRON COLLIDER

Activity 2

Use the word bank below to compose some headlines of your own. Use as many words ending with **-le** as you can.

angle	apple	wriggle	ankle	giggle	mangle	wobble	puzzle	gobble	nibble
hobble	cancel	gurgle	ripple	gargle	mingle	bramble	jumble	truffle	
chuckle	crumble	bundle	muddle	swindle	tumble	grumble	beetle		
feeble	battle	table	title	rifle	uncle	bubble	buckle	bottle	bumble

SB pages 72–73

42 Common endings: '-el' and '-al'

REMEMBER

- The **-el** ending is commonly used after the following letters:
  n: *chan**n**el* **r:** *bar**r**el* **s:** *wea**s**el* **v:** *re**v**el* **soft c**: *par**c**el* **soft g:** *an**g**el*
- **-al** is often used as an ending for an adjective (describing word): *magic**al** spell.*
- The **-al** makes the word mean 'to do with': to do with a spell.
- A few words ending in **-al** are nouns or naming words. There is no rule to tell you whether to use **-al**. For example:
  *decim**al** cathedr**al** med**al** materi**al**.*

Activity

Read this report. Unscramble the words in bold. They all end with either **-el** or **-al**. Write them into the table below the article.

Offciials Deny Cover Up of Treasure Trove

At a secret location in Switzerland archaeologists have begun digging a **tnunel** which links **lareves** chambers. It is believed that these were dug during the Second World War, to hide precious **mtela** and **ejewls**. This was done in **ttoal** secrecy. Although the government have issued a **nedail**, some believe that there may be **colsosla** stores of gold and banknotes still hidden. These rumours began to circulate when a **barerl** containing a few gold sovereigns was found, and a man with a **shlevo** dug up a silver statue of an **legan**.

It is not clear exactly where this **sepcial** place is. Fears have grown that revealing the location would make the site a magnet for **lanimirc** masterminds, keen to steal **metarial** and make a tidy sum on the black market. Whatever happens, this site is a **niontala** treasure with a **msyitcla** reputation. The story will probably run and run.

Words found ending with -al	Words found ending with -el

SB page 74

43 Common endings: '-able' and '-ible'

REMEMBER

There is no clear rule to help you choose when to use the ending **-able** (as in *un**able***) or **-ible** (as in *ined**ible***), but two things may help you.

1. More words end in **-able** than **-ible**.
2. You can sometimes hear whether the ending is **-able** or **-ible**, for example: *sens**ible*** or *break**able***.

-able endings

Activity

These words are all hidden in the puzzle below. Put them in the correct place and reveal a hidden word on the winning line.

advisable mistakable agreeable predictable admirable

desirable fashionable probable noticeable valuable

Winning line! ↓

				G		E		A		L	E			
			P		E		I		T		B		E	
				D		I		A		L				
	D		I		A		L							
	D		S		R		B		E					
		S		A			B		E					
					A	S	H				A			
		P												
									L	E				
N			I			A			E					

The hidden word is _ _ _ _ _ _ _ _ _ _.

SB pages 75–76

44 Common endings: '-ical', '-icle' and '-acle'

REMEMBER

- The **-ical** ending is often used at the end of an adjective or describing word. Further examples of the **-ical** ending are: *myst**ical**, opt**ical**, chem**ical**, econom**ical**.*
- Words ending in **-icle** and **-acle** are nouns or naming words, and they are not very common.

Activity

All the answers in this quiz end in either **-ical**, **-icle** or **-acle**. Choose your answers from the word bank and write the correct answers into the spaces provided.

vertical	umbilical	article	chronicle	cubicle	miracle	tentacle
icicle	oracle	comical	mystical	musical	obstacle	geographical
mythical	medical	barnacle	horizontal	logical	mathematical	

1 Another name for a story in a newspaper _ _ _ _ _ _ _
2 The opposite of horizontal _ _ _ _ _ _ _ _
3 An exceptional event that defies belief _ _ _ _ _ _ _
4 A spike of ice which forms in freezing weather _ _ _ _ _ _
5 Something funny which makes a person laugh _ _ _ _ _ _ _
6 A type of show which contains songs as part of the story _ _ _ _ _ _ _
7 Something which gets in the way is an… _ _ _ _ _ _ _ _
8 To do with doctors and hospitals _ _ _ _ _ _ _
9 To do with numbers and sums _ _ _ _ _ _ _ _ _ _ _ _
10 To do with the world and its places _ _ _ _ _ _ _ _ _ _ _ _
11 A limpet type creature which hangs on to rocks _ _ _ _ _ _ _ _
12 The opposite of vertical _ _ _ _ _ _ _ _ _ _
13 Something involving reason and scientific proof _ _ _ _ _ _ _
14 A word describing myths and legends _ _ _ _ _ _ _ _
15 Magical wizardry _ _ _ _ _ _ _ _
16 Cord joining mother to baby in the womb _ _ _ _ _ _ _ _ _
17 All knowing person who answers questions _ _ _ _ _ _
18 Long limb of an octopus _ _ _ _ _ _ _ _
19 Private area in a changing room _ _ _ _ _ _ _
20 A written record of historical events _ _ _ _ _ _ _ _ _

SB pages 77–78

45 Common endings: '-ence' and '-ance', '-ate' and '-ite'

REMEMBER

The word endings **-ance** (as in *glance*) and **-ence** (as in *indifference*) sound very alike. There are no rules to help you decide which ending to use.

Activity 1

Find four **-ance** and five **-ence** words in this review. Place each word in the correct column in the table.

The BBC show Strictly Come Dancing has been something of a phenomenon. It involves contestants having a dance (or a prance) each week, trying to capture the essence of a particular style and then having the skill and confidence to perform it in front of a live audience. As each week passes they gain experience and with ultimate persistence they can eventually win the contest. Most of the dances are all about romance. The key to winning a performance is being popular with the general public for it is they who phone the show and vote. It's all about making sure you beat the opposition.

Words ending with -ance	Words ending with -ence

REMEMBER

The endings **-ate** (as in *calculate*) and **-ite** (as in *appetite*) are usually quite easy to tell apart.

- The ending **-ate** is used most often, and the long vowel sound **a** can be heard very clearly: *animate*.
- The ending **-ite** usually sounds like a long vowel sound **i**: *excite*.
- In a few words the ending **-ite** sounds like a short vowel sound *i*: *favourite, opposite, granite*.

Activity 2

The words in the box below all end in **-ate** or **-ite**. Copy each word into the correct column in the table. Use a dictionary to check the meaning of any word you do not know.

terminate decorate polite favourite definite opposite
concentrate invite irritate incite granite relate

-ate ending	-ite ending with long vowel i	-ite ending with short vowel i

SB pages 81–82

Unit 7 SPELLING AND PUNCTUATION

46 Capital letters

REMEMBER

Use capital letters for the beginning of a sentence, proper nouns, brand names, words that come from proper nouns, the pronoun **I**, any abbreviations involving **I**, the first word of speech, initials, days of the week, months of the year, seasons, titles and the names of specific events.

Activity

Read the following article carefully. Put a circle around all the letters that should be capital letters. Underline all the letters that should not be capital letters.

The Finest Fool's Day Fun

The origin of April Fool's Day is unclear. even though we don't know why we play tricks on each other at this time of Year, it doesn't stop us having some fun. over the years there have been some terrific examples of pranks, japes and jokes.

In 1998, burger king ran a Newspaper advert announcing the arrival of a whopper especially for left-handed people. They said it was designed so the Ketchup would only run out of the right side. many thousands were fooled into requesting one.

The bbc programme *panorama* showed a Film supposedly showing swiss farmers harvesting Spaghetti trees. Many contacted the bbc for instructions about how to grow their own.

The german car maker bmw has claimed many new 'cutting edge' inventions on April fool's day. They include elastic windscreens to bounce off insects and tiny wipers for the BMW badge.

In 1976, british astronomer patrick moore announced on the radio a once-in-a-lifetime astronomical event at 9.47 a.m. Because pluto was passing behind jupiter, the earth's gravity would alter slightly. Listeners were told to jump in the air at this exact moment and they would experience a floating sensation. Moore later said 'hundreds rang us to report feeling the sensation'.

Residents of sitka in alaska were alarmed when a dead Volcano, mount edgecumbe, began belching out thick black smoke. A local man, porky bickar, had flown hundreds of tyres into the Volcano's crater and set fire to them.

In 1976, richard branson designed a special balloon to resemble a Space Ship. he landed in london and stepped out in a Silver suit.

SB page 83

47 Apostrophes of abbreviation

REMEMBER

The apostrophe of abbreviation shows where a letter or letters have been missed out of a word: *you are → you're.*

Activity 1

A student has had to write lines on the blackboard many times. Below are some of the things he had to write. Put in the apostrophes where they have been missed.

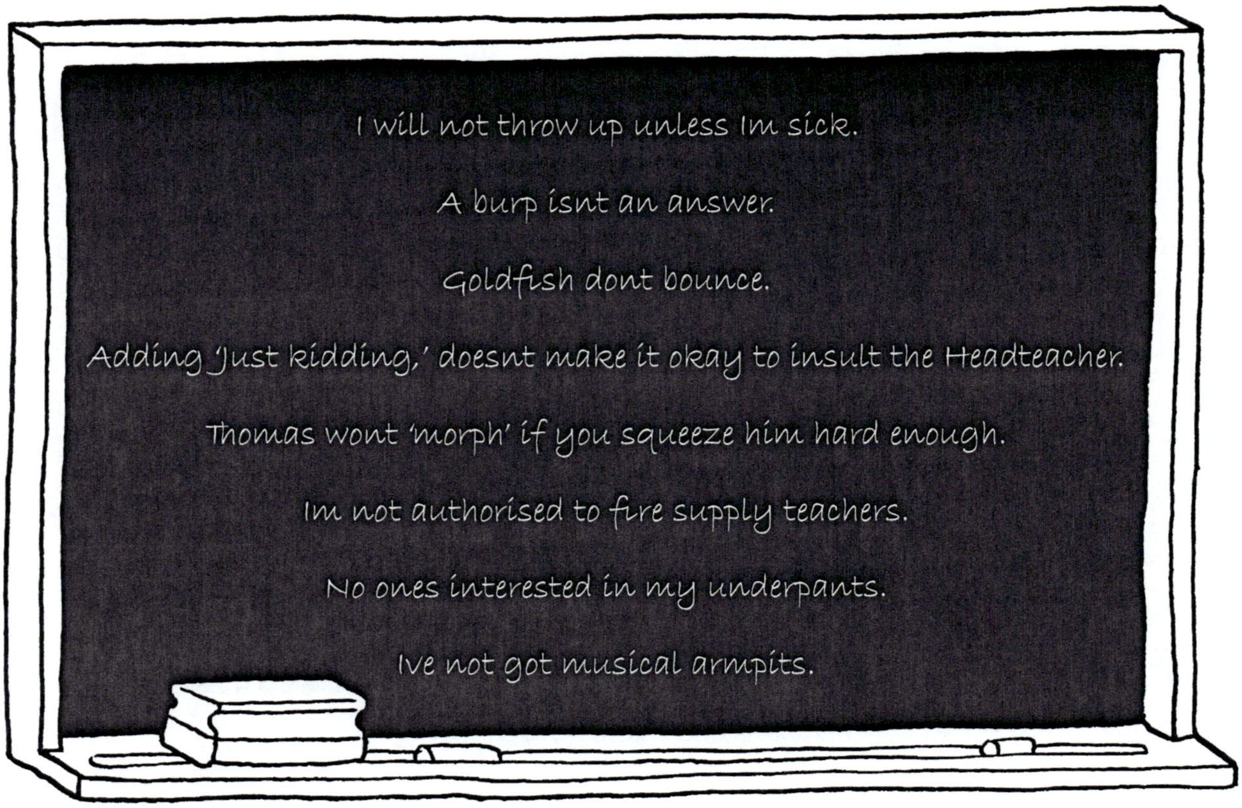

Activity 2

Turn the words below into abbreviations. Then write a sentence including each one.

1 they shall → __________ ______________________________

2 teacher has → __________ ______________________________

3 let us → __________ ______________________________

4 dare not → __________ ______________________________

5 it has → __________ ______________________________

6 dog will → __________ ______________________________

7 that has → __________ ______________________________

8 when will → __________ ______________________________

9 she would → __________ ______________________________

10 Tom is → __________ ______________________________

SB pages 84–86

48 Apostrophes of possession

REMEMBER

- If the 'owning' noun is singular, add an apostrophe and **s**: *David's Ferrari.*
- If the 'owning' noun is plural, just add an apostrophe: *nurses' union.*
- Irregular plurals need an apostrophe and **s**: *children's nursery.*

Activity 1

Apostrophes are missing from the titles of these books. Write in the apostrophes where they are needed.

Activity 2

Write a sentence for each pair of words below. It must include both words and show possession between them. The first one has been done for you.

1	country	flag	The country's flag was fluttering in the breeze.
2	classroom	door	
3	nurse	uniform	
4	farmer	tractor	
5	animals	cages	
6	King	crown	
7	people	favourite	
8	film	plot	
9	festival	atmosphere	
10	politicians	argument	

SB pages 90–91

Unit 8 MISC-SPELL-ANEOUS!

49 Homophones

REMEMBER

Homophones are words that sound the same but have different spellings and meanings: *break* / *brake*, *grown* / *groan*.

Activity 1

Write the correct word into the space to complete each sentence.

1	Be brave, stop being a ________________.	coward/cowered
2	Don't use slang, write ________________.	formerly/formally
3	The defender's ________________ in concentration cost a goal.	laps/lapse
4	He ________________ out the candles on the cake.	blue/blew
5	Don't give opinions, I want ________________.	facts/fax
6	Nothing grew at all, the land was ________________.	baron/barren
7	There were ten ________________ of chairs in the hall.	rose/rows
8	The referee sent him off for ________________.	dissent/descent
9	About the matter we ________________ last night…	disgust/discussed
10	________________ is a very dangerous drug.	Heroin/Heroine
11	The terrorists were fighting a ________________ war.	gorilla/guerrilla
12	The politician needed to ________________ support.	canvas/canvass
13	You need to ________________ your spelling.	practise/practice
14	Where are we going, your ________________ or mine?	plaice/place
15	The ________________ for the match was very poor.	attendants/attendance

Activity 2

Look back at the homophones you chose between in Activity 1. Write a sentence for ten of the homophones you DID NOT use. Use a dictionary to help you.

1 ____

2 ____

3 ____

4 ____

5 ____

6 ____

7 ____

8 ____

9 ____

10 ____

SB page 95

50 Silent letters

REMEMBER

Silent letters appear in the spelling of words but are not heard when the words are said aloud: *wi**t**ch*, ***k**nitting*, *com**b***.

Activity

Each sentence has missing silent letters. Write out each sentence correctly using the letters from the right.

		Missing letters
1	The restling exibition mach attracted many fans.	h w t
2	Were is the bucher's shop that sells the cheapest lam?	t b h
3	Wy has he put 15 garden nomes around the ege of his lawn?	d g h
4	The night presented the Princess with a wite silk hankerchief.	d k h
5	That colum is a list of gests – rite any new arrivals underneath.	w n u
6	I gess your nowledge of sychology is vast, professor?	k p u
7	The to gitarists produced a great rythm.	w u h
8	He riggled out of the car reck with barely a scrach.	w t w
9	Tying your laces in a not was pretty dum, to be onest.	b h k
10	If I don't get a receit I'll take your busness to cort and sue you!	p u i

Unit 9 THE SPELLING CHALLENGE

51 Commonly misspelled words (1)

Activity

Can you find all these words in the grid below?

blue	write	always	read	why
could	once	when	found	about
what	before	again	because	were
does	said	only	clean	goes
right	three	better	upon	these
where	would	every	eight	pretty
funny	together	today	please	fly
thank	four	myself	round	those
laugh	work	going	black	start
light	hurt	both	white	which

G	O	E	S	A	L	G	R	E	H	T	E	G	O	T	H	R	O	I	T
G	J	A	U	Y	Q	W	R	E	R	O	F	E	B	A	G	I	V	R	R
O	F	P	F	L	G	W	H	K	Q	P	Z	U	H	H	U	G	U	K	E
I	O	W	R	I	T	E	E	T	I	H	W	H	N	M	A	H	A	I	A
N	U	H	O	S	J	R	K	U	Q	B	T	U	C	N	L	T	S	P	D
Z	R	A	W	U	H	E	C	D	L	U	O	C	M	L	Y	V	C	B	Z
I	F	T	O	F	L	Y	A	B	P	T	D	T	R	A	T	S	Y	X	J
K	J	T	R	L	R	D	L	R	B	O	A	X	M	J	A	G	N	B	H
D	F	R	K	E	B	T	B	Q	S	A	Y	W	C	I	A	E	W	E	T
P	O	S	V	S	X	E	G	U	G	Y	D	H	D	W	X	H	D	C	O
L	B	E	F	Y	W	S	T	A	J	S	C	I	H	O	E	N	K	N	B
E	E	I	S	M	E	Z	I	T	U	J	L	C	H	R	V	D	G	O	Y
A	K	G	A	L	S	N	T	R	E	O	E	H	E	K	Y	L	N	O	W
S	R	N	Y	K	Y	V	C	K	M	R	A	N	B	E	T	B	W	X	E
E	F	I	Q	T	A	T	Q	Y	P	C	N	X	U	E	C	H	Y	Z	H
G	Z	O	H	D	W	H	Y	T	P	O	Y	L	F	T	C	M	G	T	Y
N	E	G	U	N	L	O	U	T	U	O	B	A	A	R	H	A	S	I	C
P	I	L	C	N	A	S	Q	E	D	R	O	U	N	D	O	A	U	T	L
E	V	E	I	D	D	E	M	R	T	H	E	S	E	X	E	L	N	S	F
N	E	H	W	W	V	N	D	P	D	E	E	R	H	T	U	W	F	K	E

52 Commonly misspelled words (2)

Activity 1

Pick a level. With a partner test each other on the words in the list. If you spell every word correctly, well done – you are a word wizard!

Level 1

people	teacher	please	purple	train
brother	children	nail	watch	wheel
night	story	helpful	giving	catch

Level 2

chair	year	great	iron	about
stopped	across	rabbit	straight	trade
racing	afternoon	afraid	doctor	doesn't

Level 3

really	almost	knife	another	laugh
everyone	balloon	because	scratch	scream
behind	lose	second	touch	birthday
flies	match	trouble	friend	should

Activity 2

Write in the missing words in the passage below. All of the missing words can be found in the lists above:

I remember the time my ________________ went mad at school. She was standing at the front of the class on a gloomy Monday ________________ when all of a sudden a boy released a live mouse! Blimey was she ________________. She let out a blood-curdling ________________ at the top of her voice and went bright ________________. She raced ________________ the room in about one ________________ flat. She ________________ knocked several desks flying and disappeared ________________ out the door. It was only when the Headmaster came in that we all finally stopped laughing! What a prank.

53 Commonly misspelled words (3)

Activity 1

caught	damage	address	interested	although
answer	disappear	quite	quiet	believe
knocked	remember	engine	enough	exciting
let's	library	breath	listen	sauce
centre	catch	whistle	changing	choice
clothing	ocean	written	squeeze	cousin
awful	helpful	until	happened	guard
highest	guest	action	decided	pleasant

Which of the words above fit into these puzzle strips? Fill in the missing letters then write out the word in full in the space provided.

r		m					r

		p	p				

			c	k		

			e	e		

i	n							e	d

			t	t		

g		a		

c					e

c		u			n

l			'	

Activity 2

Using words from the word bank above, create three of your own word strips, then test a partner with them.

54 Commonly misspelled words (4)

Activity 1

The passages below all contain spelling errors but you will need to find the mistakes yourself. Write the correct spelling of the words in the spaces beneath. Use the word bank below to help you.

Word bank

stomach	delicious	suggest	powerful	prejudiced
surprise	environment	imagine	attention	disappoint
question	beginning	represent	manufacture	treatment
memories	celebration	chocolate	favourite	fuel
science	wonderful	absence	contribute	schedule

1 My favourite delicous choclates are 'Celibrations'. They are manufatured by Cadbury's. You'll never be dissappointed when you open every wunderful pack. They are also my best suprise present for my mum, mainly because I just eat them all myself!

______ ______ ______ ______

______ ______ ______ ______

2 Scienc is my best subject. At the begining of the year we learned about the enviroment. In the second half term we learned about space and how powerfull rocket feul propels the space shuttle. I always pay atention when the teacher asks us questtions. In the future I want to be an inventor and imagin fabulous new technology.

______ ______

______ ______

______ ______

______ ______

Activity 2

Use some of the words in the word bank to create a passage to test your partner. Make some deliberate mistakes and try to catch your partner out!

55 Commonly misspelled words (5)

Activity 1

Create your own wordsearch. How many of the words below can you hide in the grid? When you have finished, pass the wordsearch to your partner. Can they find all your words?

addresses	muscle	scissors	ambulance	definite
shoulder	coupon	separately	governor	decoration
gracious	decisive	handsome	appreciate	happiness
headache	passenger	assignment	determine	description
heroes	disastrous	discriminate	beautifully	distributed
improvement	independent	maintenance	emptiness	knowledge
enormously	vacuum	excitement	experience	probably
accomplishment	exceptional	existence	acquire	fluid
unnecessary	embarrassment	harassment	mysterious	significance
fascinating	committee	nervously	frequently	occupation

56 Subject specific words – English

Activity

The answers to these quiz questions can all be found in the word bank below. Write out the answers in the spaces provided.

1. A class of words that describes actions ____________
2. Another word for a story ____________
3. Another word for a picture ____________
4. A group of letters fixed to the beginning of a stem ____________
5. A punctuation mark that looks like this ':' ____________
6. A special poem written vertically ____________
7. Type of newspaper, opposite to broadsheet ____________
8. A pair of poetry lines that rhyme ____________
9. A punctuation mark that looks like this ',' ____________
10. The opposite of non fiction ____________
11. A part of a play ____________
12. Words which sound alike at the end of poetic lines ____________
13. More than one ____________
14. A person in a play is generally called a… ____________
15. A piece from a text ____________

Word bank

verb	theme	scene	noun	speech
adverb	image	slang	drama	fact
sonnet	write	colon	discuss	contrast
ballad	ode	vowel	pun	draft
comma	quote	capital	poem	inform
comment	argue	blurb	prose	media
fiction	irony	rhyme	hyphen	analogy
emotion	summary	genre	narrative	accent
preposition	empathy	anecdote	antonym	stanza
opinion	imply	feature	article	extract
critical	clause	character	grammar	tabloid
literal	farce	phrase	singular	proverb
acrostic	simile	narrator	suffix	legend
symbolic	plural	audience	prefix	couplet
dialect	adjective	paragraph	insight	tragedy
parody	myth	persuade	pronoun	

57 Subject specific wordsearch – Mathematics

Activity

Can you find all these words in the grid below?

acute	area	degree	regular	equal
cosine	depth	factor	helix	axis
convex	compass	length	cubic	metre
litre	angle	pentagon	polygon	similar
square	chance	wrong	sine	volume
minus	width	vector	vertex	scale
calculate	centimetre	diagonal	dimension	height
horizontal	inverse	kilometre	adjacent	average
value	cylinder	distribution	ratio	isometric

E	Q	U	A	L	T	E	Z	O	X	G	C	H	A	N	C	E	G	T	Y
W	Y	R	V	D	I	S	T	R	I	B	U	T	I	O	N	J	I	H	C
A	D	G	O	H	R	A	L	I	M	I	S	C	W	A	E	V	S	E	X
X	H	L	L	P	S	B	C	P	A	K	T	Q	F	R	H	A	O	R	G
I	E	A	U	C	D	R	A	Y	E	V	R	H	U	E	U	L	M	T	L
S	L	T	M	O	N	S	V	Q	L	N	E	O	G	A	F	U	E	E	I
A	I	N	E	S	S	C	E	V	C	I	T	R	T	I	R	E	T	M	T
N	X	O	Q	I	J	A	C	S	I	P	N	A	A	C	E	E	R	O	R
G	T	Z	C	N	B	L	T	F	B	Z	I	D	G	G	A	H	I	L	E
L	S	I	N	E	M	E	O	F	U	I	K	U	E	O	E	F	C	I	V
E	C	R	J	I	Y	D	R	A	C	U	T	E	L	R	N	F	Z	K	M
D	E	O	M	E	T	R	E	W	R	B	N	O	I	S	N	E	M	I	D
I	E	H	K	W	D	M	U	I	L	C	A	L	C	U	L	A	T	E	W
A	R	O	I	T	A	R	L	D	Q	E	B	S	S	A	P	M	O	C	R
G	G	Q	X	V	P	D	Y	T	B	I	N	V	E	R	S	E	U	E	O
O	E	C	E	P	G	L	N	H	W	V	H	G	H	E	J	V	G	N	N
N	D	L	V	R	D	E	P	T	H	S	K	X	T	O	M	U	A	O	G
A	M	I	N	U	S	T	N	E	C	A	J	D	A	H	L	E	A	A	Y
L	Z	X	O	E	R	T	E	M	I	T	N	E	C	A	N	S	H	Z	W
X	O	T	C	G	N	O	G	Y	L	O	P	A	R	X	E	T	R	E	V

58 Subject specific words – Technology

Activity

Which of the words in the word bank below fit into these puzzle strips? Write out the word in the spaces provided, then copy out the completed word in the spaces beneath.

i	n								

g							s

	o						r

	r	e									

	i			

	c	c									

	e					h

	o	l			r

	a	m					e

v	e							

Word bank

computer	display	mouse	mobile	format
printer	safety	surface	grain	diet
scanner	pixel	force	icon	brief
colour	mineral	menu	fashion	vitamin
investigation	fibre	assemble	outcome	graphics
presentation	industrial	lathe	indicate	gluten
function	design	vegetable	criteria	protein
suitability	research	packaging	dyeing	preview
specification	efficiency	appearance	embroidery	elasticity
acceleration	implement	adjustable	laminate	diagram

Activity 2

Create three word strip puzzles of your own. Test them on a partner.

59 Subject specific words – Science

Activity

Create a science quiz to test your partner. Use the words below as your answers.

acid	lava	beaker	dilute	proton
plasma	funnel	digest	solvent	tissue
molten	tripod	watt	vein	voltage
sensor	joule	alcohol	artery	pigment
element	electron	extinct	density	hormone
fungus	alloy	spore	force	energy
alkaline	bacteria	oxygen	evaporation	formula
medicine	molecule	nucleus	nuclear	physics
ammeter	particle	electricity	experiment	gravity
humidity	structure	genetic	liquid	muscle

1 ______________________________ ____________

2 ______________________________ ____________

3 ______________________________ ____________

4 ______________________________ ____________

5 ______________________________ ____________

6 ______________________________ ____________

7 ______________________________ ____________

8 ______________________________ ____________

9 ______________________________ ____________

10 ______________________________ ____________

11 ______________________________ ____________

12 ______________________________ ____________

13 ______________________________ ____________

14 ______________________________ ____________

15 ______________________________ ____________

16 ______________________________ ____________

17 ______________________________ ____________

18 ______________________________ ____________

19 ______________________________ ____________

20 ______________________________ ____________

60 Subject specific words – Humanities

Activity

In the passages below, certain words have been deliberately misspelled. Write out the correct spellings in the spaces provided.

1 In Geography last term we learnt about the clymate, desserts and floods. We explored coastal erossion and how to read conturs on a map.

__________ __________ __________ __________

2 In Religious Education we learnt about Hindoo and other faiths. We were taught about the Byble, and the profets and how missonaries spread the Christian religion around the world.

__________ __________ __________ __________

3 In History last term we studied America. We started by exploring the early setlements, and the barrbaric treatment of the native American Indians. Then we moved onto the twentieth centurry and The Great Depresion. We looked at populaton growth and the growth of the car indistry.

__________ __________ __________ __________

__________ __________

Word bank

Bible	Hindu	faith	rite	saint
cause	atlas	desert	flood	iceberg
plain	pulpit	scale	gospel	moral
village	vicar	church	fault	valley
climate	condensation	erosion	continent	contour
spirit	racial	industry	depression	sediment
population	primary	abortion	refuge	secondary
settlement	Anglican	communist	civilisation	century
barbaric	typhoon	parable	missionary	festival
miracle	regional	prayer	prophet	founder
latitude	longitude	measure	algebra	diameter

Part C Answers and spelling games

Answers to Student Book activities

Unit 1 SPELLING STRATEGIES

Dictionaries and spell-checkers

Activity 2 (page 8)

table, tall, tangle, task, teeth, three, throw, tight, tired, tooth

Activity 3 (page 9)

Level 1

any, bat, deep, eat, fat, ham, jug, peel, self, team

Level 2

alert , burn, button, clear, exist, leader, light, multiply, mystery, orbit

Level 3

habit, hag, hairy, half, Halloween, hammer, hand, happy, hard, harp, hazard

Activity 4 (page 9)

I wonder whether a spell checker can find the words which I've spelled wrong?

Peer evaluation (page 9)

There are no mistakes in this newsletter because we used special software which checks your spelling. It is more or less a way to verify. However, it cannot correct errors in punctuation or usage and it will not find words which are misused but spelled right. For example, a paragraph could have many flaws but would be passed by the spell checker.

Breaking words into parts

Activity 1 (page 12)

1	nervous	=	ner/vous
2	obstruction	=	ob/struc/tion
3	fraction	=	frac/tion
4	sometimes	=	some/times
5	different	=	diff/e/rent
6	beginning	=	beg/inn/ing

Activity 2 (page 12)

replay, replaying, replayed, display, displaying, displayed, misplay, misplaying, misplayed, interplay, outplay, outplaying, outplayed, overplay, overplaying, overplayed, playful, playfully, playing, played, player

Letter patterns

Activity 2 (page 13)

Word	Start patterns	Word	Middle patterns	Word	End patterns
what	**wh-**	shu**tt**ing	**-tt-**	aw**ful**	**-ful**
knight	**kn-**	co**rr**upt	**-rr-**	wa**tch**	**-tch**
physical	**phy-**	trave**ll**er	**-ll-**	t**ough**	**-ough**
guile	**gu-**	ma**nn**ers	**-nn-**	wei**ght**	**-ght**
except	**ex-**	fi**tt**er	**-tt-**	vo**gue**	**-gue**
wrists	**wr-**	bo**bb**ed	**-bb-**	bund**le**	**-le**
		ach**ie**ve	**-ie-**		
		ch**ie**f	**-ie-**		

Proof-reading

Activity 2 (page 14)

aggression, excitement, extraordinary, manoeuvres, fierce, friends, achieve, success, surprise, incredible, beautiful, disastrous, ecstasy, opportunities, negotiate

A history of words

Activity 2 (page 15)

Possible answers

- The English language is still expanding.
- It is estimated that English is used by one-third of the world's population.
- The words 'get', 'take', husband' and 'wife' were brought into the English language in 787 when the Vikings invaded.
- When William the Conqueror led the French to invade England, the words 'castle', 'prison', 'challenge' and 'royal' were introduced into the English language.
- The first English dictionary was written in 1755 and contained over 40,000 words.

Activity 4 (page 16)

Possible answers

television

telegraph

telepathy

teleport

teletext

Peer evaluation (page 16)

Possible answers

Greek prefix	Meaning	Word found	Dictionary definition
anti	against	(anti)climax	disappointing end to something
auto	self	(auto)graph	signature of a celebrity
bio	life	(bio)logy	study of life
geo	earth	(geo)graphy	study of the earth
hydro	water	(hydro)electric	generation of electricity from water
micro	small	(micro)scope	instrument for viewing small objects
mega	big	(mega)phone	device for amplifying the voice

Activity 7 (page 17)

1. photograph
2. graph
3. triumph
4. paragraph
5. orphan
6. sphere
7. alphabet
8. earphones

Unit 2 VOWELS AND CONSONANTS

Activity 1 (page 24)

The longest and highest rollercoaster in the world is the Steel Dragon in Japan.

Activity 2 (page 24)

sink, Playstation 3, computer, football

Short vowels

Activity 1 (page 25)

Possible answers

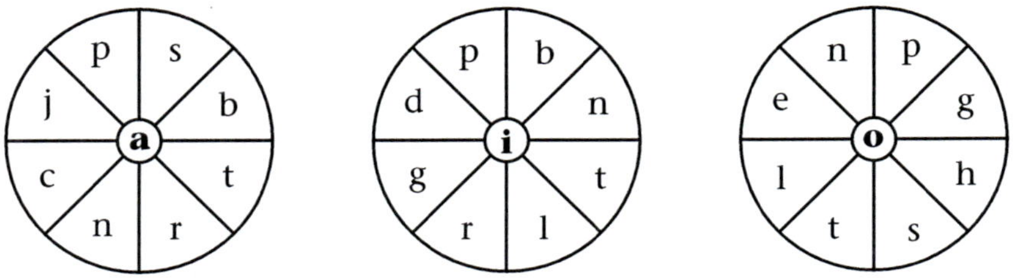

sat	jar	tip	rip	pot	lot
rat	can	pin	big	son	hop
bat	pan	lid	ring	not	ton
pat	tab	grid	pig	hot	slot
bar	nap	lip	pit	hog	got

Activity 2 (page 25)

short 'e' sound	short 'i' sound	short 'o' sound	short 'u' sound
(as in ten)	*(as in tip)*	*(as in top)*	*(as in tub)*
h**ea**d	m**y**stery	bec**au**se	g**oo**d
s**ai**d	cr**y**stal	w**a**s	br**o**ther
bag**ue**tte	ang**ui**sh	w**a**nder	t**oo**k
l**e**sson	cr**y**pt	sq**ua**bble	t**ou**gh
pl**ea**sure			r**ou**gh
fr**ie**nd			c**ou**ld

Activity 3 (page 25)

The correct letter patterns are underlined in the answer below.

Indiana Jones and the Kingdom of the Crystal Skull

(Rating: Very good)

In a crypt in ancient Peru, Indy and friends are busy keeping you on the edge of your seat. The plot should keep you guessing. A squad of zombies with missing heads makes for a pretty exciting opening. It's followed by enough brilliant action sequences to make your eyes pop out. Who said this fantastic series of films was dead? Take your mother. She'll love it.

Long vowels

Activities 1 and 2 (page 26)

Letter patterns that make the long vowel sound 'a'

Letter pattern	a (often)	ai (often)	ay (often)	ei (not often)	ey (not often)	ea (not often)
Example	fade	maid	delay	freight	they	break
	taking	afraid	away	eight		steak
	make	tailor	holiday			great
	famous		display			
	tame		play			
	amazing		delay			
	made					

Activities 4 and 5 (page 27)

Letter patterns that make the long vowel sound 'e'

Letter pattern	e (often)	ea (often)	ee (often)	ie (not often)	ei (not often)	i (not often)
Example	the	dream	wheel	grief	deceive	magazine
	we	team	steel	achievement	weird	ravines
	these	scream	feel			machine
	being		seems			
			been			
			sweep			
			feeling			

Activities 6 and 7 (page 27)

Letter patterns that make the long vowel sound 'i'

Letter pattern	i (often)	y (often)	ie (not often)	ye (not often)	uy (not often)	ey (not often)
Example	mine	hype	pie	dye	guy	eyesight
	might	flying	lies	eye	buy	
	fight	sky				
	night	dry				
	fine					
	wine					
	fines					
	crimes					
	delight					
	shines					
	bright					
	prize					

Activities 9 and 10 (page 28)

Letter patterns that make the long vowel sound 'u' as in blue

Letter pattern	u (often)	oo (often)	o (often)	ew (not often)
Example	blue	moon	move	crew
	June	soothed	who	brew
	ruby	spoon	lose	strewn
	rude	food	improved	blew
	clue	too	do	
		mood		
		loot		
		groove		
		snooker		

Letter patterns that make the long vowel sound 'u' as in cube

Letter pattern	u (often)	ue (not often)	ew (not often)	eu (not often)
Example	tune	fuel	new	feud
	tube	due	few	neutrals
	confused	Tuesday's	renew	
	pupil	argue		
	computer			
	dubious			

Unit 3 PLURALS

When to add 's' or 'es'

Activity 1 (page 30)

months, numbers, clashes, groups, parents, manufacturers, games, hundreds, meetings, speeches, hours, teenagers, consoles, supporters, monitors, illnesses, approaches, screens, kids, phones, buttons, switches, eyes, warnings, dangers, boxes, instructions

Activity 2 (page 31)

triumphs, reporters, strokes, races, hitches, things, corners, seconds, stresses, strains, problems, drivers, bunches, cars, finishes, chances

Words ending in 'f', 'ff'or 'fe'

Activity (page 32)

The correct words are underlined in the answer below.

Robin had never seen such a gang of <u>scruffs</u>, although their clothing blended perfectly with the <u>leaves</u> on the bushes and trees all around them. Without exception, they all had long <u>knives</u> hanging from their belts and looked very menacing. The men laughed loudly at him, howling like <u>wolves</u>. Robin knew he would have to call their <u>bluffs</u>. 'Who are you?' he yelled. 'Do you robbers and <u>thieves</u> have a leader?' Robin gulped as a huge man stepped forward. 'I lead these men. They call me Little John.' The atmosphere was tense as Robin asked. 'I believe this bridge is the only route over the river to Nottingham. Will you let me pass?'

'I don't care what your <u>beliefs</u> are, rich man.' He tossed a long, sturdy stick over to Robin. 'And now that we both have <u>staffs</u>, you'll have to beat me if you want to get past.'

Although the giant man smiled at him, Robin knew they'd both be fighting for their <u>lives</u>, with the loser being cast over the <u>cliffs</u> below them.

Words ending in 'y'

Activity 1 (page 33)

The correct words are underlined in the answers below.

7.30 p.m. *Eastenders*

Three different breweries are competing to buy the Queen Vic but the bins are full and the empties are piling up. The chip shop keys go missing. Can copies be cut before the Cornish pasties go off? To add to his worries, Ian realises his chimneys need rebuilding.

8.00 p.m. *Jamie Oliver – The Naked Chef*

Jamie explores a world of unusual curries and chutneys while visiting India. He also displays his versatile qualities when trying his hand at catering for wedding parties.

9.00 p.m. *The Holiday Programme*

From the luxuries found in the world's best hotels to budget getaways. The mysteries of the Norwegian Lakes are experienced on ferries while the beauties of Madagascar are explored on a range of trekking holidays. Follow the team as they cope with marauding monkeys on safari and all the novelties of a trip to Disneyland.

10.00 p.m. *Match of the Day*

Replays of today's games. Including Goal of the Month and your chance to vote for the worst penalties ever taken.

11.35 p.m. *The 50 funniest ever films*

The result of Tuesday's phone vote. What do the public think are the best comedies ever?

11.45 p.m. *Footballing dreams*

The second in this series of documentaries following young teenage footballers hoping to fulfil their dream of playing in the Premier League. The academies of the top clubs really put these young bodies through the ultimate fitness test.

Activity 2 (page 34)

The correct words are underlined in the answer below.

Dr Who: A British television institution.

Since 1963, Doctor Who has demonstrated uncanny abilities to banish bullies from different galaxies. His many enemies never quite manage to get the better of him. But even though the show is watched in countries all over the world, success has not come without many controversies.

Did you know?

- In the 1970s, moral campaigner Mary Whitehouse complained the stories were simply too scary.
- Armies of Daleks and Cybermen meant whole families watched Doctor Who from 'behind the sofa'. This phrase is now commonly used to describe TV shows with frightening content.
- A mother once complained that both her babies were terrified by the show's electronic theme music. Doctor Who was the first show to have completely electronic theme music, one of its many novelties.
- Shops in cities around the UK reported a drop in trade following an episode that showed window dummies coming to life.

Doctor Who still remains a firm date in many diaries however, even considering the many agonies we may suffer from behind the sofa.

Activity 3 (page 34)

1 motorways, ponies, injuries, jockeys
2 valleys, factories, centuries, turkeys
3 companies, allergies, policies, delays
4 varieties, strawberries, brandies, lollies
5 toys, birthdays, deliveries, emergencies

Words ending in 'o'

Activity 1 (page 35)

pianos, mangos/mangoes, igloos, radios, echoes, buffaloes, heroes, Eskimos, kangaroos, tomatoes, avocados, studios, mosquitoes, cellos, fiascos, cuckoos, tattoos, banjos

Irregular plurals

Activity 1 (page 35)

man – men	goose – geese
mouse – mice	ox – oxen
tooth – teeth	cactus – cacti

Activity 2 (page 35)

appendix – appendices
curriculum – curricula
datum – data
stimulus – stimuli
phenomenon – phenomena
oasis – oases
larva – larvae
criterion – criteria
formula – formulae
louse – lice

Unit 4 PREFIXES AND SUFFIXES

Prefixes

Activity 1 (page 37)

The stem is underlined.

uneven
antisocial
impossible
prefix
underground
misbehave
disobey
overdress
rebuild

Activity 2 (page 37)

The stem is underlined and the prefix is in bold.

preorder
preview
impossible
unsure
misbehave
overrated

Activity 3 (page 38)

misspell, misrule, misspent, immature, unnecessary, unnerve, underrated, overreact, overrated, overrule, overview, illegal, dissolve, dissent, innumerate

Activity 4 (page 38)

almost, always, mistakes, disappointment, illegal, immature, unnecessary

Activity 5 (page 38)

Not pleased or contented = dissatisfied
Completely unlike = dissimilar
Not essential or required = unnecessary
Freaked out = unnerved
Decide against somebody = overrule
Stops car from moving = immobiliser
Against the laws of nature = unnatural
Spell incorrectly = misspell
Young and not fully grown = immature
Person lives forever = immortal

Activity 6 (page 39)

The correct prefixes are in bold.

Teenagers are **under**stood to be **dis**appointed at **un**official council plans to play classical music at bus stops and other public places to **dis**courage them from hanging around them at night. **Re**searchers have **dis**covered that playing the classical tunes causes the children **dis**comfort. In other words it sends them nuts! One boy **re**acted with **dis**belief. "It's **un**necessary and an **over**reaction. People always **mis**take people my age for criminals. They think we are **im**mature vandals," he said. Council chiefs **re**fused to comment.

Peer evaluation (page 39)

disolved, disatified, imobile, unecessary, imoral, dissqualified, dissappointed, dissrepute

Suffixes

Activity 1 (page 40)

finding
landed
joyful
friendship
sickness
brightest

Activity 3 (page 40)

The stem is in bold and the suffix is underlined.

bright<u>est</u>	**price**<u>less</u>
polite<u>ly</u>	**snigger**<u>ed</u>
correct<u>ed</u>	**amuse**<u>ment</u>
teach<u>er</u>	**event**<u>ually</u>
care<u>less</u>	**ask**<u>ed</u>

Suffixes: adding -ful to stems

Activity 1 (page 41)

beautiful, colourful, delightful, wonderful, peaceful, tasteful, cheerful, helpful, thoughtful, restful, successful

Adding suffixes to stems: when to keep the 'e'

Activity 1 (page 42)

hopeful, priceless, wireless, careful, movement, darkness, goodness, advertisement

Activity 2 (page 42)

A	Z	Y	B	M	X	V	K	X	N	G	L	K
M	D	Q	R	O	O	T	N	R	Y	K	X	P
A	I	V	R	R	F	Q	O	E	X	O	C	L
N	P	O	A	T	U	O	W	C	H	O	O	C
A	O	U	L	N	H	N	L	H	N	E	U	H
G	Y	T	F	Q	T	T	E	A	O	X	R	A
E	W	R	I	M	K	A	D	R	K	I	A	N
A	G	A	K	C	M	N	G	G	W	C	G	G
B	V	G	A	X	E	X	E	E	Z	H	E	E
L	Q	E	I	F	X	A	A	A	O	U	O	A
E	A	O	N	Q	N	V	B	B	H	U	U	B
C	X	U	Y	X	D	J	L	L	S	D	S	L
Z	I	S	Z	N	T	U	E	E	E	O	X	E

manageable, outrageous, knowledgeable, chargeable, courageous, changeable, noticeable, advantageous

When to drop the 'e'

Activity 1 (page 43)

believable, believer, believing, believed, believes
creating, created, creates
disagreeable, disagreeing, disagreed, disagrees
education, educating, educated, educates
facer, facing, faced, faces
forcer, forcing, forced, forces
foreseen, foreseeable, foreseeing, foresees
lovable, lover, loving, loved, loves

Activity 2 (page 43)

amusing, careless, forceful, aching, believer, excitement, spiteful, saver, forgiveness, noticeable, management, homeless, excited, rechargeable, agreement, desirable

Suffixes and stems: doubling

Activity 1 (page 44)

Words with one syllable:

pat, feel, pay, quit, dream, treat, space, glad, bed, clap, sad, bar, pet, clip, bet, trap, stem, stop, tree, grape, train, stab, burst, tap, sky, throb, red, rid, star, fail, trek

Words with one short vowel sound:

<u>pat</u>, feel, pay, <u>quit</u>, dream, treat, space, <u>glad</u>, <u>bed</u>, <u>clap</u>, <u>sad</u>, bar, <u>pet</u>, <u>clip</u>, <u>bet</u>, <u>trap</u>, <u>stem</u>, <u>stop</u>, tree, grape, train, <u>stab</u>, burst, <u>tap</u>, sky, <u>throb</u>, <u>red</u>, <u>rid</u>, star, feel, <u>trek</u>

Words that have one consonant as the final letter:

<u>pat</u>✓, feel, pay, <u>quit</u>✓, dream, treat, space, <u>glad</u>✓, <u>bed</u>✓, <u>clap</u>✓, <u>sad</u>✓, bar, <u>pet</u>✓, <u>clip</u>✓, <u>bet</u>✓, <u>trap</u>✓, <u>stem</u>✓, <u>stop</u>✓, tree, grape, train, <u>stab</u>✓, burst, <u>tap</u>✓, sky, <u>throb</u>✓, <u>red</u>✓, <u>rid</u>✓, star, feel, <u>trek</u>✓

Activity 2 (page 45)

Possible answers:

patter, patting, patted
quitter, quitting, quitted
gladder, gladden
bedding, bedded
clapper, clapping, clapped
sadder, sadden
petting, petted
clipper, clipping, clipped
better, betting, betted
trapper, trapping, trapped
stemming, stemmed
stopper, stopping, stopped
stabber, stabbing, stabbed
tapper, tapping, tapped
throbbing, throbbed
reddish, redden
ridden
trekker, trekking, trekked

Activity 3 (page 45)

skipper, quitter, fitter, skipper, quitter, grabbed, getting, swimming, dipping, dropping, trapping, stopping, sitting, running, skipping, trekking

Peer evaluation (page 45)

1. tap, sit, quit, ship
2. fit, nap, jet
3. drip, sun, sap, mop, plop
4. pit, whip, pop, strip
5. lip, trip, fun, kit
6. rip, trap, grip, zip

Suffixes and stems: the 'l' rule

Activity 2 (page 46)

marvellous, channelled, chiselling, modelled, shovelled, compelling, cancelled, quarrelling, unrivalled, travellers, propelled

Suffixes and stems: changing 'y' to 'i'

Activity 1 (page 47)

prettiest, beautiful, happiest, envied, joyful, easily, married, employment, busier, merrily

Activity 2 (page 47)

destroyed, enemies, terrifying, mightiest, qualities, victories, injuries, abilities, enjoyment, heaviest

Unit 5 COMMON LETTER PATTERNS

Soft and hard letters

Activities 1 and 2 (page 50)

Hard 'c' words	Soft 'c' words	Hard 'g' words	Soft 'g' words
can't	certain	argue	dodgy
magic	notice	good	huge
can	per cent	get	magic
excuse		English	
actual		spelling	
fact		something	
strict		using	
		being	

Soft 'c' spellings

Activity 1 (page 51)

Hard 'c' words: can't, clever, cartoons, craziness, circus, clowns, candyfloss, reckon

Soft 'c' words: Alice, choice, certainly, cinema, fancy, circus, decision, Lucy

Activity 2 (page 51)

1. fence
2. pierce
3. vacancy
4. cinder
5. racism
6. cereal
7. menace
8. glance
9. citizen

Activity 3 (page 51)

- The words ending in **-iss** have one syllable.
- The words ending in **-ice** have more than one syllable.

Activity 4 (page 51)

1 palace
2 surface
3 populace
4 grimace
5 terrace
6 furnace

Soft 'cy', 'ce' and 'ci' spellings

Activity 1 (page 52)

1 democracy
2 lunacy
3 ecstasy
4 decency
5 pharmacy
6 prophecy
7 uneasy
8 frequency
9 supremacy
10 clumsy

Activity 2 (page 52)

The corrected words are shown in bold.

Breaking news. Click a link for more…

* **Cyanide** poison threat in supermarket **juice forces emergency** recall
* **Civil Service redundancy** problem
* **Divorce** for **celebrity** chef
* **Glaciers facing** meltdown crisis
* **Defence** lawyer blames government **complacency**

Soft 'g' spellings

Activity 1 (page 53)

- Hard 'g' words: groan, gather, dog, geography, bigger, guilt, goat, gum, flag, garden, gain
- Soft 'g' words: geography, sewage, digit, lounge, biology, ginger, voltage, gym, origin, germ

Activity 2 (page 53)

The correct words are underlined.

a Geometry genius indulges his passion for angles
b Gentle giant takes the plunge
c Jogging binges are bad for your health
d Young at heart or old for your age?
e Shortage of magicians worries magic circle
f Regional differences in language are huge
g Fragile jewel joins national museum collection

'-ge' and '-dge' endings

Activity 1 (page 54)

The correct words are underlined.

HEDGE DISPUTE CAUSES OUTRAGE

The sleepy village of Holloway erupted with savage scenes of revenge earlier this week. An argument concerning a hedge running along the edge of neighbouring cottages was at the centre of the disturbance. Chris Bigland alleges that his neighbour, Lynda Taylor, has carried out a series of attacks on his property. "She claims the hedge is too high," says Mr Bigland, "But it gives me plenty of privacy. She challenged me about it but I told her it was staying. Then strange things began to happen."

Mr. Bigland claims that Mrs Taylor has sent foul-smelling packages through the post, one of which contained rotting cabbage. In addition, thousands of pounds worth of damage was done to his car: "She stuffed sausages up the exhaust pipe and poured porridge into the petrol tank. It's completely wrecked; there's no chance of salvage."

Mrs Taylor was filled with rage when told of the accusations. "Do I look like the sort of person to h old a grudge and go on a rampage like that? I acknowledge the fact I complained about his hedge but only because he won't cut it on my side. I can't manage it at my age. I don't care how tall it is."

With neither side willing to budge, the peaceful image of this beautiful village looks likely to be ravaged for quite some time.

'ph' words

Activity 1 (page 55)

1 microphone
2 feathers
3 pharmacy
4 prophet
5 daffodil
6 physics
7 typhoon
8 perfume
9 typhoid
10 phones

Activity 2 (page 55)

The correct words are underlined.

English lessons used to be fun but now I've got a real phobia about them. Learning the alphabet was easy, but since then I've felt such a fool. Splitting my writing into paragraphs can be a bit tricky although I find that simple compared to some of the other stuff. Those apostrophes look like floating commas to me so getting those right is always a fluke. I get confused between metaphors and similes and euphemisms scare the living daylights out of me. If it was left to me I'd call a hyphen a 'dash', and homophones sound like something for sending text messages. It's just not fair!

'ei' or 'ie' spellings?

Activity 1 (page 56)

1 airfield
2 ceiling
3 Chief
4 receivership
5 piece
6 shield
7 believe
8 brief
9 deceitful
10 thief

Activity 2 (page 56)

The correct words are underlined.

Dear Laura,

I'm sorry to hear you're having so much grief with the behaviour of your niece. She sounds like a little fiend. Shrieking at the local priest like that must have been unbelievably embarrassing. You need all the support you can receive so please don't hesitate to call on me if you need relief from the situation.

Your friend,

Elizabeth

Activity 3 (page 57)

Here are some example answers with the suffixes underlined.

replied, agencies, currencies, tendencies, melodies, emergencies, injuries, frequencies, robberies

Activity 4 (page 57)

sci/ence – 2 syllables
di/et – 2 syllables
au/di/ence – 3 syllables
so/ci/e/ty – 4 syllables
con/ve/ni/ent – 4 syllables
ca/shi/er – 3 syllables
ex/pe/ri/ence – 4 syllables
pre/mi/er – 3 syllables
va/ri/e/ty – 4 syllables
in/gre/di/ent – 4 syllables

'ch' and 'tch' words

Activity 1 (page 58)

The correct words are underlined.

- New at Brumby's Butchers – top quality ostrich burgers. Try them with our special ketchup.
- Daly's dispatch riders – we fetch and carry without a hitch.
- Teach yourself archery from scratch. No previous experience required. Apply to Jo Hawkyard at P.O. box 235.

- Screeching brakes? Dodgy clutch? Engine lost its punch? Top notch repairs carried out at Belper Autos.
- Catch a quick lunch at Marple's Deli. Poached fish a speciality.
- Switch to a brand new kitchen with Lilleyman's. Ditch the old, bring in the new and watch the value of your home soar.
- Mulgrew's single malt Scotch whisky. Each purchase with free glass.
- Munch and crunch your way through a delicious packet of Calladine's crisps. There's nothing to match them.
- Private Detective agency. Suspect treachery? Searching for the truth? All research carried out in strictest confidence. Call Phil Whitney at once.

Activity 2 (page 58)

The correct words are underlined.

1. The beach is scorching hot today.
2. Approach the area carefully because of the hidden trench.
3. Can you reach up there and pass me the bleach?
4. I drew a church on my sketch pad.
5. That pitch is in terrible condition for a Premier League match.

'ch' or 'sh' words

Activity (page 59)

1. pistachio
2. shepherd
3. chauffeur
4. chandelier
5. ricochet
6. shuttlecock
7. parachute
8. moustache
9. chalet
10. nonchalant

'ch' or 'k' words

Activity (page 59)

1. monarch
2. anarchy
3. napkin
4. school
5. choir
6. melancholy
7. ankle
8. kebab
9. psychology
10. Christmas
11. schedule
12. skull
13. technique
14. orchid
15. chemical

'ou' letter patterns

Activity 1 (page 60)

The correct answers are underlined.

Teenagers banned

Strict measures have been announced that are intended to reduce the number of complaints concerning rowdy incidents in the town centre. Council leader Heather Beveridge pronounced: "We are mounting this campaign to stop crowds of louts and yobs hanging around the shopping precinct and fountain in the evenings. I'm dumbfounded that they're even allowed outside at such a late hour."

Unsurprisingly local teenagers were not impressed. Matt Boyle, aged 15, argued: "There's never any hassle. We're just hanging about with mates." Suman Sharma, 16, added: "She's just power crazy that Beveridge woman, looking for something to pounce on to grab a few headlines."

Police confirmed that the area did not cause them particular concern. "There's a bit of shouting occasionally, but that doesn't amount to much," said PC Adam Walton, community officer for the area. "Those kids know the boundaries." Councillor Beveridge stood her ground, however. "I've received a mountain of letters about a countless number of problems. We have the power to impose a ban and that's exactly what we intend to do."

Activity 2 (page 60)

1	couch	7	blouse
2	lounge	8	prowl
3	surround	9	mouse
4	frown	10	pound
5	voucher	11	gouge
6	vowel	12	rebound

Activity 3 (page 61)

1	couple	7	odious
2	curious	8	butcher
3	gullible	9	cousin
4	nourish	10	muffin
5	nougat	11	pompous
6	famous	12	precious

Peer evaluation (page 61)

The correct missing words are: trouble, serious, young, enormous, must, bogus, jealous, furious, would, trouble, various, obvious, envious.

'w' letter patterns

Activity 1 (page 62)

The correct answers are underlined.

1. My wrist-<u>watch</u> has broken. I <u>want</u> a new one for my birthday.
2. <u>What</u> was that awful smell that came <u>wafting</u> through here?
3. <u>Was</u> it a <u>wasp</u> or a bee that stung you?

Activity 2 (page 62)

The correct answers are underlined.

Terrorist <u>warmonger</u> <u>warned</u> by UN

<u>Lukewarm</u> weather causes locust <u>swarm</u>

Traffic <u>warden</u> receives safety <u>award</u>

Students <u>thwart</u> early <u>warning</u> scheme

Move <u>toward</u> postal elections brings no <u>rewards</u>

Activity 3 (page 62)

1. worm
2. worthy
3. work
4. world
5. worst
6. worship

'q' letter patterns

Activity 1 (page 63)

The correct answers are underlined.

1. The <u>mosquito</u> bite made me feel <u>queasy</u>.
2. The peach <u>liqueur</u> did not <u>quench</u> my thirst.
3. Did you <u>acquire</u> tickets for the <u>banquet</u>?
4. The speaker was <u>eloquent</u> but <u>quickly</u> put me to sleep.
5. That <u>turquoise</u> dress is <u>exquisite</u>.

Activity 2 (page 63)

1. quadruple
2. quarantine
3. squander
4. squalor
5. qualify

Activity 3 (page 63)

The correct answers are underlined.

A <u>freak</u> event occurred during a visit to a local <u>mosque</u> yesterday afternoon. Visiting <u>monks</u> had travelled from Tibet to admire <u>antique</u> paintings and other <u>unique</u> works of art, when a golden <u>plaque</u> fell from a wall, striking one of the visitors on the head. Luckily the injury was not serious, although a <u>mark</u> was left on the fallen object.

Unit 6 COMMON ENDINGS

'-ough', '-ought' and '-aught' endings

Activity 1 (page 66)

Rhymes with:	stuff	show	scoff	now
	tough	though	cough	plough
	rough	dough	trough	bough
	enough	although		

Activity 3 (page 66)

The correct answers are underlined.

1. My mum bought me a gift. I never thought it would be an iPhone.
2. I ought to tell my dad I got nought in my maths exam.
3. Boxers are taught to be tough!

'-ous', '-ious' and '-eous' endings

Activity 1 (page 67)

Dangerous, fabulous, famous, enormous, joyous, nervous, marvellous, generous, monstrous, poisonous, venomous, jealous, ridiculous

Activity 3 (page 68)

precious, devious, mysterious, serious, glorious, ambitious, infectious, ingenious

Activity 4 (page 68)

'shus' sound following 't', 'c' or 'x'

precious
ambitious
infectious

'i' as a syllable heard on its own:

devious
mysterious
serious
glorious
ingenious

Activity 5 (page 68)

gorgeous, outrageous, courageous, spontaneous, courteous, hideous

'-tion', '-ssion', '-cian' and '-sion' endings

Activities 1 and 2 (page 69)

action, relaxation, sensation, exhilaration, destruction, domination, competition, opposition, addition, promotion, accommodation, instruction, tuition, solutions, revolution

-tion (long vowel before 'shun' sound)	-tion (consonant before 'shun' sound)	-tion (after short vowel 'i' sound doesn't end mission)
sensation relaxation exhilaration domination promotion accommodation solution revolution	*instruction* action destruction	*tuition* competition opposition addition

Activity 3 (page 70)

obsession, profession, impression, discussion, aggression, compassion, admission, depression, permission, confession

Activity 4 (page 70)

1. opposition
2. tradition
3. procession
4. definition
5. ambition
6. percussion
7. discussion
8. compassion
9. competition
10. obsession
11. consolation
12. permission
13. condition
14. relaxation
15. submission
16. destruction

Activity 6 (page 71)

The correct answers are underlined.

1. The tension towards the end of the match was unbearable.
2. My granddad is 65, so now he's started collecting his pension.
3. A mirage is an illusion in the desert.
4. Getting a person to do something is called the art of persuasion.
5. My holiday was a brilliant occasion.
6. There's never anything on television.
7. When I make a decision I stick to it.

Activity 7 (page 71)

The correct answers are underlined.

Most people love watching fast-action animation films like *Shrek* or *Wallace and Grommit* at the cinema or on television. But did you know that these days animation is within reach of anyone with a computer, decent software and the ambition? If you have the vision and the passion, you can create wonderful stop-motion films and become a technician of the artform. The decision is yours to create a perfect expression of your imagination. You decide the location, the story, the conclusion. Whatever your intention, give it a try!

'-le', '-el' and '-al' endings

Activity 1 (page 72)

bubble, able, fable, double, circle, eagle, buckle, cackle, rifle, table, beetle, dazzle, bottle

Activity 4 (page 73)

paranormal, sceptical, supernatural, magical, mystical, trial, mental, ancestral, brutal, historical, survival, unconventional, unusual, special, total, exceptional, hysterical, normal, national

'-able' and '-ible' endings

Activity 1 (page 74)

dependable, unreasonable, fashionable, unsuitable, miserable, syllable, preferable, avoidable, reasonable, predictable

Activity 3 (page 74)

1. sensible
2. incredible
3. audible
4. impossible
5. accessible
6. horrible
7. invisible

'-ical', '-icle' and '-acle' endings

Activity 1 (page 75)

Science and Technology	Arts and Humanities
medical	alphabetical
logical	lyrical
biological	metaphorical
optical	musical
practical	historical
technical	geographical
mechanical	physical
electrical	biblical
chemical	political
clinical	critical
astronomical	classical

Activity 3 (page 75)

Medical miracle in optical hospital

Critical chemical leak at electrical factory

Political scandal hits government

Classical musical flops

Mechanical fault causes technical failure

Fake painting identical to original

Activities 4 and 5 (page 76)

-acle	**-icle**
tentacle	icicle
barnacle	particle
miracle	chronicle
oracle	article
obstacle	vehicle
spectacle	
manacle	
pinnacle	

Activity 7 (page 76)

The correct spellings are underlined.

According to a recent article a new miracle cure for baldness has just been announced by medical experts. It's a chemical that has been proved in clinical trials. Patients were critical at first but now say it works. Doctors say it is effective because it strengthens every individual hair follicle.

'-ence' and '-ance' endings

Activity 1 (page 77)

1. A group of words which start with a capital letter and end with a full stop = sentence
2. To move forward = advance
3. The quality of being outstanding or superior = excellence
4. The space separating two things = distance
5. A novel or film with love as its theme = romance
6. Another word for money = finance
7. A door or gate that people enter through = entrance

Activity 2 (page 77)

-ence	-ance
defence	dominance
violence	advance
residence	admittance
	entrance
	instance

Activity 3 (page 77)

The corrected answers are underlined.

When 'Evil the Weavel' ace stunt rider tried to jump a new record-breaking distance last week, he ended up in an ambulance. He tried to make a clearance of 52 double-decker buses but his unsuccessful performance shocked the audience. There's no doubt about his usual competence on the bike: he's got so much experience, but in this instance he lost his balance and slam dunked!

'-ate' and '-ite' endings

Activity 1 (page 78)

1	Straight away	immediate
2	Work as a team	cooperate
3	Determined not to agree with others	obstinate
4	To find the best route to somewhere	navigate
5	To produce energy	generate
6	To do up a property	renovate
7	To speed up	accelerate
8	To put up with something	tolerate
9	The very best	ultimate
10	To oil moving parts	lubricate
11	To enjoy	appreciate
12	Put into another language	translate
13	An approximate calculation	estimate
14	Unlucky	unfortunate

The secret message is: I congratulate u

Activity 2 (page 78)

'-ite' sounding like a short vowel 'i'	'-ite' sounding like a long vowel 'i'
favourite	dynamite
petite	write
	white
	satellite
	unite

Unit 7 SPELLING AND PUNCTUATION

Capital letters

Activity 1 (page 81)

1. When Stoke City play Notts County on Sunday, the two oldest football teams in the globe are facing each other.
2. The man said, "Do you know what Tom? I'm really proud to be a Londoner and I can't wait for the Olympic Games to start here."
3. Even though Shaakirah loved Pepsi, she had a soft spot for Dr Pepper too.
4. Adam asked, "Are you watching Coronation Street on TV tonight?" Sam replied, "No, I'm going into Manchester to see my Uncle Eric."

Activity 2 (page 82)

Corrections are underlined.

Star Wars is probably the most successful film franchise of all time. The first film, *Episode IV: A New Hope*, was released in 1977. Since then, a further six films have been released, earning approximately $2.5 billion in the USA alone. Characters such as Darth Vader and Yoda are recognised around the entire world and the cultural impact of the films is huge. 390,000 English fans even named the Jedi 'faith' as their official religion, according to a census taken in 2001.

When the actor Alec Guinness said "May the force be with you," little did he know that, years later, this short line would become the source of the religion's 'official' day of celebration. 'May the force' sounds very similar to 'May the 4th,' and so this day was adopted by fans. Don't be surprised to hear the following conversation in early summer:

"Happy Star Wars day!"

"What?"

"May the 4th be with you!"

Apostrophes of abbreviation

Activity (page 83)

The answers are underlined.

I can't believe it. I really didn't think I'd a chance of winning. It's the greatest moment of my life. Of course you don't win an award like this on your own. There are so many others I'd like to give my thanks to. First, huge hugs and kisses to my director. Steven's a remarkable man, he's just so dedicated. Then there's my stylist Candelabra; she's got such awesome talent with a mascara brush. I would also like to praise Stella who's the greatest designer ever, and Lucille, who had a real job organising my hectic life for me. Last, of course, I'd like to thank Mum and Dad; they're simply the best. And of course there's you, my adoring fans. You're the greatest. I love you all!

Apostrophes of possession

Activity 1 (page 84)

Here are some possible answers.

The **car's tyre** had a puncture.

The **teapot's spout** was broken.

The **victim's injury** was painful.

The **footballers' luxury homes** were expensive.

The **decorator's paint** was white.

The **old lady's handbag** got stolen.

The **students' party** was very noisy.

The **politician's opinion** was biased.

The **warriors' battle-cry** was fierce.

The **rap star's CD** sold a million copies.

Activity 2 (page 85)

Dad's Army

National Lampoon's Animal House

Monty Python's Life of Brian

Breakfast at Tiffany's

The Simpsons' Halloween Episodes
Harry Potter and The Philosopher's Stone
Billy Connolly's World Tour of Australia
A Bug's Life
Pirates of The Caribbean: Dead Man's Chest
Ocean's Eleven
One Flew Over the Cuckoo's Nest
William Shakespeare's Romeo and Juliet
The Flintstones' Christmas Party
Peter Kay's Phoenix Nights
Wayne's World
My Best Friend's Wedding
A History of the Champions' League
Charlotte's Web
Dr. Seuss' How The Grinch Stole Christmas

Activity 3 (page 86)

- **a** **Saturdays** only
- **b** Local **Businesses**
- **c** **Desserts**
- **d** There are no strangers here. Just **friends** that haven't met yet!!!
- **e** **Families** dining are welcome until 6pm
- **f** Part Time **Chefs/Cooks** Required

Activity 4 (page 86)

- Elephants are the only mammal that can't jump.
- Like fingerprints, everyone's tongue prints are different.
- A hedgehog's heart sometimes beats 300 times a minute.
- Camels have three eyelids to protect them from sand storms.
- Cows' milk causes more allergies than any other food.
- Ostriches' eyes are bigger than their brains.
- Bananas aren't really fruits, they're berries.
- Men's noses and ears never stop growing.
- Don't burp or sneeze in churches in Nebraska, USA: it's against the law!
- There's a Stockholm restaurant that only sells garlic products. It's even got garlic cheesecake!

Hyphens

Activity (page 87)

Possible answers

1 I will *resign* from my job at the end of the month.
The caretaker will need to *re-sign* the toilets more clearly.

2 *Man eating tiger* caught on camera! (newspaper headline)
The *man-eating tiger* prowled around the forest.

3 You will need to *reserve* a table at the restaurant.
He can *re-serve* the leftovers with dinner.

4 The broken arm will *recover* fully.
She needs to remember to *re-cover* the food after serving.

5 *Used car salesman* stands trial
I bought my old car from a *used-car salesman.*

6 There were more than *50 year-old* puppies in the shop.
50-year-old puppies defy science (newspaper headline)

How many words?

Activity (page 87)

1. There's a lot of noise.
2. I had already finished.
3. My room is upstairs.
4. Move a bit to the left.
5. I'm going as well.
6. She's in front of me.
7. No one will talk to me.
8. It's underneath the rug.

Unit 8 MISC-SPELL-ANEOUS!

Homophones

Activity 1 (page 90)

The correct words are underlined.

1. There's a hole in the floor where a cold draught is blowing in.
2. Don't steal from shops, you'll get caught by store detectives.
3. The price of that tomato sauce is very cheap.
4. After that long walk my feet are extremely sore.
5. I don't really like black jeans, only blue ones.

Activity 4 (page 91)

The correct words are underlined.

Dear Sir,

I have the need to write to you following a painful experience I suffered in your restaurant last week.

I knew things were going to be poor right from the start as the table was extremely dirty. The bread on the table did not look fresh. In fact I broke a tooth when I tried to bite it. The main course was not cooked properly because the steak was raw. It also took an hour to arrive. The pears in the sweet were still frozen. The wine tasted like vinegar and the staff ignored my complaints.

I have been to many restaurants all over the world, but I have never seen such dreadful food. Do you think a guest should be treated like this? Would you put up with such awful service? Everything I ate made me want to be sick.

I would be grateful for a full explanation as soon as possible.

Yours faithfully,

'there', 'their' and 'they're'

Activity (page 92)

The correct answers are underlined.

1. If that's their idea of a good time, they're crazy?
2. If there was a different route, their information was incorrect.
3. They're looking in the wrong place, it's over there.
4. If they're well-behaved, I'll increase their pocket money soon.
5. I'll take their photographs when they're looking this way.

'its' and 'it's'

Activity (page 92)

The correct answers are underlined.

1. Because the house is damp, it's going to lose some of its value.
2. It's a simple game but only when you know its rules.
3. My laptop lost its Internet connection so it's been difficult to work.
4. It's going to take a while but I'll let you know when it's finished.
5. Its poor service meant the hotel couldn't improve its reputation.

'to', 'too' and 'two'; 'your' and 'you're'

Activity 1 (page 93)

The correct answers are underlined.

1. If you want to feel ill, drink too many milkshakes.
2. She needed two attempts to get the right answer.
3. Whenever I go to see friends, my sister has to come too.
4. It's far too early for me to do anything energetic.
5. She needs to understand that it's happened too often.
6. We need to get there by two o'clock.

7 Those directions to the park aren't too clear.

8 I'm going to the doctor as I can't get to sleep at night.

9 If you want to be successful, learn to organise yourself.

10 The library was too quiet for Sarah; she wanted to giggle!

Activity 2 (page 93)

The correct answers are underlined.

1 To improve your image, you're going to have to work very hard.

2 Your best friend is one you're sure you can trust.

3 You'll find your bag underneath your bed.

4 I hope you're certain that it wasn't your fault.

5 I think you're wrong. Your English teacher is much better than mine.

6 When you're in a better mood you can have your pocket money.

7 If you're listening carefully you're going to understand more.

8 Your biggest fault is you're always late.

9 You're being very generous but the credit is all yours.

10 I would like your opinion if you're sure you have the time.

'past' and 'passed'

Activity 2 (page 94)

The correct answers are underlined.

1 A worried look passed between them as they walked past the hospital.

2 It's nearly a quarter past four. If he'd passed he'd have rung by now.

3 He strolled past his old home without sorrow. The heartache was firmly in the past now.

4 He passed ten GCSEs, all with top grades.

5 I passed the shop without realising it.

'off' and 'of'

Activity 1 (page 94)

The correct answers are underlined.

1 He got off the bus and grabbed a cup of coffee.

2 One of the best ways of getting slim is to work off the calories with exercise.

3 Turning things off at the mains will save lots of money.

4 On the fifth of November you'll hear many fireworks going off.

5 You're out of luck: the milk has gone off.

Silent letters

Activity 1 (page 95)

The corrected words are underlined.

Dear Madam,

Last Wednesday I spoke to one of your staff concerning when my mortgage would be confirmed. I spent an hour being reassured that as soon as I signed the papers everything would be completed by the start of February. The letter I received today now says that early autumn is the best I can expect. Do you know why this is? The owners of the building I want to buy are becoming impatient and I feel guilty about messing them about.

Please write immediately as I'm having doubts about the whole thing.

Yours faithfully,

Activity 2 (page 95)

The corrected words are underlined.

1 The church organist was playing a solemn hymn.

2 I'm not so handsome now I've got so many wrinkles.

3 I often go climbing at the weekend.

4 The cupboard was full of biscuit crumbs.

5 Knock three times and the castle guard will let you pass.

Answers to Student Book self-tests

Unit 2 VOWELS AND CONSONANTS

Self-test 1 (page 29)

1. f**u**zz *(short vowel sound 'u')*
2. t**ea**ch *(long vowel sound 'e')*
3. b**i**n *(short vowel sound 'i')*
4. ch**ai**n *(long vowel sound 'a')*
5. wh**y** *(long vowel sound 'i')*

Self-test 2 (page 29)

1. I feel gr**ea**t. *(long 'a')*
2. I can't stop sn**ee**zing. *(long 'e')*
3. That's a brilliant new t**u**ne. *(long 'u')*
4. Have you had a flu vacc**i**ne? *(long 'e')*
5. I prefer beer to w**i**ne. *(long 'i')*

Self-test 3 (page 29)

Long vowel sound 'a'

1. fake
2. relay
3. stain
4. obey
5. break
6. freight

Long vowel sound 'e'

7. neat
8. sheet
9. deceive
10. achieve
11. complete
12. Pauline

Long vowel sound 'i'

13. dye
14. sigh
15. eye
16. sky
17. Guy
18. pie

Long vowel sound 'o'

19. dough
20. boat
21. throw
22. spoken
23. sew

Long vowel sound 'u' (oo, as in rude)

24. balloon
25. true
26. crew
27. do

Long vowel sound 'u' (yoo, as in tune)

28. argument
29. in lieu
30. iTunes
31. few

Unit 3 PLURALS

Self-test 1 (page 36)

1. rollerblades
2. cigarettes
3. drinks
4. taxes
5. witches
6. jokes
7. flashes
8. catches
9. dinosaurs
10. bosses

Self-test 2 (page 36)

1. radios
2. tattoos
3. cellos
4. stereos
5. buffaloes
6. torpedoes
7. patios
8. dingoes
9. Eskimos
10. rodeos

Self-test 3 (page 36)

1 midwives
2 sunroofs
3 lives
4 tariffs
5 giraffes
6 bluffs
7 thieves
8 chiefs
9 dwarfs
10 sheaves

Self-test 4 (page 36)

1 motorways
2 cowboys
3 armies
4 essays
5 lorries
6 assemblies
7 puppies
8 volleys
9 communities
10 ponies

Unit 4 PREFIXES AND SUFFIXES

Prefixes: Self-test 1 (page 48)

1 almost
2 immature
3 misbehave
4 overruled
5 innumerable
6 disagree
7 underrated
8 dissatisfied
9 disallowed
10 unnerving

Suffixes: Self-test 2 (page 48)

a suffixes that start with a vowel: -ing, -able
b suffixes that start with a consonant: -ment, -less, -ful, -ness, -ship

Suffixes: Self-test 3 (page 48)

1 The trick worked **brilliantly**!
2 The **relaxing** holiday did us good.
3 He's so **boastful**, I'm sick of it.
4 This **friendship** means an awful lot to me.
5 The local **reporter** writes rubbish.
6 That was an **outrageous** foul.
7 That **footballer** gets paid far too much.
8 The **Darkness** is a brilliant band.
9 That bed was so **comfortable**.
10 The operation was very **painful**.

Suffixes: Self-test 4 (page 48)

1 Treasure Island is about **buried** treasure.
2 That goal has been disallowed. The celebrations will have to be **delayed**.
3 Kitty was well known for her **clumsiness**.
4 **Carrying** heavy weights incorrectly can damage your back.
5 I find boy bands very **annoying**.
6 I spent all my birthday money and now I'm **penniless**.
7 That joke is the **funniest** I've ever heard.
8 What a **beautiful** car. How much did you pay for it?
9 Some schools have a problem with **bullying**.
10 She's the **brainiest** girl in the class but she's not a genius.

Suffixes: Self-test 5 (page 49)

1 My dad can't wait for his **retirement**.
2 The girl **politely** helped the boy pick up his papers.
3 Sunburn has caused **soreness**.
4 **Ageing** affects people in different ways.
5 You're **unbelieveable**!
6 When did you change the **arrangement** for the hols?
7 I **forced** the back door open.
8 I'm **closely** watching the football results.
9 **Lateness** will lead to detention in this school.
10 Your cruel actions are **unforgivable**!

Suffixes: Self-test 6 (page 49)

1. **Cheerfulness** is a valuable personality trait.
2. **Cancelling** the holiday will incur charges.
3. Does swearing at a teacher get you **expelled**?
4. The **traveller** had never had a proper job.
5. What a **marvellous** teacher he is.
6. **Signalling** failures cause most late trains.
7. The French Revolution was a massive **rebellion**.
8. Product **labelling** now shows how healthy foods are.
9. **Controlling** this remote control plane is difficult.
10. Moles are known for their **tunnelling** skills.

Suffixes: Self-test 7 (page 49)

1. What a **chatty** old gossip that woman is.
2. My new brace was **fitted** yesterday.
3. **Stopping** smoking will improve your health.
4. The weather is **sunny** today.
5. The dog has never been **wetter**.
6. I've been **running** in preparation for the marathon.
7. I've been **treated** really badly by my best friend.
8. These energy saving bulbs are **dimmer** than normal ones.
9. The **jogger** is in training for a triathlon.
10. **Hidden** caves were recently discovered.

Unit 5 COMMON LETTER PATTERNS

Self-test 1 (page 64)

1. I have a tendency to ignore advice.
2. I have been given notice to quit my tenancy.
3. Walking through wet cement was clumsy of me.
4. You must spell with precise accuracy.
5. Cruise liners are safe from piracy.
6. The agency was in the centre of town.
7. Let's celebrate a successful result.
8. The fire was certainly a case of arson.
9. The cygnets were sitting beneath the cedar tree.
10. Cycling through the city saves time.

Self-test 2 (page 64)

The correct answers are underlined.

1. Your gems and jewels make me jealous.
2. I managed to eat the cabbage.
3. I left my baggage in the train carriage.
4. The general feeling is we must give an apology.
5. The jury listened to the statement from the hostage.

Self-test 3 (page 64)

1. I trudged through the snow with my sledge.
2. The monkey sat on a ledge at the back of the cage.
3. I don't have the courage to make my own fudge.
4. There's no charge for crossing the bridge.
5. The garage will replace the badge on your car.

Self-test 4 (page 64)

1	pamphlet	6	fury
2	foreign	7	triumph
3	phrase	8	pheasant
4	phantom	9	nephew
5	cellophane	10	orphan

Self-test 5 (page 64)

1. field
2. conceit
3. brazier
4. yield
5. retrieve
6. sufficient
7. grieve
8. gradient
9. perceive
10. belief

Self-test 6 (page 65)

1. blotch
2. scratch
3. bench
4. porch
5. drench
6. staunch
7. hutch
8. coach
9. crutch
10. wretched

Self-test 7 (page 65)

1. machine
2. sachet
3. shovel
4. charade
5. chord
6. chrysalis
7. chaos
8. kayak
9. chemist
10. chronic

Self-test 8 (page 65)

1. pouch
2. found
3. browse
4. pout
5. bound
6. allowance
7. counsel
8. counter
9. gouge
10. frown

Self-test 9 (page 65)

1. courier
2. cactus
3. glorious
4. devious
5. trouble
6. blunt
7. lump
8. nervous
9. double
10. joyous

Self-test 10 (page 65)

1. The swan swam toward the river bank.
2. You should have forewarned me about the swamp.
3. You need a wash; you smell like a warthog!
4. You must work your way upwards from the bottom.
5. The smell of warm waffles drifted past them.

Self-test 11 (page 65)

1. square
2. equal
3. teak
4. acquaintance
5. squid
6. quote
7. require
8. adequate
9. beak
10. request

Unit 6 COMMON ENDINGS

Self-test 1 (page 79)

1. tedious
2. gorgeous
3. courteous
4. dangerous
5. ingenious
6. precious
7. curious
8. courageous
9. famous
10. delicious
11. poisonous
12. hideous
13. scrumptious
14. obvious

Self-test 2 (page 79)

1. potion
2. adoration
3. possession
4. aggression
5. completion
6. motion
7. instruction
8. emotion
9. exhibition
10. emission

Self-test 3 (page 79)

1. The worst thing about exams is the <u>revision</u>.
2. The <u>beautician</u> made an ugly woman beautiful.
3. The best penalty kicks are taken with <u>precision</u>.
4. Coastal <u>erosion</u> is a serious problem on the East coast.
5. The <u>mathematician</u> solved a difficult equation.
6. The <u>explosion</u> brought the derelict building down.
7. I watch <u>television</u> for about six hours each day.
8. The <u>electrician</u> has rewired our house.
9. I live in a <u>mansion</u> with 15 rooms.
10. An <u>optician</u> tests people's eyesight.

Self-test 4 (page 80)

	Words ending in -le or -el		Words ending in -le or -al
1	bangle	1	doodle
2	uncle	2	metal
3	beetle	3	fizzle
4	jewel	4	royal
5	bottle	5	final
6	label	6	gamble
7	rustle	7	giggle
8	cackle	8	actual
9	dazzle	9	global
10	towel	10	normal

Self-test 5 (page 80)

1. icicle
2. geographical
3. comical
4. biblical
5. medical
6. chronicle
7. logical
8. particle
9. tentacle
10. cubicle

Self-test 6 (page 80)

1. intelligence
2. silence
3. evidence
4. sentence
5. appearance

Self-test 7 (page 80)

1. indefinite
2. invite
3. favourite
4. opposite
5. definite

Unit 7 SPELLING AND PUNCTUATION

Self-test 1 (page 88)

1. If I put a coin in a glass of Pepsi on Tuesday, will it be shiny by Wednesday?
2. Did you know there is a city called Smackover in Arkansas, USA?
3. In the United States and France, one out of every three families has a pet dog.
4. The wheelbarrow, kites and fireworks were invented by the Chinese.
5. The 71 million packets of biscuits sold every year by United Biscuits, owner of Mcvitie's, creates 125 tons of crumbs.
6. All the Smarties eaten in a year would stretch around the Earth's equator nearly three times.
7. When he was the American president, George W Bush once said, 'Most imports are from outside of the country.'
8. A Channel 4 poll voted The Simpsons as the greatest cartoon of all time.
9. In 1884 Dr Hervey D Thatcher invented the milk bottle. In 1971 Prime Minister Margaret Thatcher earned the nickname of Milk-snatcher.
10. The name of Wendy was invented for the book *Peter Pan*, by JM Barrie.

Self-test 2 (page 88)

1. After being given detention on Monday, Sandeep snarled, 'I hate Mr Godkin. He's evil.'
2. The NHS is always very busy during the period around Bonfire Night.
3. Computer games have come a long way since Space Invaders and Pac-Man.
4. George asked, 'Can we go to KFC now that I've finished my homework?'
5. 'Because he has antlers at Christmas, Rudolph must be a girl!' laughed Ali.
6. 'You should see these old pictures of my dad. Look at his hair,' sniggered Sam.
7. Over a million people have attended garden parties at Buckingham Palace during the reign of Queen Elizabeth II.
8. 'Come on, I'm starving. Is that Tesco near you open 24 hours a day?' asked Reese.
9. 'The camp site we stayed on had lots of French and Dutch tourists staying there,' said Aaron.
10. The teacher, Mrs Nadal, explained that the Spanish trip was only for Sixth Form students.

Self-test 3 (pages 88–89)

1. Gemma's patience was running out with Luke's immature behaviour.
2. 'My phone's been nicked, I'm gutted,' sighed Alex.
3. I can't understand why those companies' logos are identical.
4. You'll never get a decent grade when you're behaving like a real loser.
5. It was the boys' fault the windows were smashed. They shouldn't have been throwing the ball.
6. 'She's going to be there later. I'll see you at Lee's,' said Oli.
7. Mr Morris' lessons are painfully boring. He's an awful teacher.
8. Many visitors turned up and the demonstrations were a great success.
9. 'Your car's a piece of junk,' laughed Charlie. 'It'll never pass its MOT.'
10. If you're travelling by plane, don't leave your luggage unattended.

Self-test 4 (page 89)

1. 'That's Kim's phone. She's been looking everywhere for it,' said Jay.
2. 'I'm afraid the hard-drive's had it,' said the technician.
3. How's your spelling coming on? With this book's help you ought to improve.

4 The team's attitude was appalling. They'd given up after the ref's poor decision.

5 They're not coming with us. They'll cause trouble and guess who'll get blamed as well?

6 'It's the people's choice who they elect,' declared the Prime Minister.

7 'Chris, let's get a MacDonald's and go. It'll be a laugh if we're early,' said Ashley.

8 The cows' tongues are covered in blisters. Do you think they've got foot and mouth disease?

9 I won't go, I've no reason to. I'll be embarrassed won't I?

10 The drive-through's intercom was terrible. They couldn't hear your order.

Self-test 5 (page 89)

'You've got to be kidding, it's the most boring game in the world,' sighed Ed.

'Well that's what we're doing for Lewis' birthday bash. He wants to spend the day at a cricket match.' The unfortunate Ed didn't know whether to laugh or cry.

'This has got to be your mates' doing hasn't it? You'll have put them up to this, I reckon,' he said, accusingly. Ian looked a little guilty as he replied.

'Well...I may have had a bit to do with it. I suppose I just might have mentioned that I can get free tickets, and it is an England versus Australia game. They're always great to watch.'

Ed was becoming angry. 'For you perhaps, but it'll be a nightmare for everyone else. And it's on a Saturday. We'll be bored to death. So how many people's fun have you ruined with this idea?' Ian decided to take a different approach.

'There'll be about twenty-odd mates going and I've got it all sorted. We've got the best seats; the view's brilliant. All the food's free, because Mark's uncle works for Sky TV and he can get us into the hospitality suite.' Ed's face brightened at the mention of free food. 'I've even got us a lift to and from the ground from Mick in his parents' car.'

Unit 8 MISC-SPELL-ANEOUS!

Self-test 1 (page 96)

1 You're not allowed in there.
2 The window pane was cracked.
3 I heard a strange noise.
4 I think I've got flu.
5 I made a real fuss.
6 The chocolate mousse is great.
7 He knows what you mean.
8 A loaf of bread.
9 I need to flee the country.
10 The postman brings the mail.

Self-test 2 (page 96)

1 It was a minor accident.
2 A glass of wine.
3 My hair is a mess.
4 Which lesson is next?
5 A queen sits on a throne.
6 That was a weak effort.
7 Karate is a martial art.
8 Send up a distress flare.
9 I play bass guitar.
10 I'm going to dye my hair.

Self-test 3 (page 96)

1. A hare looks similar to a rabbit.
2. The stuntman sighed with relief.
3. The soldiers went back to their base.
4. The prison cell didn't look cosy.
5. She rode a white stallion.
6. I have changed my mind.
7. How much profit did you make?
8. I need to hire a car.
9. There's a crack in the ceiling.
10. Make sure you've packed your case.

Self-test 4 (page 97)

1. You look worn out.
2. I build houses for a living.
3. The bells were rung loudly.
4. I paid him a compliment.
5. The creak came from the old door.
6. The bald man wore a wig.
7. The colours were bright and bold.
8. Only three laps to go.
9. I guessed the answer.
10. The red rose smelled delightful.

Self-test 5 (page 97)

1. You got that answer correct.
2. You need a plumber to fix that leak.
3. That's a very sharp knife.
4. Fasten all your shirt buttons.
5. After summer comes autumn.
6. That hedge needs trimming.
7. My feet are numb with cold.
8. Fresh salmon tastes better than tinned.
9. Those jeans are so out of fashion.
10. I wrote you a letter.

Self-test 6 (page 97)

1. I knew I was right.
2. I have paid off my debts.
3. I could design a better car than that.
4. I need to wrap that present.
5. I could have pneumonia.
6. I must listen more carefully.
7. I can play guitar.
8. I have hurt my wrist.
9. I'm as white as a ghost.
10. I have a blister on my tongue.

Spelling games

Word chains

Students create word chains where the last two letters of a word form the first two letters of the next. For example:

CAPTAIN → INSIDE → DECIMAL → ALPHABET → ETHNIC

The game helps students to recognise possible letter patterns and improves their ability to predict the spelling of words that are new to them.

Scoring

- 2 points for each letter used
- 1 point for each letter used if a dictionary is used
- If a player believes their opponent will be unable to follow their own word, a challenge can be issued. If successful, the opponent loses their score for the word and forfeits their turn.

Typical scoring chain

PENCIL	Chosen by Janet as a start word. *No score*
ILLUSION	No dictionary used by John. *Score 16*
ONEROUS	Janet used a dictionary. *Score 7*
USED	No dictionary used by John. *Score 8*
EDUCATION	No dictionary used by Janet. *Score 18*
ONLY	John scores 8. Janet challenges. John is unable to name a word starting 'ly'. John loses his 8 points. Janet has a chance to replace only with another 'on' word.
ONCE	No dictionary used by Janet. *Score 8*

You can refine the game by adding strict time limitations on dictionary use.

Word squares

This is a game for a single player.

Begin with an empty grid of squares. The example below uses a 7 x 7 grid, although any size will suffice.

Begin by writing a word across the top row of squares. The last two letters of the word must become the first two letters of the next. The object is to fill the entire grid, in a clockwise direction, forming a spiral.

The following example begins with the word 'butter'. The words used are:

B	U	T	T	E	R	A
P	E	R	A	T	U	S
M	N	T	E	R	R	E
E	E	C	H	T	E	D
T	P	N	I	A	F	I
A	O	H	S	E	R	B
M	I	T	I	G	E	L

The words used are:

BUTTER → ERASED → EDIBLE → LEGITIMATE → TEMPERATURE → REFRESH → SHOP → OPEN → ENTERTAIN → INCH

Students learn to recognise letter patterns because they must choose words whose last two letters make new word formation possible.

Jumbles

This is a game for two students.

The players decide on the number of letters their words will have, for example six. They then write down ten words, each must contain exactly six letters, but they must jumble the letters up. For example, a student may think of the word 'target' but they would write down 'gettar'. The students then swap their words and attempt to write the proper word next to the jumbled version. The first to finish is the winner.

Keep it in the family

This is a whole class activity and an excellent starter.

Students are given a word and asked to write down as many words as they can from the same family. For example, the word play could result in:

PLAYS, PLAYED, PLAYING, PLAYFUL, PLAYER, PLAYERS, REPLAY, REPLAYS, REPLAYING, REPLAYED, PLAYABLE, PLAYFULLY, PLAYFULNESS

A strict time limit with countdown increases the fun.

Euler's day off

This is a game for those who enjoy anagrams.

Begin by drawing a 5 x 5 grid for each participating player. Twenty-five letters must then be randomly selected. This can be done simply by closing your eyes and pointing in a book.

The object of the game is to arrange these 25 letters within the grid to form as many horizontal and vertical words as possible. A point is scored for each letter of the words that are formed. Only words of three letters or more are allowed. The maximum possible score is 50.

The player with the most points wins. In the event of a tie, the player with the most five letter words wins. If this is a tie as well, the player with the most four letter words is the victor. The same points and the same number of five and four letter words mean a genuine tie.

The game starts as soon as the letters are selected and a time limit should be imposed.

AA

This is a game for single players or small teams.

The object is to write prose consisting of words that start with the same letter. The letter used can be chosen at random.

For example: *An Australian acrobat achieved awesome acts as an aircraft architect, arranging all aspects around an amazing artificial airfield.*

Add on

This is a game for two or more players. In fact, a whole class can be involved.

The object is to build a story with each player adding a single word at a time. A refinement can be if a player chooses to add punctuation. For example:

Tom:	*The*	Suman:	*was*
Kelly:	*morning*	James:	*exciting*
Eve:	*that*	Sarah:	*Full-stop*
Sam:	*school*	Joe:	*It*
Jane:	*exploded*	Michael:	*started...* (etc.)

Detective

One player is designated as 'Sherlock'. Their task is to question the other players. Sherlock chooses a letter of the alphabet but does not reveal his choice to the others. This letter is now 'taboo'. Sherlock now asks questions of the others, who respond with single word answers. Each time a player gives an answer that contains one of the taboo letters, a life is lost. Anyone losing three lives is out of the game. Any player who guesses the taboo letter is Sherlock in the next round.

For example:

Dan (who has secretly chosen the letter P):	*What is your favourite colour?*
Louise:	*Yellow*
Dan:	*How old are you?*
Cameron:	*Fourteen*
Dan:	*What is the capital of France?*
Anna:	*Paris.*
Dan:	*You lose a life. What sort of letter starts a sentence?*
Ben:	*Capital*
Dan:	*You lose a life. What is the opposite of rich?*
Raveena:	*Poor. I think the answer is P.*
Dan:	*Correct. How did you know?*
Raveena:	*P is the only letter common to Paris, capital and poor.*

Adverbs

This is a game for two or more players, but is better with larger groups.

The object of the game is to guess an adverb from the manner competitors carry out an assigned action.

The game can be played by individual players or in teams. An adverb is secretly chosen then competing players ask for an action to be carried out 'in the manner of the word'. Alternatively, questions can be answered in 'the manner of the word'.

Consequences

The object of the game is to create stories composed of completely separate contributions from each player.

Each competing player is given a sheet of paper. The game begins by writing an adjective at the top of the paper that describes a male person. The paper is folded to hide the adjective from the next player, and then passed on. The next player then writes a male name. The paper continues to be folded and passed from player to player, with statements written in the following order:

- An adjective describing a male
- A male name
- An adjective describing a female
- A female name
- Where they met
- What he said to her
- The reply she made
- What the consequence of this conversation was
- What others said about them

Once the list of phrases is completed, players spend a little time writing the phrases up into complete sentences.

For example:

A grotesquely obese David Beckham met one-eyed Prunella Clackersthorpe at Alton Towers. He asked her, 'Do you whistle in your sleep when you've eaten smoky bacon crisps?' She replied, 'Please help me find my Aunty Gladys.' The consequence of this meeting was that he began to send flowers to her on a daily basis. Friends commented that she intended to call a plumber to get rid of the problem.

Alternative versions of the game can be simply played by adding different or extra categories, such as what they did, what they gave to each other, when they met, etc.

A literary variant of the game is building a book or film review. The categories are:

- The title
- The subtitle
- The author's name or the main stars
- A short review
- A cliff-hanger
- How critics have received the book/film
- Where it can be bought/watched

Definition poetry

This is an entertaining dictionary exercise that replaces well-known texts and phrases with their dictionary definitions. It can be carried out as a paired or whole class activity.

Keeping the texts private means that students can attempt to guess the original.

For example:

An apple a day keeps the doctor away. = *The round edible fruit of a small tree each rotation of the Earth prevents the physician attending.*

It is important to have a bank of well-known excerpts to give to the students. Any very familiar, recognisable phrase is acceptable (for example, advertising slogans, film quotations, famous first lines) but proverbs are a good starting point. A bank is included below.

- Actions speak louder than words.
- A bird in the hand is worth two in the bush.
- Don't cry over spilt milk.
- Better late than never.
- A miss is as good as a mile.
- An eye for an eye and a tooth for a tooth.
- Curiosity killed the cat.
- Don't put all your eggs in one basket.
- You can lead a horse to water but you can't make it drink.
- First come, first served.
- Don't throw out the baby with the bathwater.
- People who live in glass houses shouldn't throw stones.
- Don't count your chickens before they're hatched.
- You can't judge a book by its cover.
- A watched kettle never boils.
- Life begins at forty.
- Love is blind.
- Rules are made to be broken.
- Sticks and stones may break my bones but words will never hurt me.
- Home is where the heart is.
- Don't make a mountain out of a molehill.
- Blood is thicker than water.

Catchword

This is a game involving quick thinking that can be played in teams or individually.

Players are required to think of words containing three specific letters. A random sequence of three letters is chosen. Within a given time limit, players must write down as many words as possible containing those letters. Many variations of this basic concept are possible:

- One of the chosen letters must be at the start or end of the word.
- The letters must appear in a particular order.
- A single point could be awarded for each word written down. Alternatively a six letter word would be worth 6 points.
- Bonus points can be awarded for the longest word from each round.

A good rule to enforce is that only a single word from a word family is allowed.

Missing vowels

This is a team game where the object is to guess words that have their vowels left out of them.

One team thinks of a word and spells it with the vowels omitted. If necessary, the team can give a clue (for example, an animal, a plant, an item of furniture). The opposing team then have to attempt to spell the word in full.

Two points are given if the actual word is spelled. A single point is awarded for all other words that fit the letter pattern, even if they are not the word originally intended. A time limit may be imposed if required.

Website games

There are many spelling games available online. With access to the Internet, the following websites carry a range of entertaining, interactive and educational spelling games.

www.funbrain.com/spell/index.html

www.gamequarium.com/spelling.html

www.bbc.co.uk/schools/spellits/ad_menu_flash.shtml

www.crickweb.co.uk/ks2literacy.html

www.english-online.org.uk/games/gamezone2.htm

www.kidsspell.com/

www.britishcouncil.org/kids-games-balloon-xmas.htm

www.freegames4all.net/play-20238.html

www.bbc.co.uk/skillswise/games/

www.surefish.co.uk/CULTURE/games/2008/0208_games.htm

www.teachingenglish.org.uk/try/links/free-english-gamescom

www.spellingcity.com/

Part D Additional resources

Student self-assessment tables

Unit 2: Vowels and consonants

How confident are you about the skills you have practised on pages 24–28 of the Student Book? Assess yourself using the grid below.

	I can't do this ✓	I think I can mostly do this ✓	I can always do this ✓
I understand the difference between, and can identify, long and short vowel sounds.			
I understand the different ways that long and short vowels can be spelled.			

Unit 3: Plurals

How confident are you about the skills you have practised on pages 30–35 of the Student Book? Assess yourself using the grid below.

	I can't do this ✓	I think I can mostly do this ✓	I can always do this ✓
I can add the right ending to a word to make plurals.			
I can correctly use apostrophes.			

Unit 4: Prefixes and suffixes

How confident are you about the skills you have practised on pages 37–47 of the Student Book? Assess yourself using the grid below.

	I can't do this ✓	I think I can mostly do this ✓	I can always do this ✓
I can correctly label prefixes, stems and suffixes.			
I can correctly add prefixes to stems to spell new words.			
I can correctly add the suffix **-ful** to words.			
I know when to keep the **e** and when to drop the **e** when adding suffixes to stems.			
I can remember the steps for the ONE, ONE, ONE rule and understand when to double consonants.			
I know when to double the **l** when adding a suffix.			
I know when to change **y** to **i** when adding a suffix.			

Unit 5: Common letter patterns

How confident are you about the skills you have practised on pages 50–63 of the Student Book? Assess yourself using the grid below.

	I can't do this ✓	I think I can mostly do this ✓	I can always do this ✓
I know what soft and hard letter sounds are.			
I know when to use a **-ge** or **-dge** at the end of words.			
I know why some **f** sounds are spelled **ph**.			
I know the **i** before **e** rule.			
I know when to use **ch** or **tch**.			
I know how **ou** letter patterns are used.			
I know how **w** changes the sound of the vowel that follows it.			
I know the rule about the letter **q**.			

Unit 6: Common endings

How confident are you about the skills you have practised on pages 66–78 of the Student Book? Assess yourself using the grid below.

	I can't do this ✓	I think I can mostly do this ✓	I can always do this ✓
I can choose the correct ending from **-ous**, **-ious** or **-eous**.			
I can choose the correct ending from **-tion**, **-ssion**, **-cian** or **-sion**.			
I can choose the correct ending from **-le**, **-el** and **-al** endings.			
I can choose the correct ending from **-able** and **-ible** endings.			
I can choose the correct ending from **-ical**, **-icle** and **-acle**.			
I can choose the correct ending from **-ance** and **-ence**.			
I can choose the correct ending from **-ate** and **-ite**.			

Unit 7: Spelling and punctuation

How confident are you about the skills you have practised on pages 81–87 of the Student Book? Assess yourself using the grid below.

	I can't do this ✓	I think I can mostly do this ✓	I can always do this ✓
I can correctly use capital letters.			
I can correctly use the apostrophe of abbreviation.			
I can correctly use the apostrophe of possession.			
I do not use apostrophes in simple plural words.			
I can use hyphens correctly.			
I know when to use one word or two.			

Unit 8: Misc-spell-aneous!

How confident are you about the skills you have practised on pages 90–95 of the Student Book? Assess yourself using the grid below.

	I can't do this ✓	I think I can mostly do this ✓	I can always do this ✓
I know what homophones are.			
I do not confuse common homophones.			
I know what silent letters are.			
I do not miss out common silent letters when spelling.			

Extra self-tests

Unit 2 VOWELS AND CONSONANTS

Self-test 1: long or short vowel sound?

Write down whether each word has a long vowel sound or a short vowel sound.

1 f**u**n *(short vowel sound 'u')*
2 sp**ee**ch
3 p**i**n
4 p**ai**n
5 m**y**
6 b**ea**m
7 s**ay**

Self-test 2: long vowel sounds

Write down which long vowel sound is made by the letters in bold.

1 I love st**ea**k. *(long 'a')*
2 The weather is fr**ee**zing.
3 The pr**u**ne is a dried fruit.
4 Washing mach**i**nes are noisy.
5 Are you coming to our house to d**i**ne?
6 The animals in the zoo are t**a**me.
7 Thr**ow** me the football.

Self-test 3: long vowel sounds

The answers to the clues below have letters missing. Choose the correct letter pattern for each gap from those given in bold above each set of clues.

Long vowel sound 'a'

a ai ay ei ey ea

1	Get from someone	t_ke	4	Kneel down and...	pr_ _
2	Press to hear	pl_ _	5	Word for fantastic	gr_ _t
3	Vehicle on rails	tr_ _n	6	Bodybuilders lift...	w_ _ghts

Long vowel sound 'e'

e ea ee ie ei i

7	Sit on this	s_ _t	10	Do well	ach_ _ve
8	Walk on these	f_ _t	11	Use up something	depl_te
9	Take delivery	rec_ _ve	12	Washing...	mach_ne

Long vowel sound 'i'

i y ie ye uy ey

13	Tell untruth	l_ _	16	Build up expectation	h_pe
14	Happiness	del_ght	17	Mr Fawkes – first name	G_ _
15	Use to see	_ _e	18	Type of graph or chart	p_ _

Long vowel sound 'o'

o oa ow ough ew

19	Slimy like frog	t_ _d	22	Not working	br_ken
20	Surrounds castle	m_ _t	23	Stitch clothes	s_ _
21	Fire arrow with	b_ _			

Long vowel sound 'u' (oo, as in rude)

u oo o ew

24 Eat soup with sp_ _n

25 Colour bl_e

26 The beanstalk... gr_ _

27 Wear on feet sh_e

Long vowel sound 'u' (yoo, as in tune)

u ue ew eu

28 Day of the week T_ _sday

29 Impartial judge n_ _tral

30 Whistle a happy... t_ne

31 The west wind... bl_ _

Unit 3 PLURALS

Self-test 1: 's' or 'es'?

Write down the plural form of the words in bold.

1. I got two identical **brooch** for Christmas.
2. Please close those **window**.
3. Have you ever played **dart**?
4. He's had several **illness** this year.
5. The mirror had many **blemish**.
6. My **reflex** are pretty good.
7. The **supporter** cheered the goal.
8. How many **guess** do you need?
9. Her hair was tied in **bunch**.
10. All my **class** are boring today.

Self-test 2: plurals and words ending in 'o'

Write down the plural form of the words in bold.

1. The **desperado** rode into the sunset.
2. Add a couple of **zero** to the end of that number.
3. How many different **scenario** can you imagine?
4. The **flamingo** were perched on one leg.
5. It had been a week of **fiasco**.
6. You can buy **gazebo** at garden centres.
7. I'm not fond of **avocado**.
8. Did you buy any **memento** on holiday?
9. The film contained several excellent **cameo**.
10. There are many **casino** in Las Vegas.

Self-test 3: 'f', 'ff', 'fe' endings

Write down the plural form of the words in bold.

1. He's made too many **gaff** recently.
2. **Jacknife** can be very dangerous.
3. Those two are always having **tiff**.
4. The restaurant offered different **aperitif**.
5. Those **scarf** are too expensive.
6. That bank contains five huge **safe**.
7. Those ear **muff** look silly.
8. The horse had sore **hoof**.
9. Did you bring your **waterproof**?
10. Car **thief** operate in this area.

Self-test 4: words ending in 'y'

Write down the plural form of the words in bold.

1. Are you enjoying the Christmas **festivity**?
2. Several **survey** had been taken.
3. Unfortunately many **redundancy** were announced.
4. The doctor offered some promising **remedy**.
5. You can get all sorts of **accessory** for it.
6. History is just a series of **yesterday**.
7. I read three **biography** on holiday.
8. He sweeps **chimney** for a living.
9. Three **sentry** were on guard at the palace.
10. He went to prison for committing many **robbery**.

Unit 4 PREFIXES AND SUFFIXES

Self-test 1: prefixes

Choose the correct spelling of the words below. Write down the correctly spelled word.

1. distasteful/disstasteful
2. imature/immature
3. misspell/mispell
4. override/overide
5. unnatural/unatural
6. dissimilar/disimilar
7. underated/underrated
8. dissatisfaction/disatisfaction
9. dissallow/disallow
10. unerving/unnerving

Self-test 2: suffixes

Make two lists of the suffixes in the words below:

- **a** suffixes that start with a vowel
- **b** suffixes that start with a consonant.

1. amazement
2. caring
3. wonderment
4. priceless
5. beautiful
6. hopeless
7. wonderful
8. curable
9. fondness
10. authorship

Self-test 3: suffixes

Add a suffix to each word in bold below, so that each sentence makes sense. Write out the new word.

1. The sun shone **bright**_____!
2. I'm the **care**_____ one in the family.
3. I'm sitting in a **comfort**_____ chair.
4. **Citizen**_____ is now taught in schools.
5. The local **football**_____ scored twice.
6. The most **courage**_____ usually win.
7. That **paint**_____ charges a reasonable price.
8. He is a **brain**_____ clot.
9. Careful, that vase is **break**_____.
10. The butterfly is **wonder**_____.

Self-test 4: suffixes and stems – 'y' to 'i' rule

Add a suffix to each word in bold below, so that each sentence makes sense. Write out the new word.

1 The Caribbean is famous for **curry**_____ goat.
2 I'm **enjoy**_____ the new challenge.
3 That boy **copy**_____ every single answer.
4 The motorist sustained some **injury**_____.
5 The monk spent five hours a day **pray**_____.
6 She set about her work **lazy**_____.
7 That's the **heavy**_____ turkey in the shop.
8 The criminal committed several **burglary**_____.
9 The school now has an anti **bully**_____ policy in place.
10 The magician had very mysterious **ability**_____.

Self-test 5: suffixes and stems – 'e' rule

Add a suffix to each word in bold below, so that each sentence makes sense. Write out the new word.

1 That treasure is **price**_____.
2 The comedian was **amuse**_____.
3 I ask you for **forgive**_____.
4 I'm so **excite**_____ about Christmas.
5 Are you giving me an **invite**_____ to your party?
6 When did you change the **arrange**_____s?
7 The kitten was **adore**_____.
8 **Unfortunate**_____ your team lost.
9 My teacher hates **late**_____.
10 You are a **hope**_____ darts player!

Self-test 6: suffixes and stems – 'l' rule

Choose the correct spelling of the words below. Write down the correctly spelled word.

1 cancelation/cancellation
2 cancelling/canceling
3 rebelling/rebeling
4 traveling/travelling
5 spiralling/spiraling
6 marveling/marvelling
7 rebellion/rebelion
8 traveller/traveler
9 modeling/modelling
10 installation/instalation

Self-test 7: suffixes and stems – doubling

Choose the correct spelling of the words below. Write down the correctly spelled word.

1 grabing/grabbing
2 puting/putting
3 patting/pating
4 stealing/stealling
5 stepping/steping
6 quiting/quitting
7 swiming/swimming
8 beting/betting
9 dipping/diping
10 tripping/triping

Unit 5 COMMON LETTER PATTERNS

Self-test 1: soft 'c'

Write down the words in bold that are spelled correctly.

1 The dress has sequins/cequins arranged in a sircle/circle.
2 Isn't it chansy/chancy walking through a semetary/cemetery at night?
3 His competensy/competency is shocking: he's a dunse/dunce.
4 I'd like a simple/cimple diamond necklase/necklace please.
5 I'm on a diet: salad/calad and sereal/cereal for me.
6 I remember when the sinema/cinema cost twenty pense/pence to get in.
7 The situation/cituation is becoming severe/cevere.
8 It was so easy/eacy under different circumstanses/sircumstances.
9 It was very noisy/noicy: over 120 desibells/decibels.
10 That fantasy/fantacy film is good enough for a sequel/cequel.

Self-test 2: soft 'g'

Write down the words in bold that are spelled correctly.

1 Teenagers/teenajers think anyone over 30 is geriatric/jeriatric.
2 Gesus/Jesus appears in many religions/relijions.
3 Those gentlemen/jentlemen are due an apology/apolojy.
4 He won the gavelin/javelin competition by a large/larje margin/marjin.
5 This strategy/stratejy could put the world in geopardy/jeopardy.

Self-test 3: 'ge' or 'dge' endings?

Write down the words in bold that are spelled correctly.

1 The café sold various beverages/beveradges and enormous weges/wedges of cake.
2 I think I'll indulge/induldge in a little roast partriege/partridge.
3 What percentage/percentadge of adults speak a foreign language/languadge?
4 I'd exchange/exchandge my college/colledge place for a good job.
5 The whole voyage/voyadge was on a barge/bardge, not a cruise liner!

Self-test 4: 'ph' words

Write down the words that are spelled correctly.

1 phigment/figment
2 sphere/sfere
3 telegraph/telegraf
4 phailure/failure
5 emphasis/emfasis
6 phony/fony
7 phamine/famine
8 phormula/formula
9 phenomenon/fenomenon
10 photography/photografy/fotography/fotografy

Self-test 5: 'ei' or 'ie'?

Write down the words that are spelled correctly.

1 gradient/gradeint
2 retrieve/retreive
3 recieversship/receivership
4 unwieldy/unweildy
5 patience/pateince
6 believes/beleives
7 experience/expereince
8 retrieves/retreives
9 ambeince/ambience
10 medieval/medeival

Self-test 6: 'ch' and 'tch'

Write down the words that are spelled correctly.

1 urchin/urtchin
2 branch/brantch
3 wretched/wreched
4 hatchet/hachet
5 pouch/poutch
6 ranch/rantch
7 twich/twitch
8 pichfork/pitchfork
9 encroach/encroatch
10 arch/artch

Self-test 7: 'sh' or 'ch' and 'k' or 'ch'?

Write down the words that are spelled correctly.

1 crochet/croshet
2 chimmering/shimmering
3 schooner/skooner
4 schizophrenia/skizophrenia
5 cherbet/sherbet
6 hierarchy/hierarky
7 archive/arkive
8 machete/mashete
9 leprechaun/leprekaun
10 franchise/franshise

Self-test 8: 'ou'/'ow'

Write down the words that are spelled correctly.

1 louse/lowse
2 touel/towel
3 vouel/vowel
4 bounty/bownty
5 joust/jowst
6 foundation/fowndation
7 broun/brown
8 boundary/bowndary
9 trouel/trowel
10 pouder/powder

Self-test 9: 'ou'/'u'

Write down the words that are spelled correctly.

1 famous/famus
2 surplous/surplus
3 various/varius
4 viciously/vicously
5 gorgeous/gorgus
6 octopous/octopus
7 odious/odius
8 anxious/anxius
9 chorous/chorus
10 impetous/impetus

Self-test 10: 'w' letter patterns

Write down the words that are spelled correctly.

1 worker/werker
2 unworthy/unwerthy
3 waddle/woddle
4 water/worter
5 wordrobe/wardrobe
6 worden/warden
7 wod/wad
8 warfare/worfare
9 wersen/worsen
10 power/powor

Self-test 11: 'q' letter patterns

Write down the words that are spelled correctly.

1 masque/maskue
2 larque/lark
3 equator/ekwator
4 steaque/steak
5 conquer/conkuer
6 enquire/enkwire
7 neque/neck
8 tanque/tank
9 plaque/plak
10 quilt/kwilt

Unit 6 COMMON ENDINGS

Self-test 1: -ous, -ious, -eous

Each word below ends in **-ous**, **-ious** or **-eous** and means the same as the word in brackets. Write out each word correctly.

1 cur_____ (interested in something)
2 mountain_____ (very high terrain)
3 outrag_____ (shocking)
4 hilar_____ (very funny)
5 nox_____ (nasty and poisonous)
6 hid_____ (very ugly)
7 obv_____ (very clear)
8 fabul_____ (amazing)
9 marvell_____ (very special)
10 spontan_____ (instant act)
11 simultan_____ (done at the same time)
12 plent_____ (lots of something)
13 ser_____ (grave)
14 fam_____ (celebrity)

Self-test 2: -tion, -ssion

Each word below ends in **-tion** or **-ssion** and means the same as the word in brackets. Write out each word correctly.

1 competit_____ (contest)
2 progre_____ (move forward)
3 promo_____ (career move)
4 profe_____ (job)
5 emo_____ (feeling)
6 po_____ (magical liquid)
7 distribu_____ (moving products from place to place)
8 expre_____ (facial pose)
9 exhibi_____ (show or event)
10 compa_____ (kind hearted act)

Self-test 3: -cian, -sion

Each word below ends in **-cian** or **-sion**. Write out each word correctly.

1 The electri_____ rewired my house.
2 The beauti_____ has a nail salon in town.
3 BMWs contain preci_____ engineering.
4 The explo_____ destroyed the building.
5 I love that musi_____.
6 I detest that televi_____ programme.
7 The politi_____ is very unpopular.
8 I have an aver_____ to custard.
9 My ver_____ of the truth is correct.
10 I play a percus_____ instrument.

Self-test 4: -le, -el, -al

Each word below ends in **-le**, **-el** or **-al**. Write out each word correctly.

1 decim_ _
2 manu_ _
3 benefici_ _
4 jew_ _
5 purp_ _
6 sensib_ _
7 funer_ _
8 crack_ _
9 dazz_ _
10 barr_ _

Self-test 5: -ical, -icle, -acle

Each word below ends in **-ical**, **-icle** or **-acle** and is the answer to the clue in brackets. Write out each word correctly.

1	phys_ _ _ _	(hard manual work)
2	art_ _ _ _	(might appear in a newspaper)
3	mus_ _ _ _	(to do with music)
4	bibl_ _ _ _	(to do with the bible)
5	pract_ _ _ _	(science experiment)
6	part_ _ _ _	(tiny speck of matter)
7	mir_ _ _ _	(wonderous act)
8	barn_ _ _ _	(shelled creature attached to ship's hull)
9	chem_ _ _ _	(used by chemist)
10	crit_ _ _ _	(disparaging comment)

Self-test 6: -ate, -ite

Each word below ends in **-ate** or **-ite**. Write down the word correctly.

1 indic_ _ _
2 oppos_ _ _
3 irrit_ _ _
4 cooper_ _ _
5 navig_ _ _
6 imperson_ _ _

Self-test 7: -ance, -ence

Each word below ends in **-ance** or **-ence**. Write down the word correctly.

1 excell_ _ _ _
2 brilli_ _ _ _
3 audi_ _ _ _
4 ambul_ _ _ _
5 perform_ _ _ _
6 depend_ _ _ _

Unit 7 SPELLING AND PUNCTUATION

Self-test 1: capital letters

Write out the following sentences putting in the missing capital letters.

1 one of the longest english words is praetertranssubstantiationalistically.
2 in america they have a national celebration called thanksgiving.
3 years ago, snickers bars were called marathons.
4 he sighed loudly saying, 'help me because i'm totally clueless.'
5 before they're two years old, the average baby crawls 150 km.
6 a desert in chile, called atacama, saw no rain in 400 years.
7 a vomit comet is a training plane used by the nasa space programme.
8 'the olympic games are held every four years, not three,' said jason.
9 'believe me, accrington stanley will win the champions league one day,' said nigel.
10 the bell in the tower of christ church cathedral, oxford, is called the old tom.

Self-test 2: apostrophes

Write out the following sentences adding apostrophes where they are needed, and removing them where they are not.

1 If youre ready wel'l get going. Marks' mum has been waiting for age's.
2 I do'nt really understand apostrophe's, theyre a hassle and give me real problem's.
3 I'm going to ask my brother's girlfriend to get me a date with one of her friends.
4 When he leaned on the rail it collapsed. The Doctors verdict was two broken finger's.
5 If you wont help me I cant go to the Leavers Party. Don't let me down.
6 The student's were angry as their grade's were poor. They blamed the teachers'.
7 My cars broken down. Its engine blew up and the tyre's caught fire.
8 Childrens' parties are great fun, but not if you're a parent, then theyre a nightmare.
9 I promise my minds made up. Im not joining Daves band and that's that!
10 She's frightened of dog's so don't let your's off it's lead.

Unit 8 MISC-SPELL-ANEOUS!

Self-test 1: homophones

Write down the words that are spelled correctly.

1 I saw a faint/feint light in the distance.
2 I need to earn/urn some money.
3 Martial/marshal law was imposed.
4 What sort/sought of cheese is it?
5 It was my first draft/draught of the essay.
6 Income tacks/tax has gone up again.
7 I've a nasty brews/bruise on my leg.
8 He let out a loud groan/grown.
9 I made a pact/packed to give up smoking.
10 It's a toad/towed, not a frog.

Self-test 2: homophones

Choose the correct word for each sentence to make sense. Write down the complete sentence.

1 If your/you're correct you've past/passed the test.
2 Its/It's the last day of/off the sale today.
3 I think your/you're jeans are great, they're/there/their really cool.
4 I'm going to/too the park if Sam is there/their/they're.
5 At half past/passed ten it's/its time for bed.
6 I've eaten too/two/to much dinner and its/it's making me feel sick.
7 The leader of/off the expedition thought it too/to/two dangerous for climbing.
8 Once you're/your there/they're/their you'll have a great time.
9 I walked too/to/two far, right past/passed the meeting place.
10 It's/Its lucky that your/you're lottery numbers came up.

Self-test 3: homophones

Choose the correct word for each sentence to make sense. Write down the complete sentence.

1. A vein/vane/vain carries blood around the body.
2. I scent/sent him a birthday card.
3. The assembly was in the main hall/haul.
4. He shouted himself horse/hoarse.
5. I knead/need a new computer.
6. The descent/dissent down the mountain was tricky.
7. Without a real/reel, a fishing rod isn't much use.
8. You must warn/worn her of the danger.
9. He mode/mowed the lawn yesterday.
10. The cat had really soft fir/fur.

Self-test 4: homophones

Choose the correct word for each sentence to make sense. Write down the complete sentence.

1. It was sheer/shear luck that goal went in.
2. The bells rung/wrung out loudly.
3. Can I have tomato source/sauce on my chips?
4. The blue dye/die ran in the wash.
5. Have you got a licence/license for that gun?
6. Train fairs/fares are getting more expensive.
7. The tractor was pulling hay bales/bails.
8. I can't bear/bare it any longer.
9. He broke the speeding limit and was find/fined.
10. It was an amazing feat/feet to break the world record.

Self-test 5: silent letters

Write out the words in bold with their missing silent letter.

1. You need to put a **com** through your messy hair.
2. **nats** are very small, annoying insects.
3. You haven't quite got the **nack** yet.
4. That **neumatic** drill outside woke me up this morning.
5. The **Ile** of Arran is off the West coast of Scotland.
6. I'm not sure **wether** to go or not.
7. I think I'll read **wile** I wait for my flight.
8. I've got a blister on my **tonge**.
9. The door **nob** fell off in my hand.
10. Fabric conditioner is meant to **sofen** clothes during washing.

Contents

The Photocopy Masters are of three levels of difficulty,

- • basic work
- •• for all children
- ••• enrichment and extension

Name ______________________________

Place £1, 10p and 1p coins to match each amount.

1. 342p

2. 469p

3. 261p

4. 347p

5. 146p

6. 431p

7. 102p

8. 555p

Name ______________________________

Hundreds, tens and units

Here are 100 cubes.

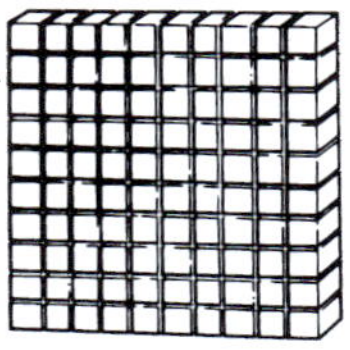

Here are 10 cubes.

Write how many cubes in each set.

1.

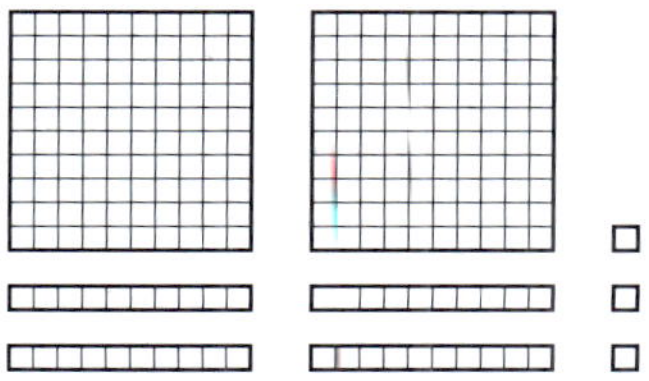

243

2.

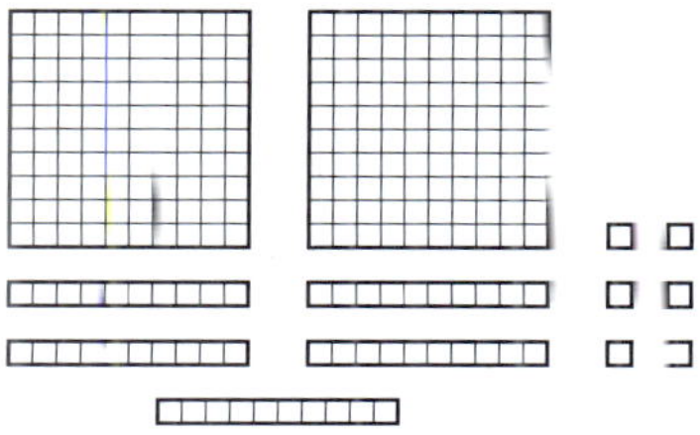

3.

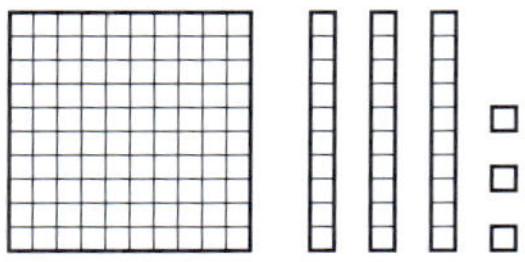

4.

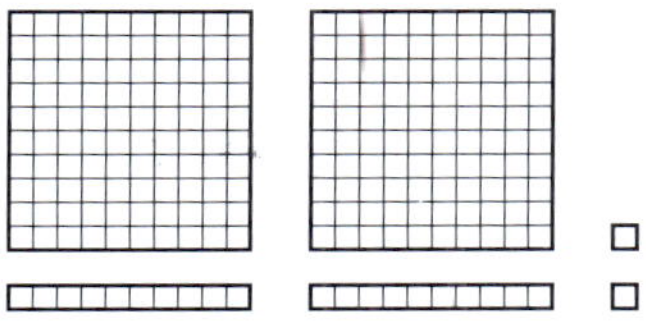

5.

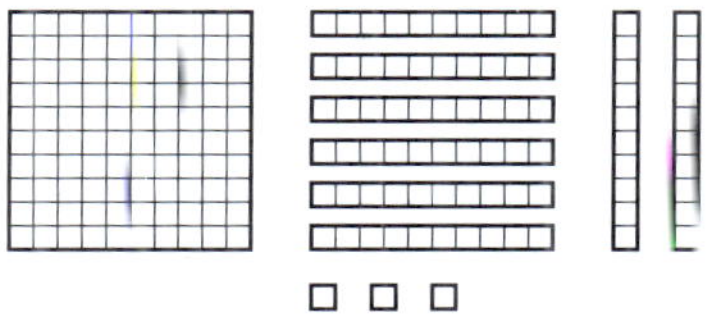

6.

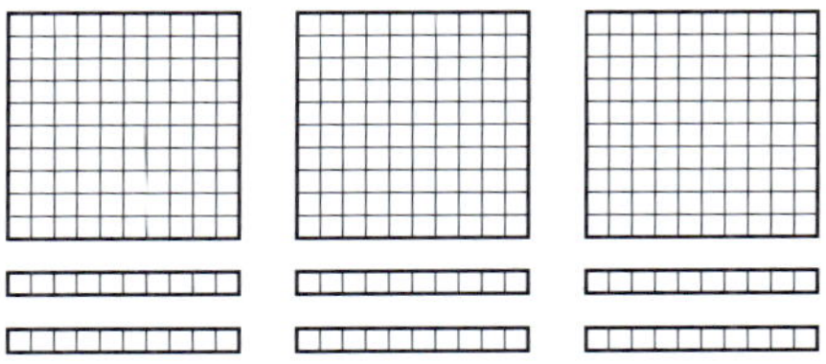

7.

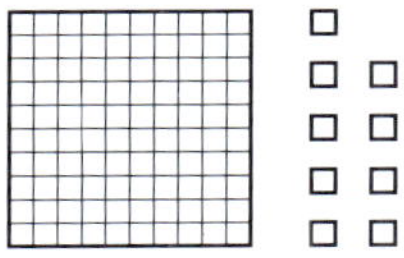

8.

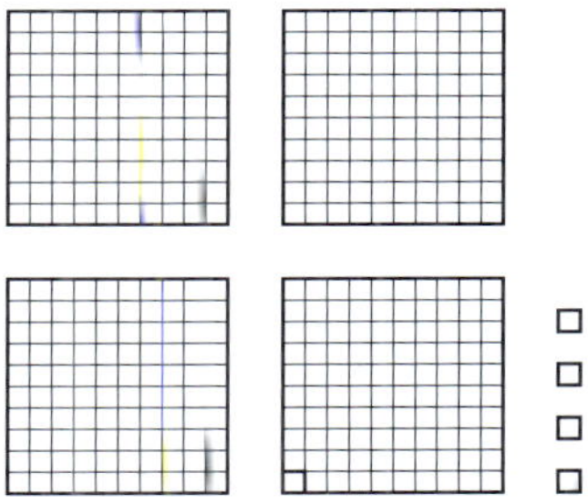

9.

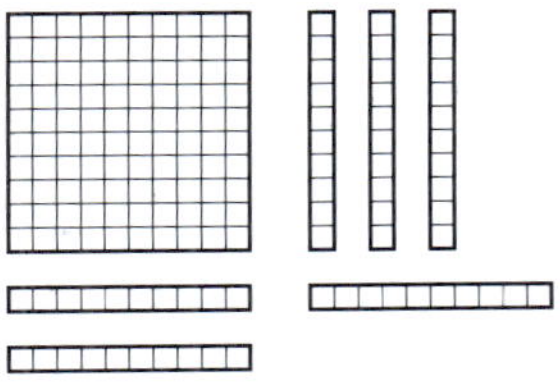

10.

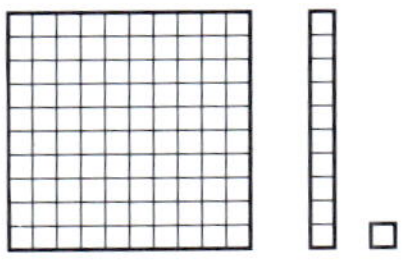

11.

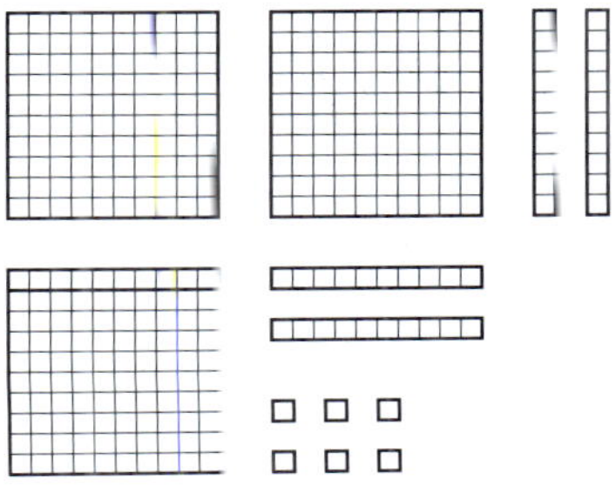

Name ____________________

Hundreds, tens and units

Write the missing numbers.

1. 245, 246, 247
2. 308, ___, 310
3. 289, ___, 291
4. 970, ___, 972
5. 997, ___, 999
6. 110, ___, 112
7. 443, ___, 445
8. 239, ___, 241
9. 330, ___, 332
10. 888, ___, 890
11. 900, ___, 902
12. 666, ___, 668
13. 476, ___, 478
14. 561, ___, 563
15. 400, ___, 402

Name ______________________________

3-digit numbers

Write a different number from 1 to 9 in each blank.

Cut out the strips.

Explore how many 3-digit numbers you can make.

	0	0

	0	0

	0	0

	0

	0

Name ______________________________

Adding to 20

Join pairs of flowers that make 20.

Name ______________________________

Adding to 20

Write the numbers to make 20.

1.

2.

3.

4.

5.

6.

7.

8.

9.

10.

11.

Name ______________________________

Adding several numbers

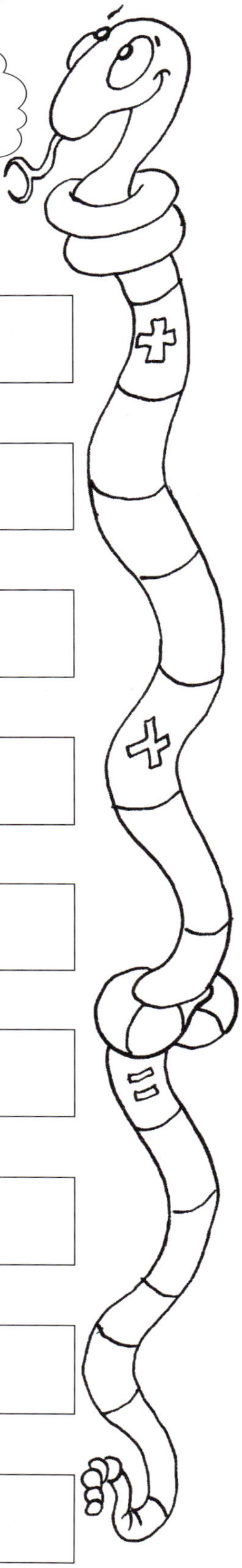

Look for 10s.

1. 5 + 5 + 3 = 13

2. 4 + 6 + 7 = ☐

3. 4 + 8 + 6 = ☐

4. 7 + 3 + 3 = ☐

5. 2 + 8 + 9 = ☐

6. 8 + 6 + 2 = ☐

7. 7 + 8 + 3 = ☐

8. 10 + 7 + 0 = ☐

9. 1 + 7 + 9 = ☐

10. 9 + 3 + 1 = ☐

11. 1 + 1 + 9 = ☐

12. 7 + 5 + 3 = ☐

13. 4 + 4 + 6 = ☐

14. 8 + 2 + 2 = ☐

15. 12 + 8 + 6 = ☐

16. 5 + 4 + 5 = ☐

17. 6 + 6 + 4 = ☐

18. 2 + 8 + 3 = ☐

19. 3 + 7 + 6 = ☐

20. 5 + 6 + 5 = ☐

Name ______________________________

Adding

Add all the next-door numbers.

Write the total above.

1.

21	13	
12	9	4

2.

6	14	8

3.

15	3	5

4.

13	9	4

5.

8	12	9

6.

10	11	9

7.

7	6	13

8.

12	8	9

Write your own numbers along the bottom.

What are the top numbers?

9.

10.

11.

12.

13.

14.

Name ______________________

Fewest coins

Write the value of the fewest coins needed to make each amount.

- 13p
- 16p
- 35p
- 42p
- 19p
- 27p
- 53p
- 67p
- 78p
- 81p
- 38p
- 49p

Name ______________________________

The next ten

Write the position of each pointer, and add to each to make the next ten.

1. 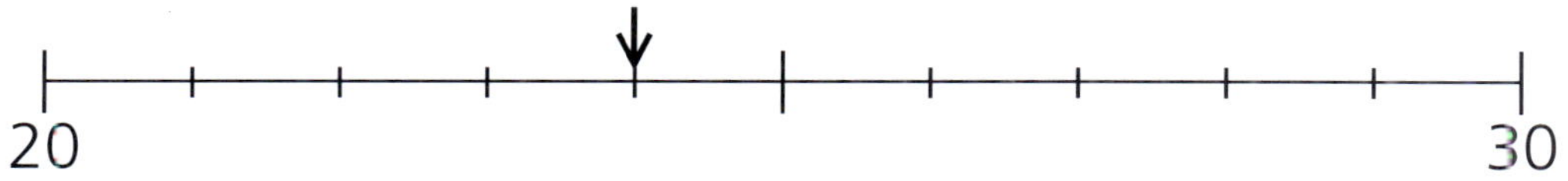

24 + 6 = 30

2. 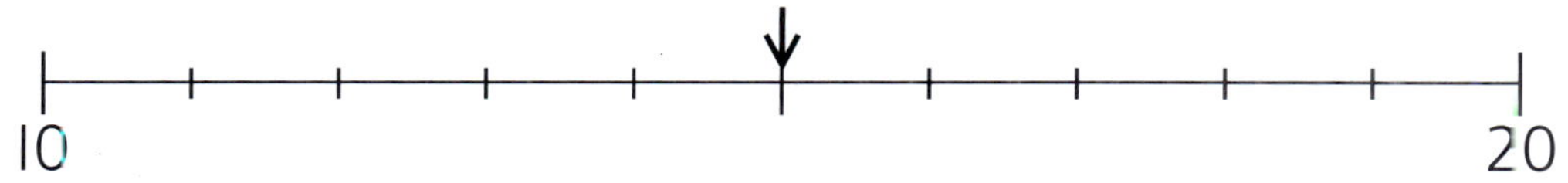

____

3. 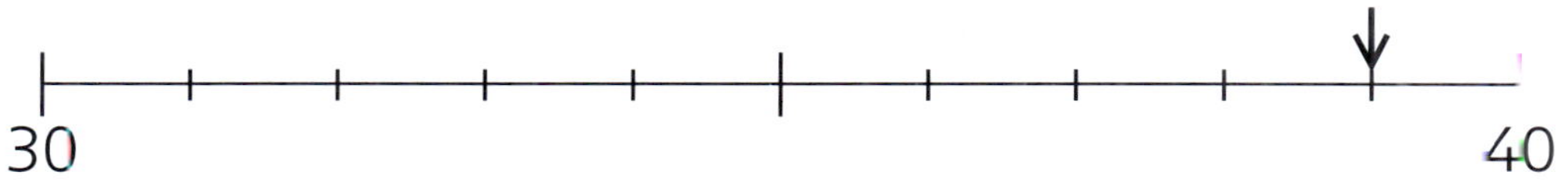

____

4. 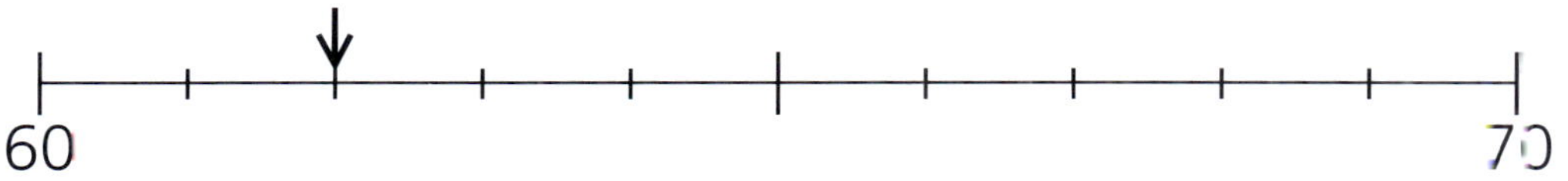

____

5. 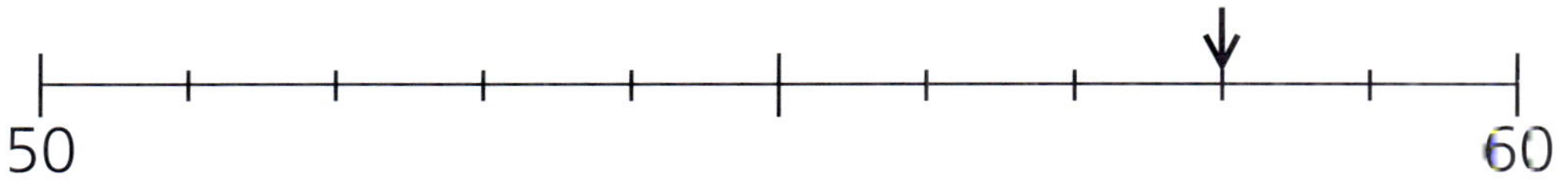

____

6. 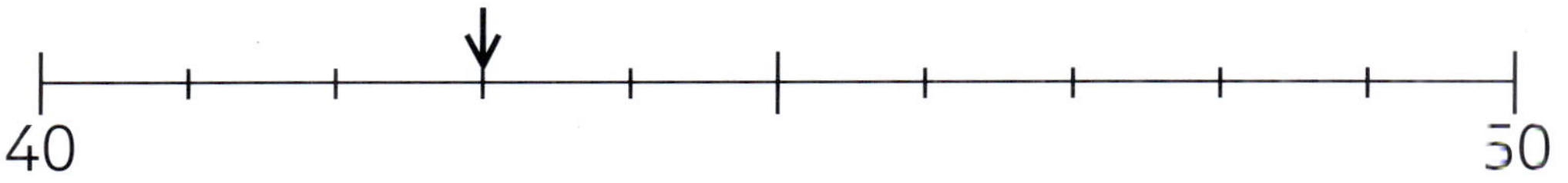

____

7. 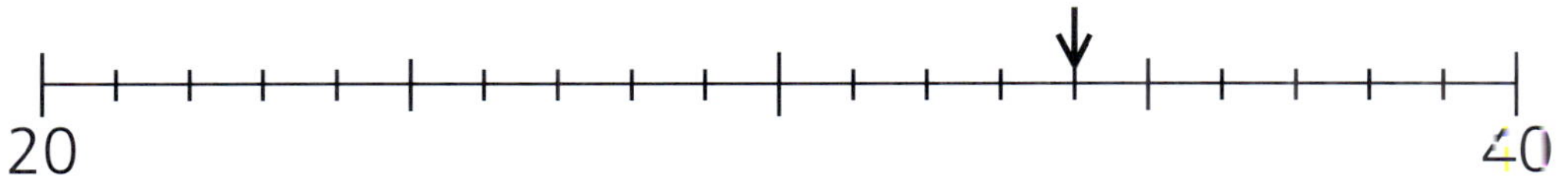

____

8. 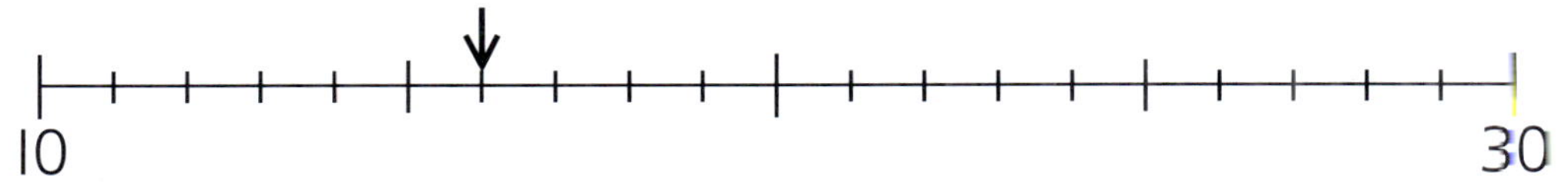

____

9. 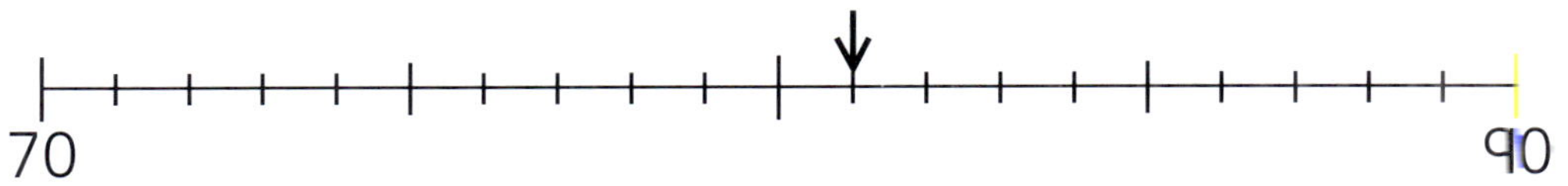

____

10. 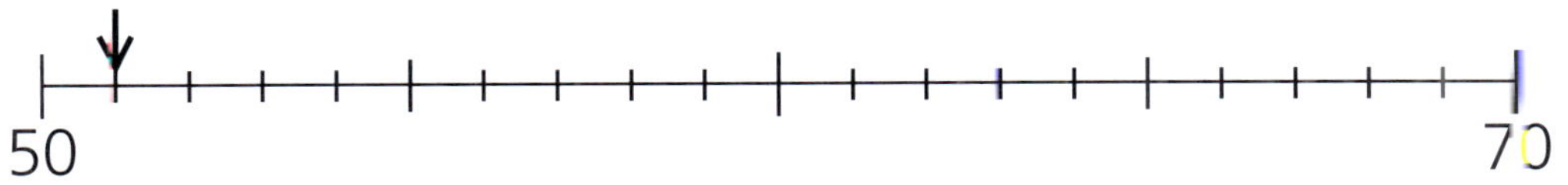

____

Name ______________________

Adding

1 2 3 4 5 6 7 8 9 10 11 12 13 14 15 16 17 18 19 20 21 22 23 24 25 26 27 28 29 30 31 32 33 34 35 36 37 38 39 40 41

Complete these.

Use the number track to help.

1. 16 + 4 =
2. 24 + 6 =
3. 13 + 5 =
4. 16 + 3 =
5. 20 + 4 =
6. 23 + 5 =
7. 24 + 4 =
8. 23 + 3 =
9. 31 + 5 =
10. 40 + 1 =
11. 20 + 9 =
12. 22 + 5 =
13. 23 + 4 =
14. 31 + 7 =
15. 23 + 6 =
16. 22 + 7 =
17. 21 + 9 =
18. 33 + 5 =
19. 31 + 9 =
20. 33 + 4 =
21. 14 + 6 =
22. 21 + 3 =
23. 33 + 6 =
24. 33 + 7 =
25. 25 + 5 =
26. 21 + 6 =
27. 31 + 8 =
28. 24 + 5 =
29. 11 + 7 =
30. 25 + 4 =

Name ______________________________

Problem page

1. Gary saves 13p, and is then given another 3p. How much has he altogether?

2. Anna buys a comic for 23p and a pen for 6p. How much does she spend altogether?

3. Jen has 5p more than Safa, who has 13p. How much does Jen have?

4. Lenny has a score of 22 points. After his next round he has a total of 26 points. How many points did he score in the round?

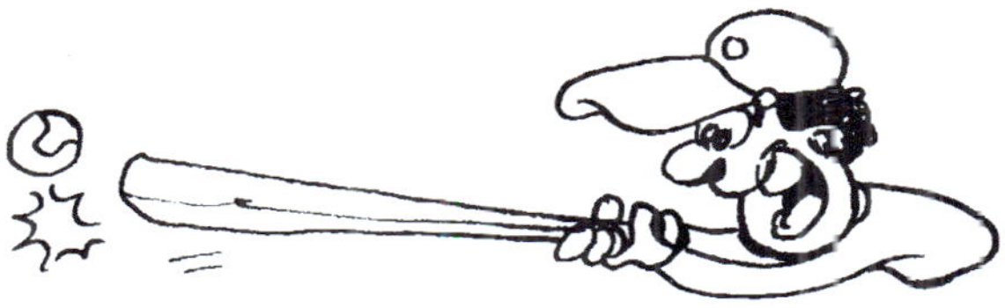

5. Alan is 5 years older than Kylie. Kylie is 13 years old. How old is Alan?

6. Lorna is 6 years younger than David, who is 28 years old. How old is Lorna?

7. The time is 10:20. What time will it be in 5 minutes time?

8. One number is 6 more than another. If the larger number is 17, what is the smaller number?

Name ______________________________

Subtracting

1. 25 − 5 = ☐

2. 36 − 6 = ☐

3. 18 − 8 = ☐

4. 47 − 7 = ☐

5. 29 − 9 = ☐

6. 54 − 4 = ☐

7. 26 − ☐ = 20

8. 38 − ☐ = 30

9. 19 − ☐ = 10

10. 42 − ☐ = 40

11 55 − ☐ = 50

12. 34 − ☐ = 30

13. ☐ − 6 = 30

14. ☐ − 5 = 70

15. ☐ − 7 = 50

16. ☐ − 4 = 20

17. ☐ − 3 = 40

18. ☐ − 8 = 90

Name ______________________________

Subtracting

1 2 3 4 5 6 7 8 9 10 11 12 13 14 15 16 17 18 19 20 21 22 23 24 25 26 27 28 29 30 31 32 33 34 35 36 37 38 39 40

1. 18 – 6 = ☐
2. 15 – 5 = ☐
3. 26 – 4 = ☐
4. 18 – 4 = ☐
5. 29 – 8 = ☐
6. 29 – 6 = ☐
7. 15 – 3 = ☐
8. 25 – 10 = ☐
9. 16 – 5 = ☐
10. 23 – 3 = ☐
11. 27 – 4 = ☐
12. 18 – 7 = ☐
13. 28 – 8 = ☐
14. 29 – 9 = ☐
15. 17 – 6 = ☐
16. 34 – 4 = ☐
17. 35 – 5 = ☐
18. 39 – 8 = ☐
19. 27 – 3 = ☐
20. 26 – 5 = ☐

Name ______________________________

Problems page

1. Jenny won 26 points, then lost 4 points. How many points has she now?

2. There are 35 people on the bus. At the next stop, two people get off. How many people are left on the bus?

3. Sumi has 6p less than Sophie, who has 18p. How much does Sumi have?

4. I went to the post-office with 29p in my purse, and came out with 22p. How much did I spend?

5. The cost of an orange juice has been cut by 5p. It used to be 27p. How much is it now?

6. Dad is 38 years old, and his brother is 6 years younger. How old is Dad's brother?

7. Stephen has 17p, and John has 4p less. How much do they have between them?

8. Milly spent 4p. She had 22p left. How much did she start with?

9. Terri cut a 5 cm piece from her ribbon. It was 37 cm long. How long is it now?

10. The sponsored walk is 19 miles long. There are 7 miles to go. How far have we walked?

Name ______________________________

Counting in ones

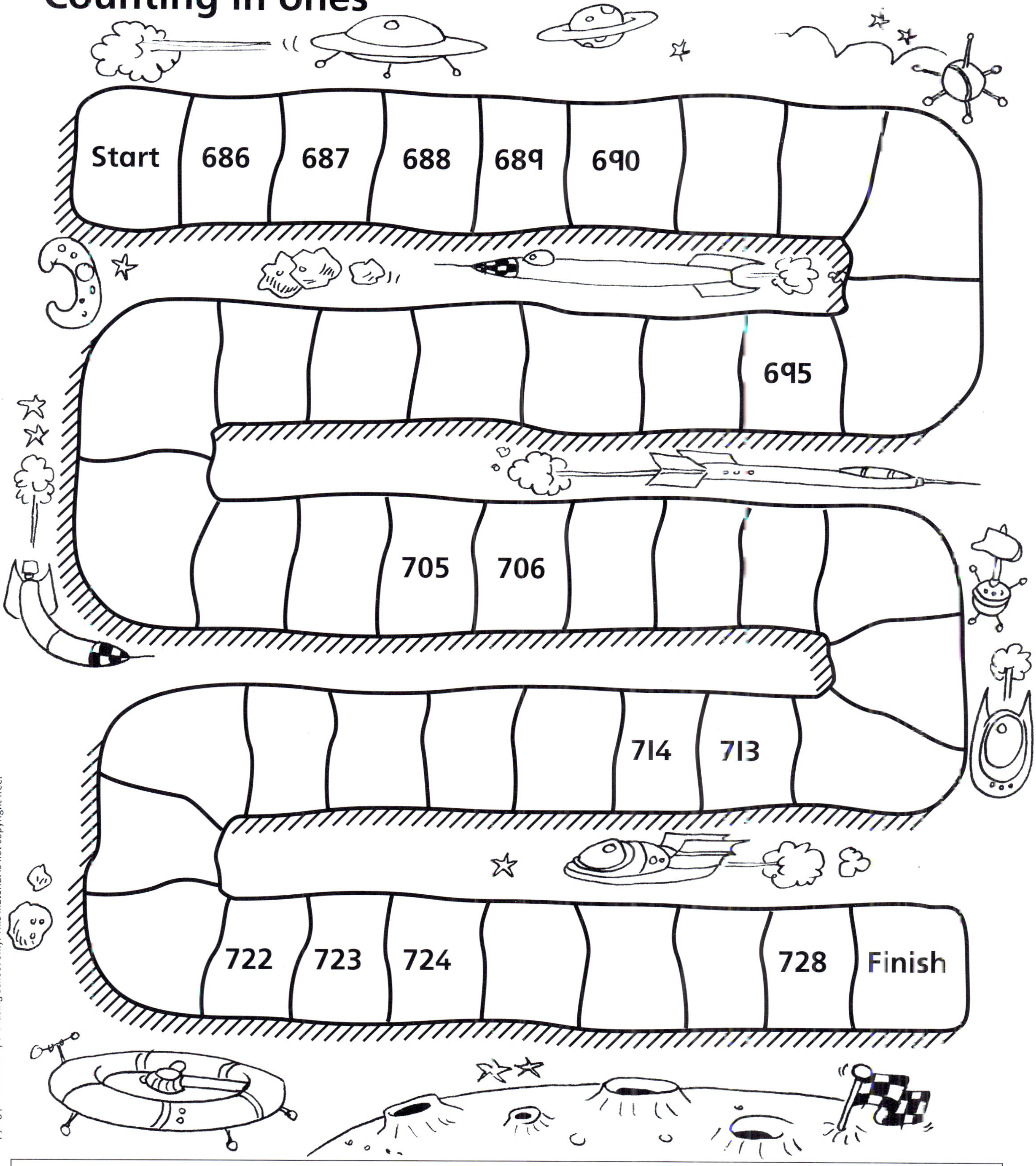

Teacher's instructions
A game for two players. Write the missing numbers.
Take turns to throw the dice and move your counter along the track.
Say aloud each number you land on.
The winner is the one who reaches the finish first.
Colour the odd and even numbers different colours.

Materials
A dice
Counters

Name ______________________________

Counting in tens

Count in tens along each track. Write the missing numbers.

1.

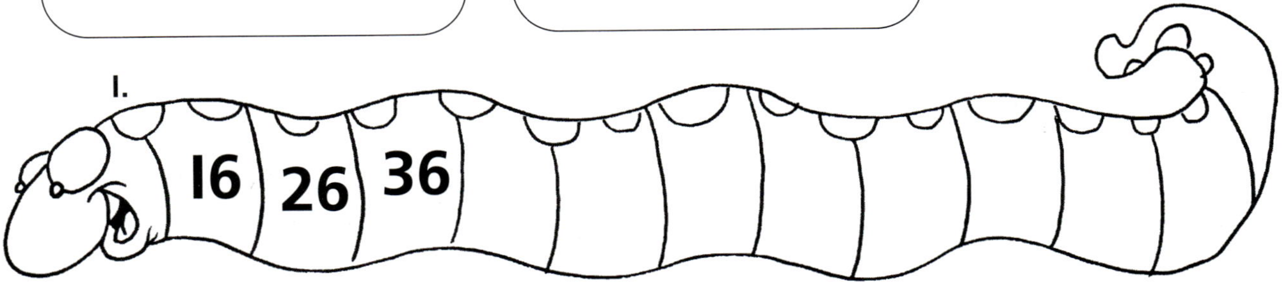

2.

3.

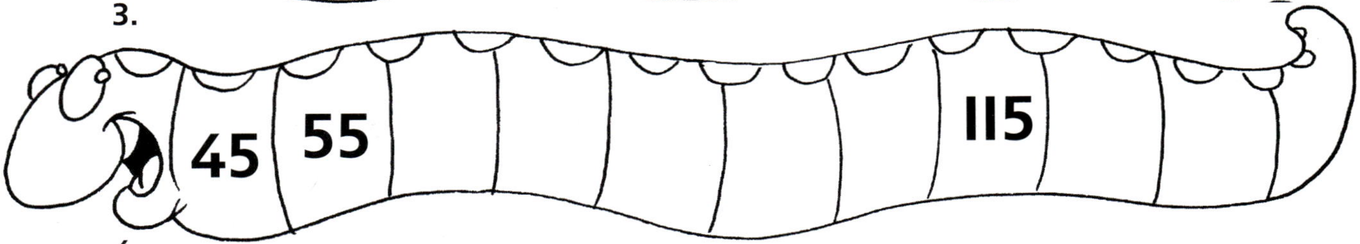

4.

5.

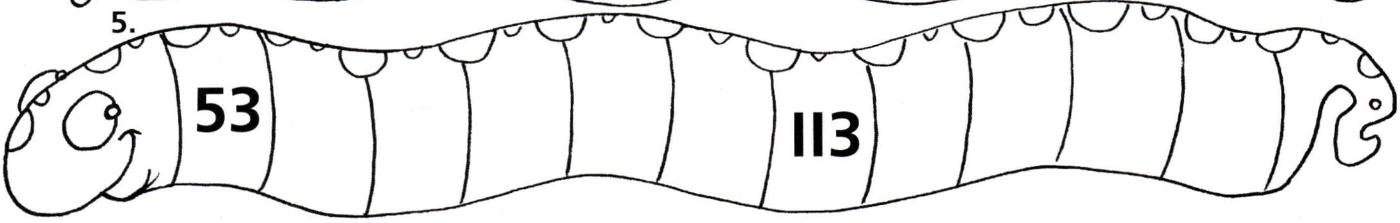

6.

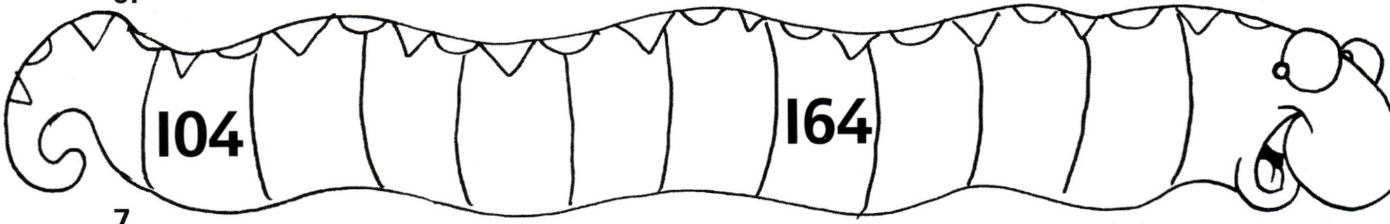

7.

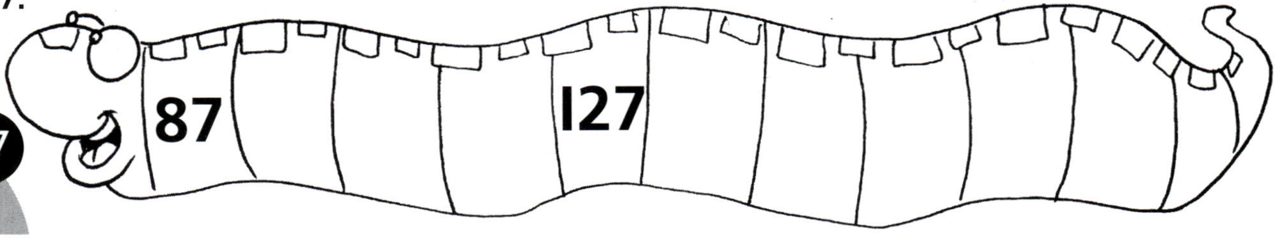

Name ______________________

Counting back in tens

Count back in tens along each line.

Write the hidden numbers.

1.

2.

3.

4.

5.

6.

7.

Ten more, ten less

Write the numbers ten less and ten more.

1. 342 | 352 | 362
2. ☐ | 654 | ☐
3. ☐ | 458 | ☐
4. ☐ | 500 | ☐
5. ☐ | 832 | ☐
6. ☐ | 187 | ☐
7. ☐ | 602 | ☐
8. ☐ | 230 | ☐
9. ☐ | 300 | ☐
10. ☐ | 729 | ☐
11. ☐ | 527 | ☐
12. ☐ | 540 | ☐
13. ☐ | 329 | ☐
14. ☐ | 871 | ☐
15. ☐ | 299 | ☐

Name ____________________

100 more, 100 less

Write the numbers 100 more or 100 less.

327 → 100 more → ___

416 → 100 more → ___

158 → 100 less → ___

273 → 100 more → ___

495 → 100 less → ___

627 → 100 less → ___

235 → 100 more → ___

348 → 100 less → ___

↑ 100 less ↑

192	276	355	619	734	428

↓ 100 more ↓

Name ______________________

Twos

Write the missing numbers.

1.

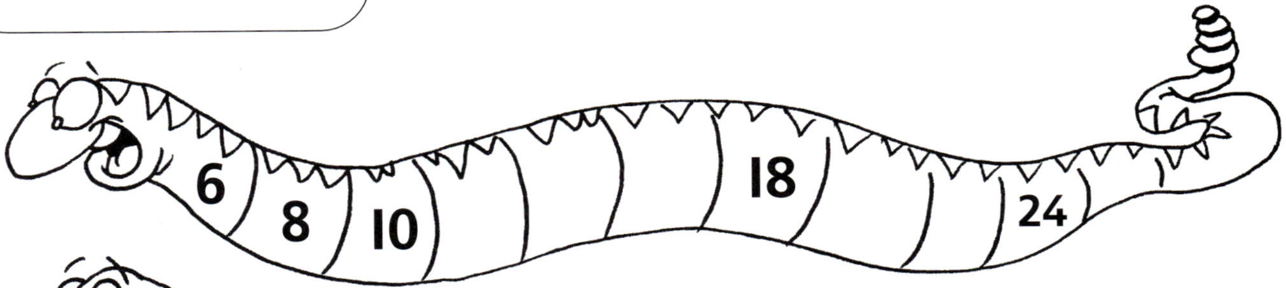

2.

3.

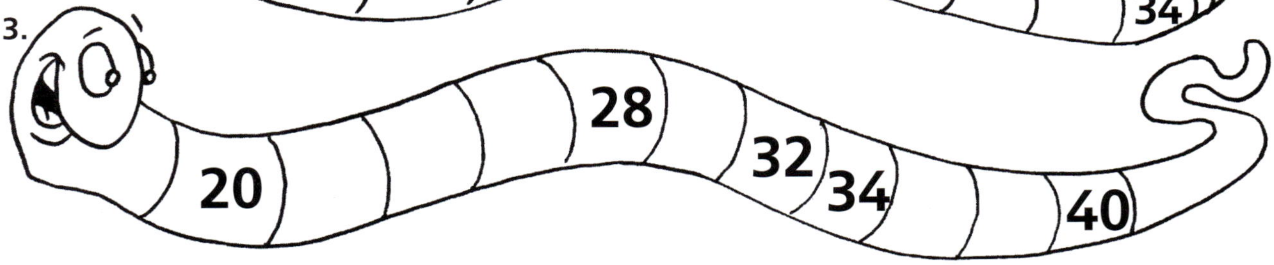

4.

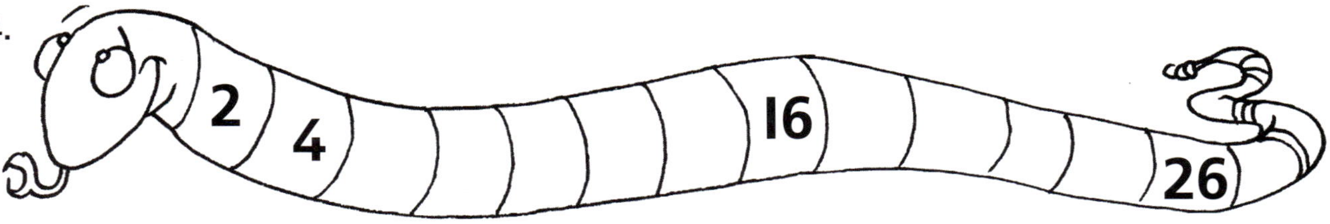

5.

6.

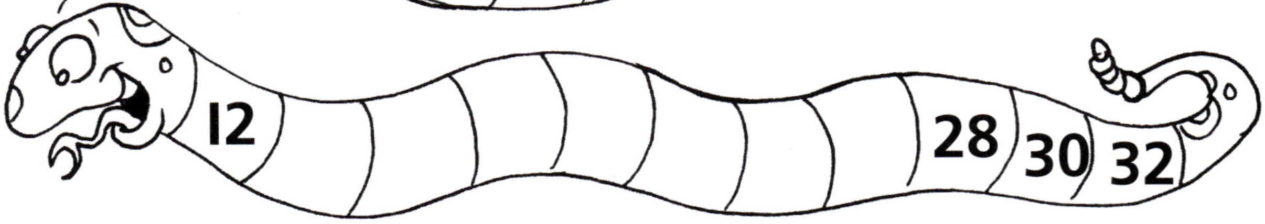

7.

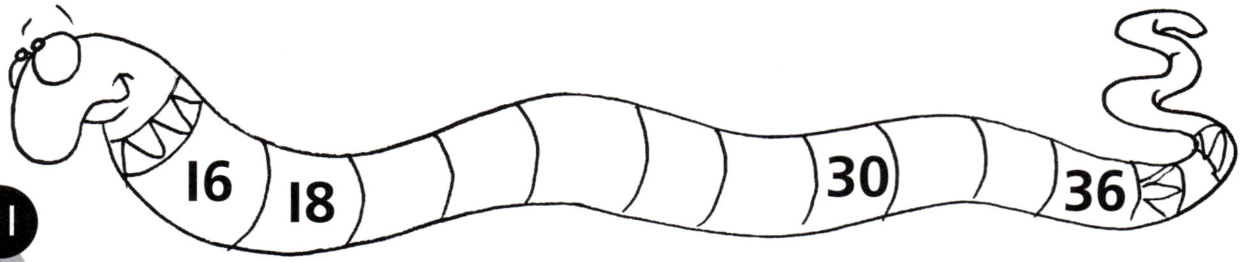

Name ______________________________

Twos

Write the missing numbers.

1. ___ × 2 = 8

2. ___ × 2 = 16

3. ___ × 2 = 18

4. ___ × 2 = 20

5. ___ × 2 = 4

6. ___ × 2 = 10

7. ___ × 2 = 6

8. ___ × 2 = 2

9. ___ × 2 = 12

10. ___ × 2 = 14

11. 11 × 2 = ___

12. 12 × 2 = ___

13. ___ × 2 = 100

Name ______________________________

Multiplying and dividing

Write a multiplication and a division for each set.

1.

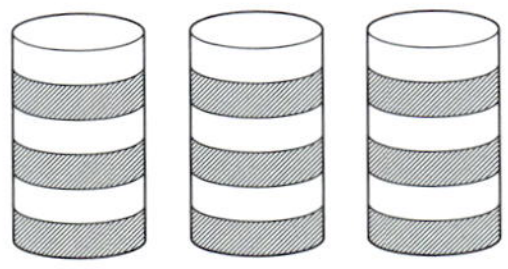

3 x 6 = 18

18 ÷ 3 = 6

2.

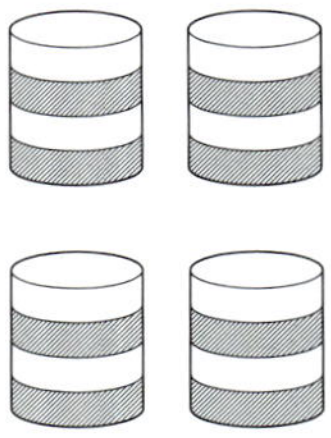

□ x □ = □

□ ÷ □ = □

3.

□ x □ = □

□ ÷ □ = □

4.

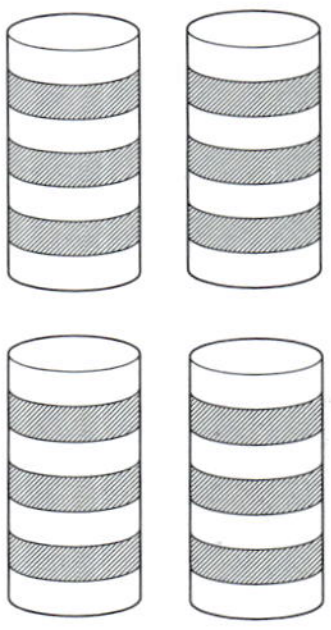

□ x □ = □

□ ÷ □ = □

5.

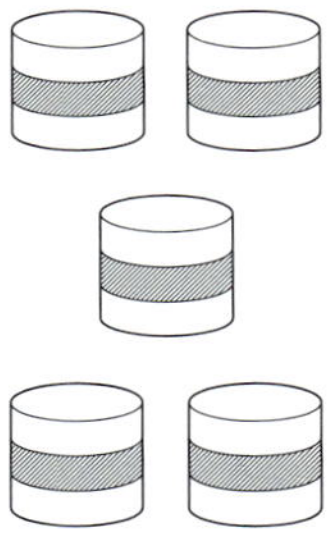

□ x □ = □

□ ÷ □ = □

6.

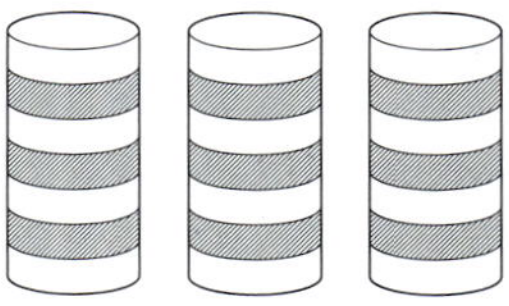

□ x □ = □

□ ÷ □ = □

7.

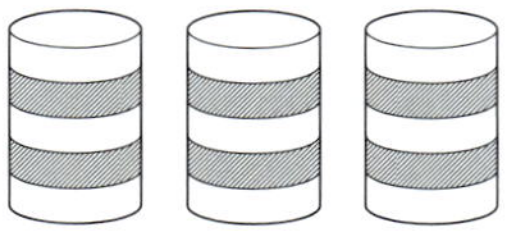

□ x □ = □

□ ÷ □ = □

Name ______________________________

Multiplying and dividing

1. 3 × ___ = 15
   15 ÷ 5 = ___

2. 4 × ___ = 12
   12 ÷ 3 = ___

3. 2 × 4 = ___
   8 ÷ 4 = ___

4. 5 × 4 = ___
   20 ÷ ___ = 5

5. ___ × 5 = 20
   20 ÷ ___ = 4

6. 7 × ___ = 21
   21 ÷ 3 = ___

7. ___ × 2 = 16
   ___ ÷ 2 = 8

8. 1 × ___ = 3
   3 ÷ ___ = 1

9. 6 × ___ = 60
   60 ÷ ___ = 6

10. 9 × 2 = ___
    18 ÷ ___ = 9

Name ____________________

Doubling

Colour each rocket and the planet that is double.

Use one colour for each pair.

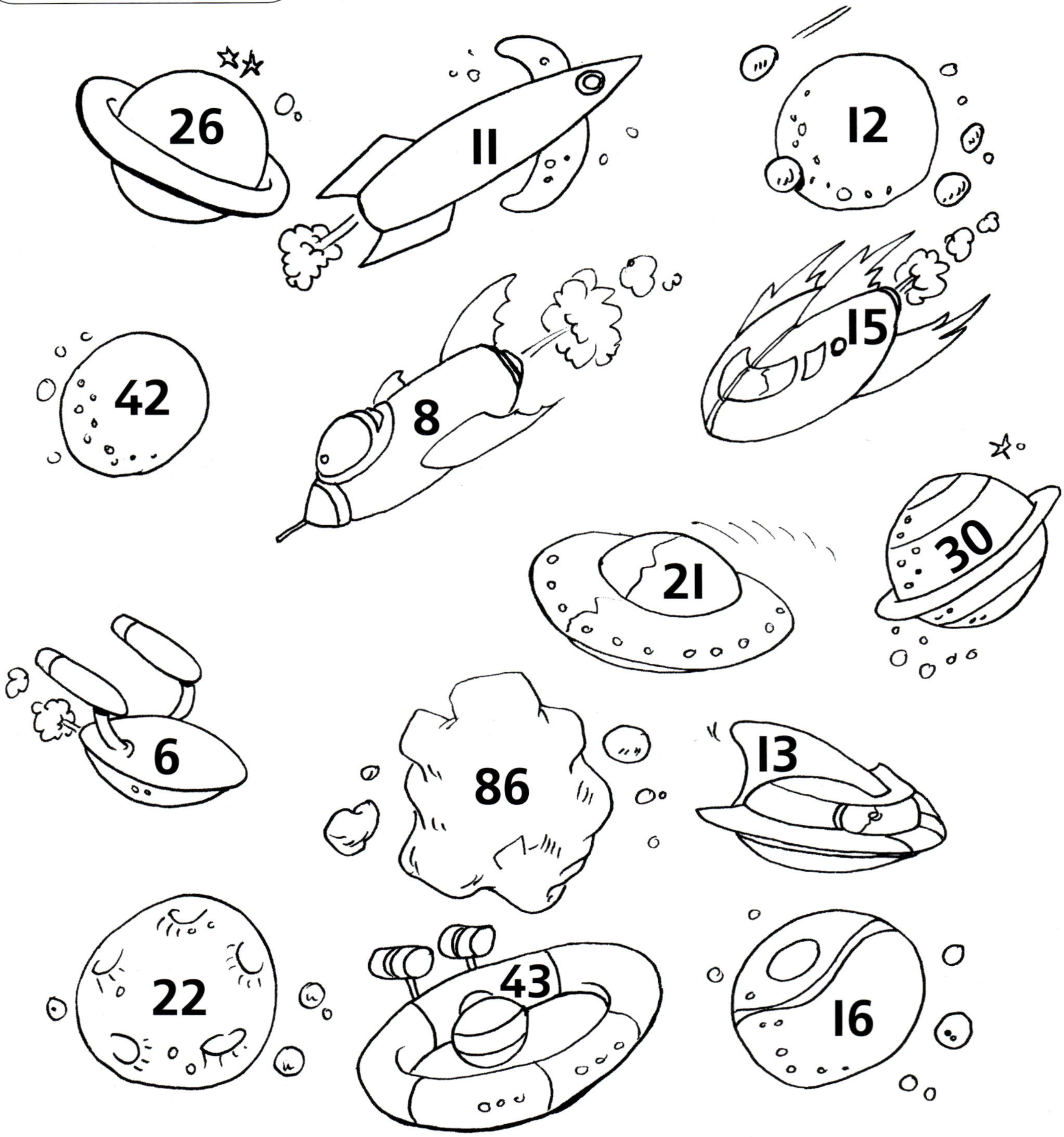

Name ____________________

Doubling and halving

Write the missing numbers.

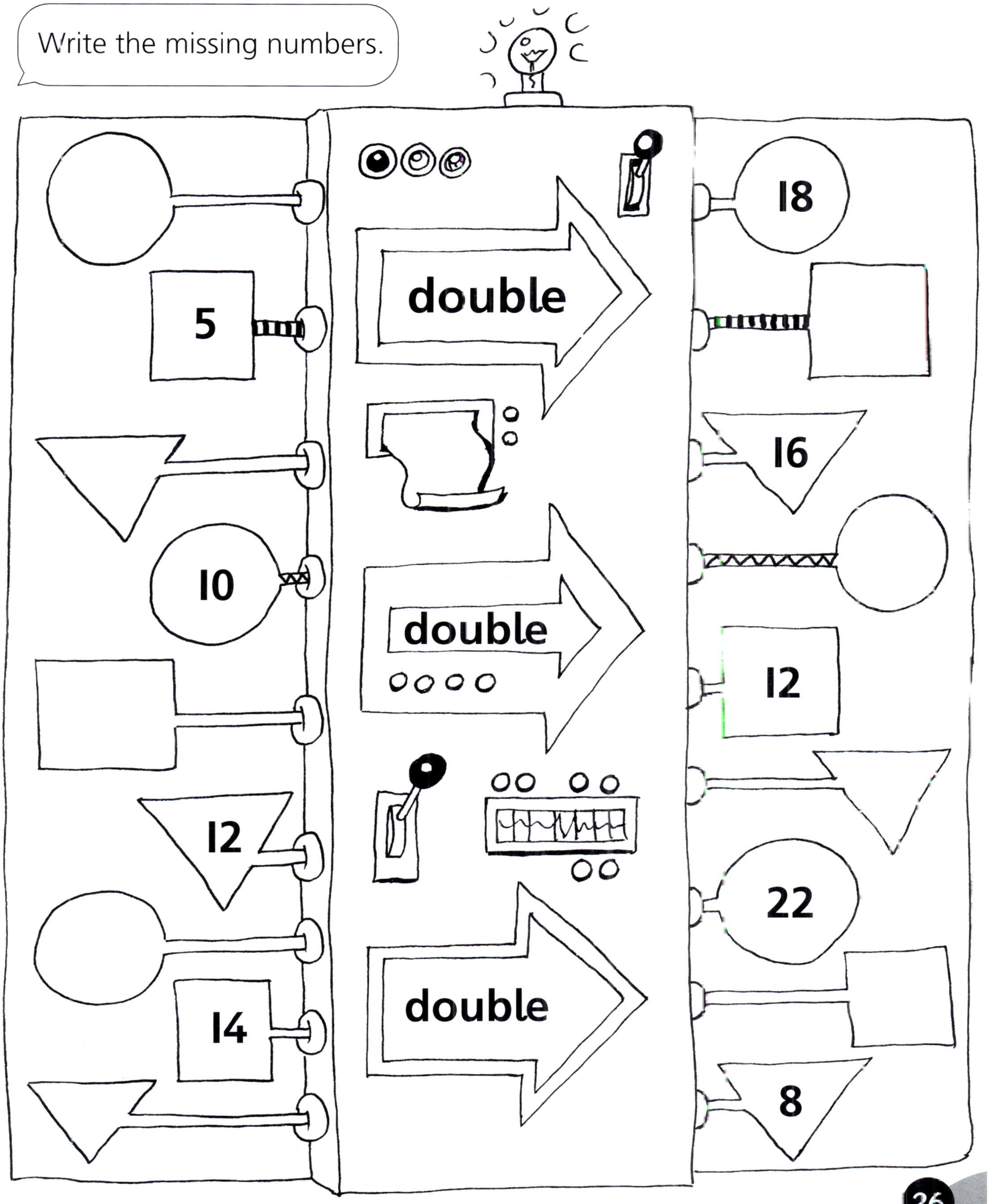

Name ______________________________

Halves, quarters and eighths

For each shape colour one half red, one quarter blue, and one eighth yellow.

1.

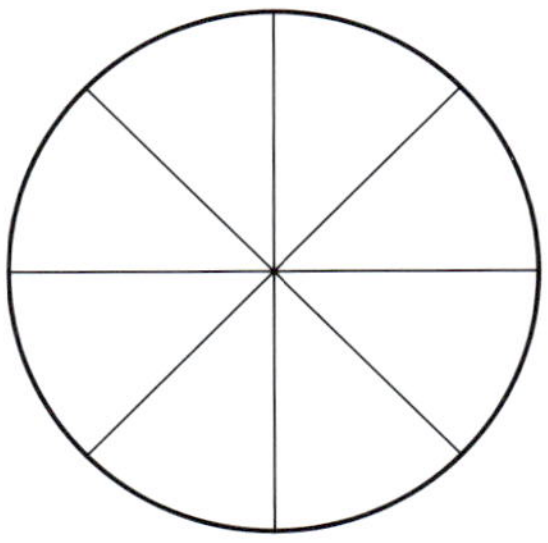

2.

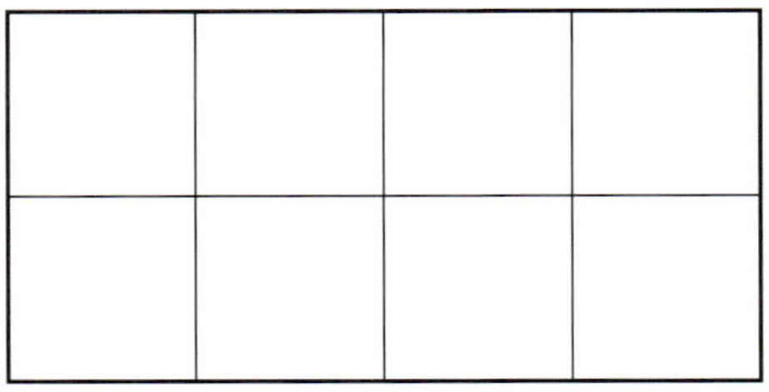

3.

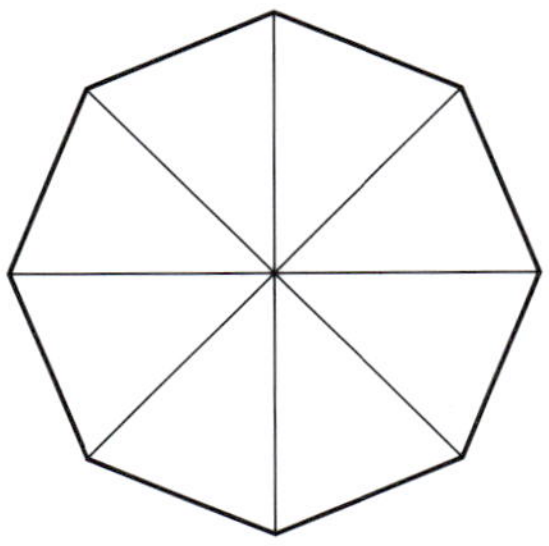

4.

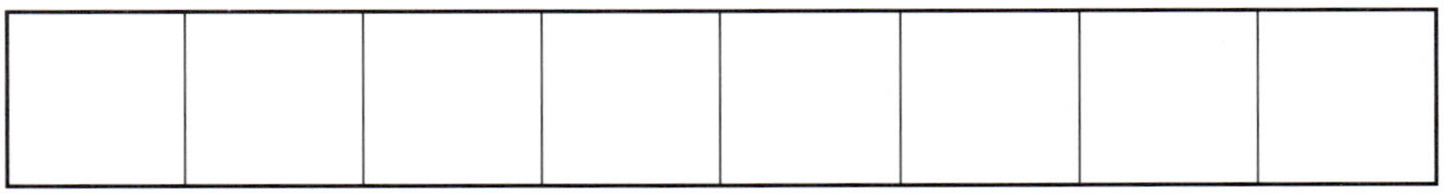

5.

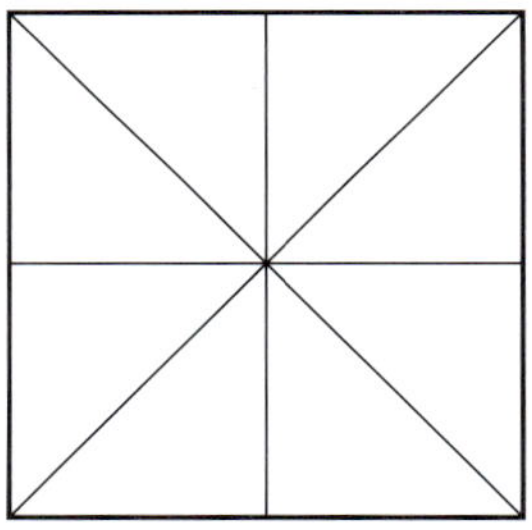

6.

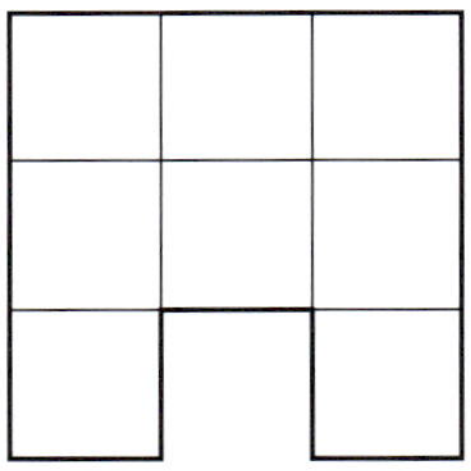

7.

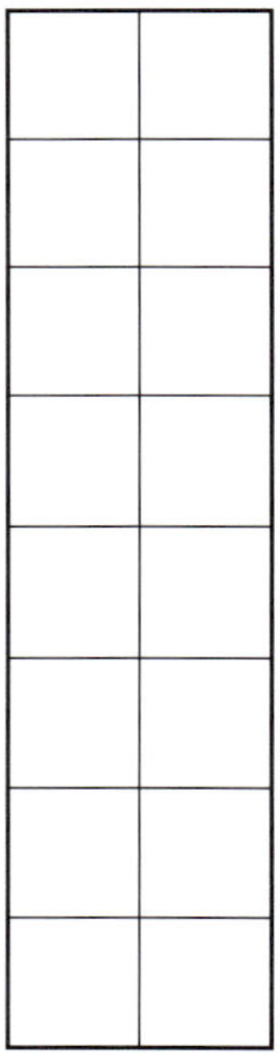

8.

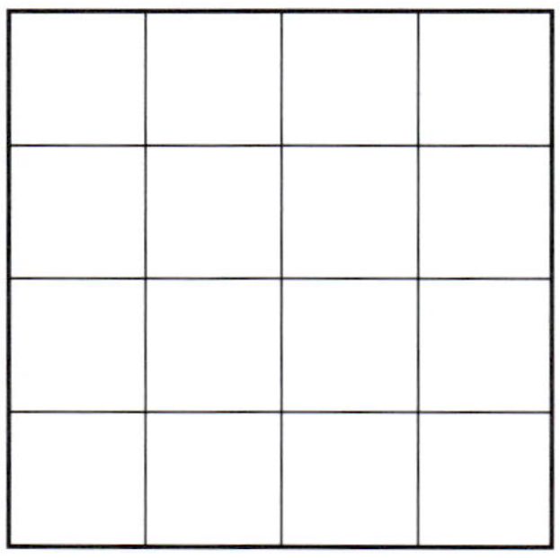

Name ______________________________

Fractions

Write the missing numbers to show how much of each set is shaded.

1.

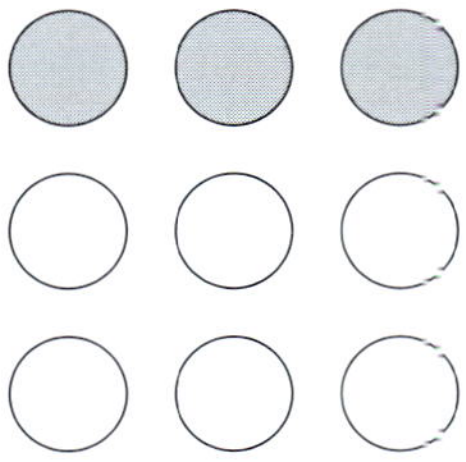

$\frac{1}{3}$ of 9 = 3

2.

☐ of 8 = ☐

3.

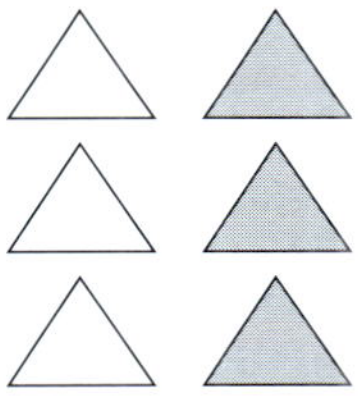

☐ of 6 = ☐

4.

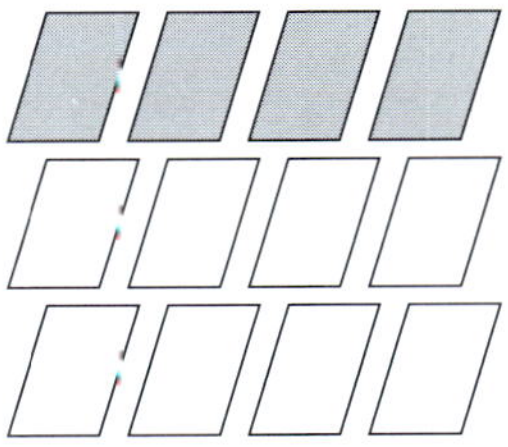

☐ of 12 = ☐

5.

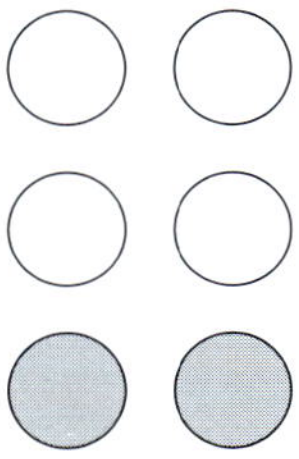

☐ of 6 = ☐

6.

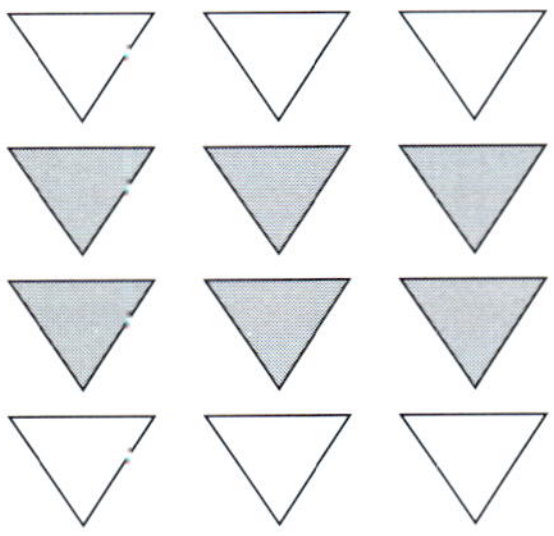

☐ of 12 = ☐

7.

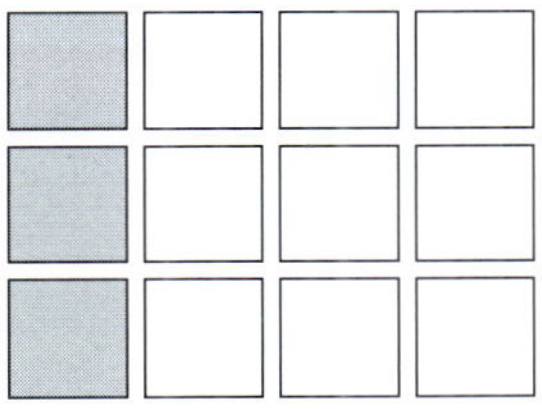

☐ of 12 = ☐

8.

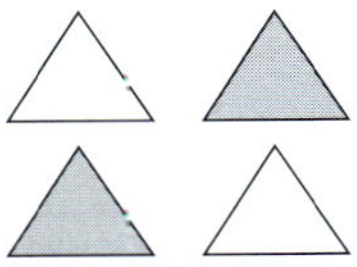

☐ of 4 = ☐

9.

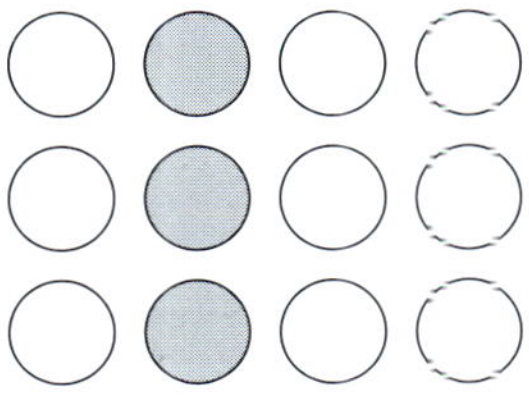

☐ of 16 = ☐

Name ____________________

Fractions

1. $\frac{1}{2}$ of 6 = 3

2. $\frac{1}{3}$ of 9 = 3

3. $\frac{1}{4}$ of 12 = ☐

4. $\frac{1}{2}$ of 20 = ☐

5. $\frac{1}{2}$ of 50 = ☐

6. $\frac{1}{4}$ of 24 = ☐

7. $\frac{1}{4}$ of 20 = ☐

8. $\frac{1}{3}$ of 21 = ☐

9. $\frac{1}{2}$ of 30 = ☐

10. $\frac{1}{3}$ of 27 = ☐

11. $\frac{1}{3}$ of 60 = ☐

12. $\frac{1}{4}$ of 100 = ☐

13. $\frac{1}{3}$ of 30 = ☐

14. $\frac{1}{2}$ of 14 = ☐

15. $\frac{1}{4}$ of 32 = ☐

16. $\frac{1}{2}$ of 18 = ☐

Name ______________________________

Adding multiples of 10

Add the next-door numbers.

Write the total above.

1.

20		60

2.

40		50

3.

70		10

4.

60		30

5.

30		20		40

6.

10		60		20

7.

40		30		50

8.

20		40		30

Write 30, 40, 50 in different orders along the bottom.

What are the top numbers?

9.

	70		90	
30		40		50

10.

30		50		40

11.

12.

13.

14.

Name ________________________________

Adding

Complete these addition grids.

+	5	10	15	20
5				
10				
15				
20				

+	10	20	30	40
25				
35				
45				
55				

+	35	45	55	65
5				
10				
15				
20				

+	15	25	35	45
25				
35				
45				
55				

Name ______________________________

Subtracting multiples of ten

Throw a dice each time to subtract a matching multiple of 10, e.g. 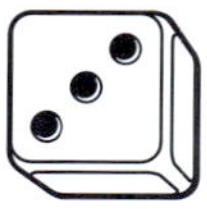 means subtract 30.

1. 65 − ☐ = ☐
2. 70 − ☐ = ☐
3. 85 − ☐ = ☐
4. 60 − ☐ = ☐
5. 80 − ☐ = ☐
6. 95 − ☐ = ☐
7. 90 − ☐ = ☐
8. 75 − ☐ = ☐
9. 100 − ☐ = ☐
10. 120 − ☐ = ☐
11. 105 − ☐ = ☐
12. 115 − ☐ = ☐
13. 270 − ☐ = ☐
14. 180 − ☐ = ☐
15. 350 − ☐ = ☐
16. 290 − ☐ = ☐

Name ______________________________

Adding to 100

For each grid, write the numbers of squares that are shaded, and the numbers that are clear.

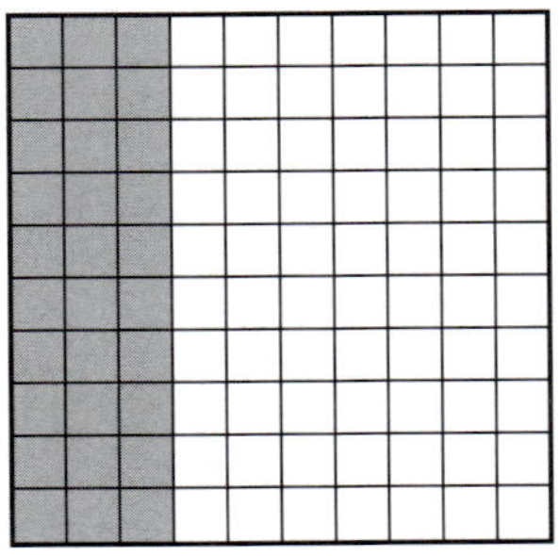

1. ____ + ____ = 100

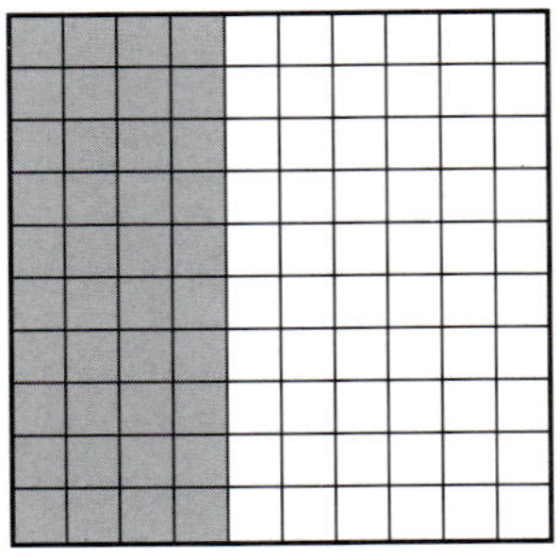

2. ____ + ____ = 100

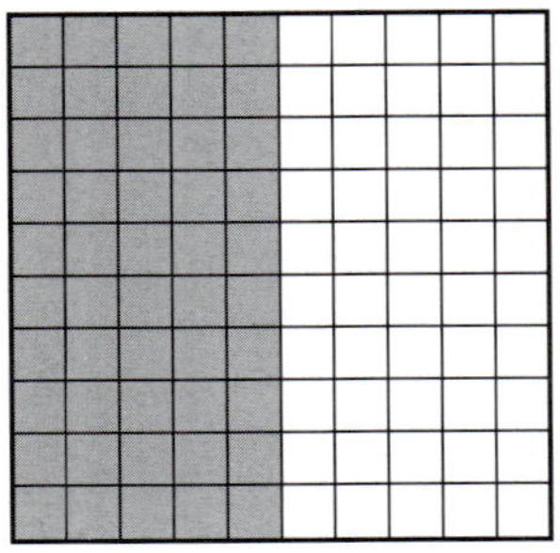

3. ____ + ____ = 100

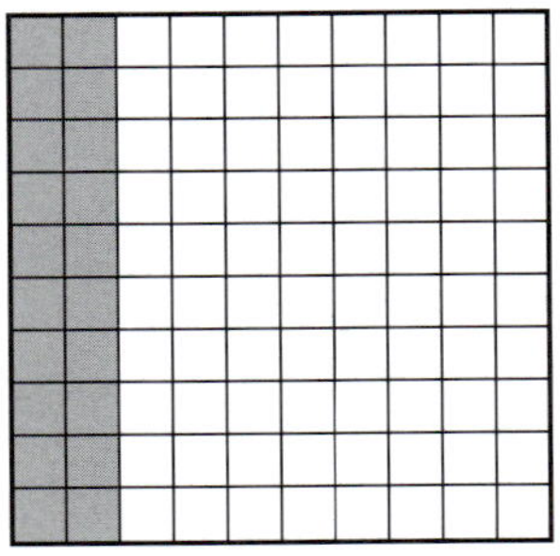

4. ____ + ____ = 100

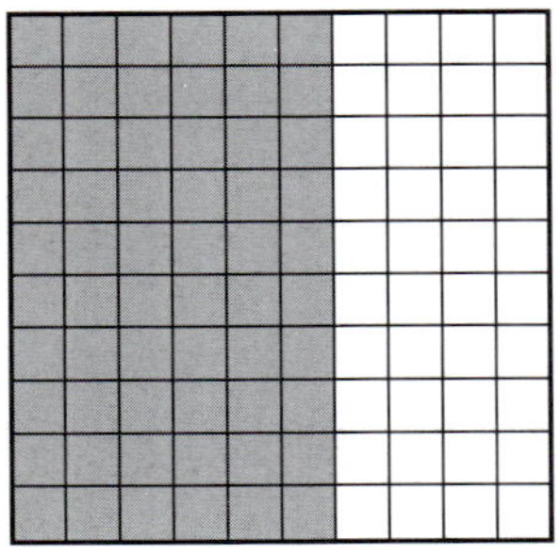

5. ____ + ____ = 100

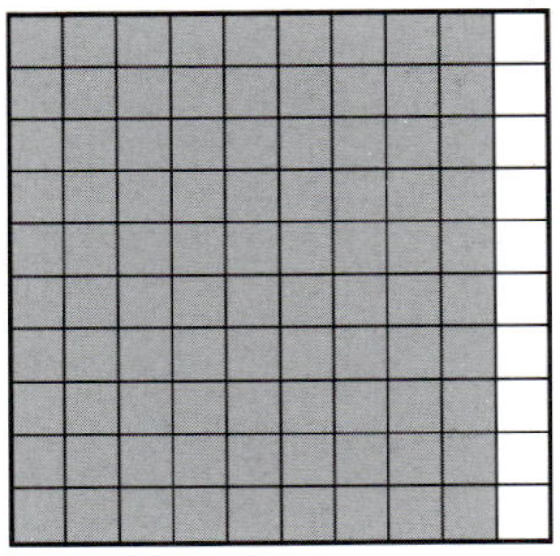

6. ____ + ____ = 100

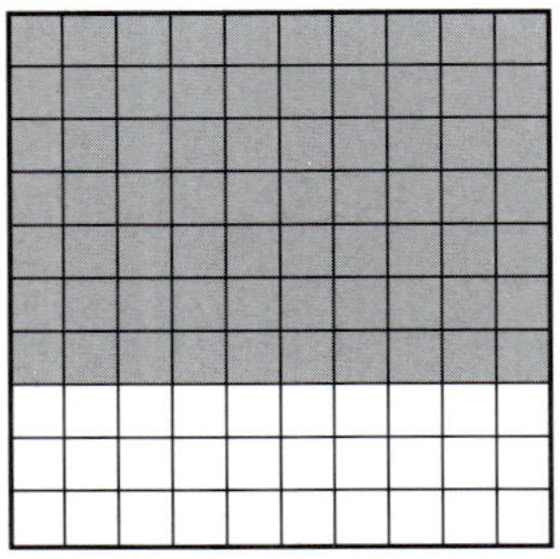

7. ____ + ____ = 100

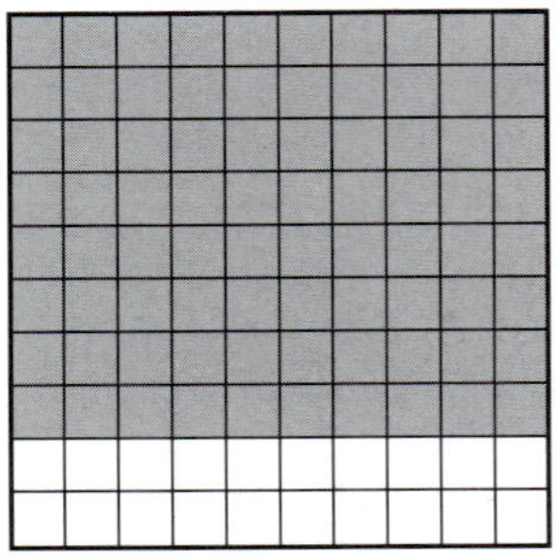

8. ____ + ____ = 100

Name ______________________

Adding to 100

The numbers in each pair total 100.

Write the missing numbers.

1. [ ] [10]
2. [80] [ ]
3. [ ] [50]
4. [ ] [60]
5. [95] [ ]
6. [20] [ ]
7. [35] [ ]
8. [ ] [45]
9. [ ] [75]
10. [ ] [85]
11. [40] [ ]
12. [70] [ ]
13. [ ] [15]
14. [ ] [55]
15. [ ] [65]
16. [ ] [30]
17. [25] [ ]
18. [ ] [5]

Name ______________________________

Numbers to 1000

Write the number at each arrow.

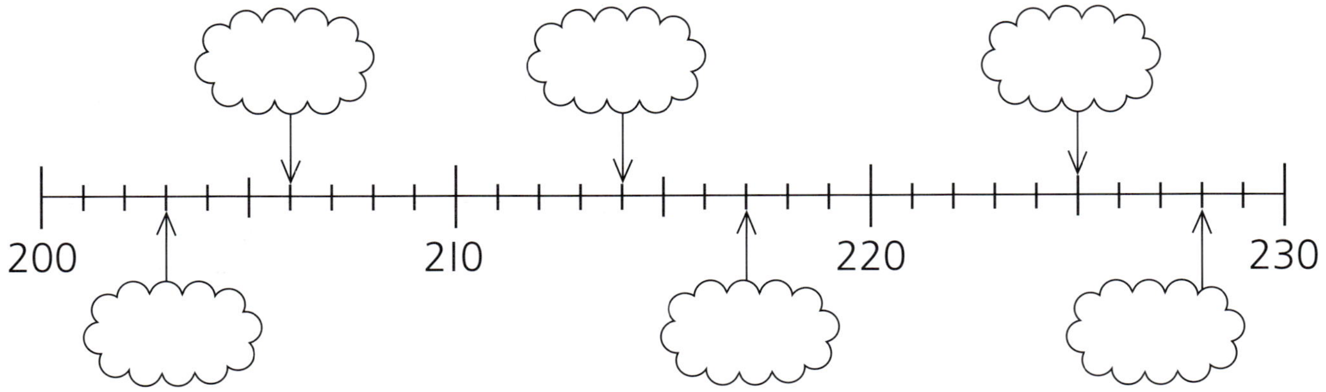

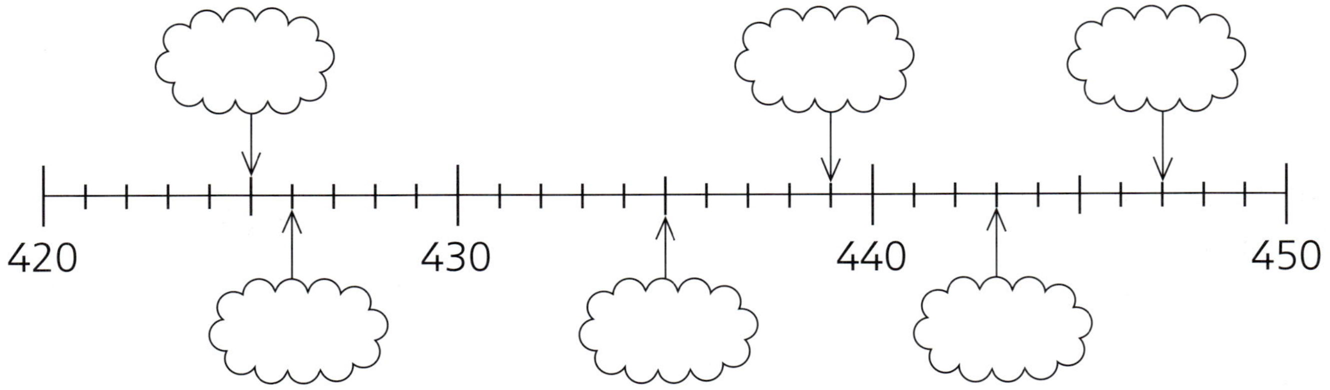

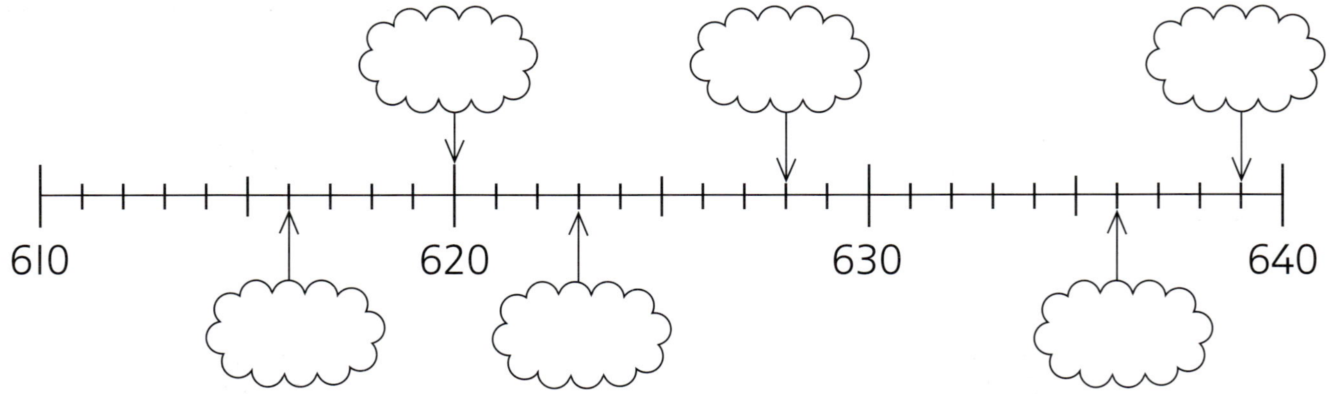

Name ______________________________

More and less

Write the numbers one less and one more.

1.

	230	

2.

	146	

3.

	759	

4.

	800	

5.

	325	

6.

	164	

7.

	999	

Write the numbers 100 less and 100 more.

8.

	243	

9.

	186	

10.

	902	

11.

	874	

12.

	761	

13.

	555	

14.

	438	

Name ______________________________

3-digit numbers

round 1 [ ][ ][ ]

score

round 2 [ ][ ][ ]

score

round 3 [ ][ ][ ]

score

round 4 [ ][ ][ ]

score

round 5 [ ][ ][ ]

score

round 6 [ ][ ][ ]

score

total score [ ]

Teacher's instructions
A game for two or more players, each with a copy of this scoresheet.
Shuffle the number cards and place them face down in a pile.
The top card is revealed, and all players write the number in one of their boxes.
After 3 cards have been revealed, the player with the largest number scores 5 points, the next largest 4 points, and so on.
The winner is the one with the most points after six rounds.

Materials
Number cards (0 to 9)

Name ____________________

The next ten

1. 16 + ☐ = 20	2. 23 + ☐ = 30
3. 34 + ☐ = 40	4. 48 + ☐ = 50
5. 68 + 2 = ☐	6. 55 + ☐ = 60
7. 21 + ☐ = 30	8. 46 + 4 = ☐
9. 76 + ☐ = 80	10. 89 + ☐ = 90
11. 38 + 2 = ☐	12. 36 + ☐ = 40
13. 22 + 8 = ☐	14. 17 + ☐ = 20
15. 91 + ☐ = 100	16. 33 + ☐ = ☐

Name ______________________________

Adding machines

Complete the tables for these adding machines.

in	23	29	38	17	46	19	28	37
out								

in	37	26	18	45	59	26	35	17
out								

in	13	37	24	48	66	34	55	79
out								

Name ______________________________

Missing numbers

Write the missing numbers.

1.	27 + 4 = ☐	2.	35 + 7 = ☐
3.	16 + ☐ = 22	4.	28 + ☐ = 32
5.	☐ + 5 = 42	6.	☐ + 7 = 53
7.	19 + ☐ = 23	8.	☐ + 5 = 32
9.	3 + 18 = ☐	10.	7 + 25 = ☐
11	6 + ☐ = 33	12.	☐ + 38 = 43
13.	☐ + 18 = 22	14.	3 + ☐ = 32
15.	5 + 49 = ☐	16.	4 + ☐ = 41

Name ______________________

Differences

Write the difference between each pair of ringed numbers.

1. 15 **(16)** 17 18 19 **(20)** 21 d = 4

2. 22 **(23)** 24 25 26 27 28 29 30 **(31)** 32 d = ☐

3. 35 **(36)** 37 38 39 40 41 42 43 44 **(45)** 46 d = ☐

4. 57 58 **(59)** 60 61 62 63 64 65 **(66)** 67 68 d = ☐

5. 60 **(61)** 62 63 64 65 66 67 68 **(69)** 70 71 d = ☐

6. 2 **(3)** 4 5 6 7 8 9 10 11 12 **(13)** 14 d = ☐

7. 96 97 **(98)** 99 100 101 102 103 104 105 **(106)** 107 108 109 d = ☐

8. 69 70 71 **(72)** 73 74 75 76 77 78 **(79)** 80 81 82 83 d = ☐

Name ______________________________

Differences

Teacher's instructions
A game for two players. Choose where to place your counter.
Take turns to throw the dice and move your counter. Take cubes to match the difference between your number and the other player's.
The winner is the first to collect 50 cubes.
Find pairs of numbers on the track with a difference of 5.

Materials
A dice
Counters
Cubes

Name ______________________________

Problem page

1. Two numbers have a difference of 5, and a total of 11. What are the numbers?

2. Leo has saved 27p, and Jen has saved 34p. How much more does Jen have than Leo?

3. Karen ran round the garden in 42 seconds. It took Penny 38 seconds. What is the difference between the two times?

4. A sticker costs 23p, but Peter only has 19p left in his pocket. How much more does he need?

5. Ali has scored 5 points less than Mary. Ali has 27 points. How many points do they have between them?

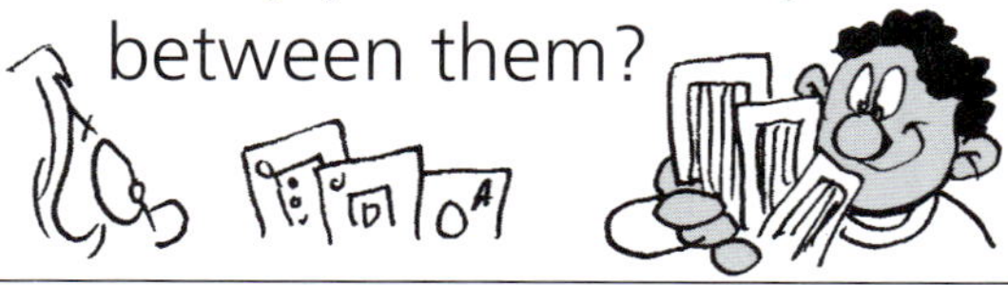

6. My cat is 21 cm tall, and my rabbit is 16 cm tall. What is the difference in height?

7. Tickets cost 25p for adults and 18p for children. What is the difference in price?

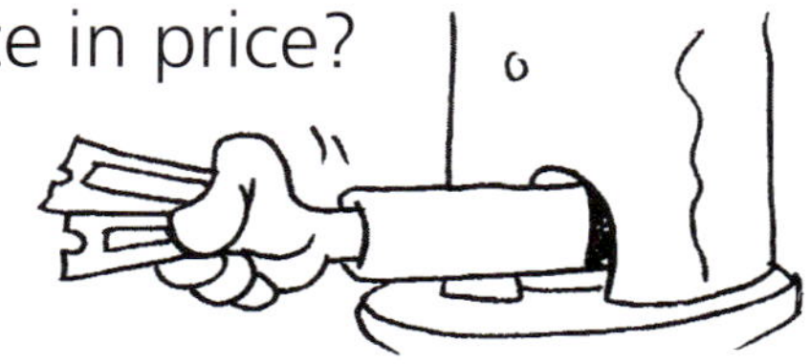

8. Two pieces of ribbon have a difference in length of 7 cm. The longer piece is 105 cm. What is the length of the shorter piece?

9. The difference between two numbers is 5. The smaller number is 57. What is the larger number?

10. The digits of a 2-digit number have a difference of 3. The number is in the ×5 table. What could it be?

Name ______________________________

Adding money

Ann

Ben

Kenji

Dean

Fay

Aziz

Hamish

Ivan

Write the total savings between:

1. Ann and Kenji __________
2. Ivan and Dean __________
3. Dean and Aziz __________
4. Ben and Fay __________
5. Hamish and Ann __________
6. Kenji and Ivan __________
7. Aziz and Fay __________
8. Ben and Kenji __________
9. Ann and Dean __________
10. Aziz and Hamish __________

Name ______________________________

Subtracting money

Write the new prices.

	20p off	50p off	30p off
 £1.75	£1.55		
 £2.65			
 £3.99			
 £1.89			
 £4.55			
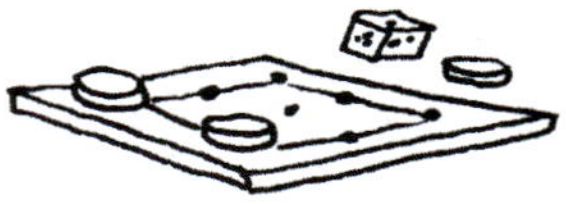 £2.85			
 £5.75			
 85p			

Name ______________________________

Problems page

1. Jim saved £1.65, and was given 30p for cleaning the car. How much has he got now?

2. Jigsaw puzzles were £1.85 each. They are now 20p off. How much do they cost now?

3. When Sara has saved another 20p, she can buy an annual which costs £3.95. How much has she got now?

4. Posters cost £4.55 with 40p off for club members. How much does a member pay?

5. Kevin sent for a team photo. It costs £5.60 and 30p for postage. How much altogether?

6. Children's cinema seats were £3.20 last year. This year they are 30p more. How much are they?

7. Boat rides this year are £4.40. Last year they were £4.70. How much has the price gone down?

8. Flippers have been reduced by 10p from £5.70. How much are they?

9. Amit has £6.70 of his holiday money left. He pays 40p for a bus ride. How much does he have left?

10. Guy spent £5.10 on a train ticket to London, and bought a 50p drink. How much did the journey cost altogether?

Name ______________________

Adding two 2-digit numbers`

1. 43 + 25 = 68
2. 31 + 45 = ☐
3. 26 + 32 = ☐
4. 18 + 21 = ☐
5. 43 + 55 = ☐
6. 27 + 52 = ☐
7. 36 + 26 = ☐
8. 58 + 25 = ☐
9. 18 + 34 = ☐
10. 27 + 16 = ☐
11. 73 + 19 = ☐
12. 45 + 46 = ☐
13. 53 + 28 = ☐
14. 27 + 37 = ☐
15. 45 + 28 = ☐
16. 35 + 45 = ☐
17. 67 + 23 = ☐
18. 73 + 18 = ☐
19. 24 + 49 = ☐
20. 57 + 36 = ☐

Name ______________________

Buying

Write how much is left after buying one of these pens.

2lp

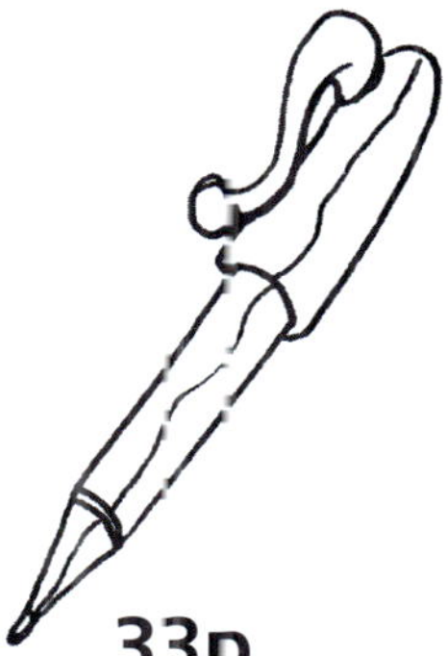
33p

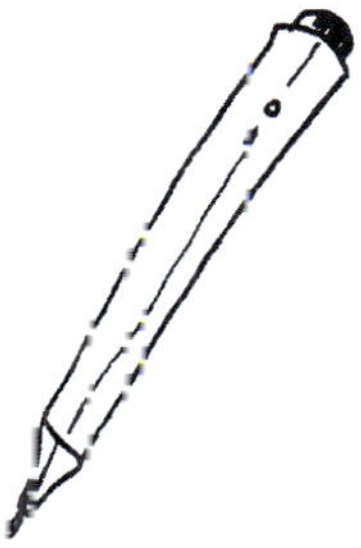
15p

______ ______ ______

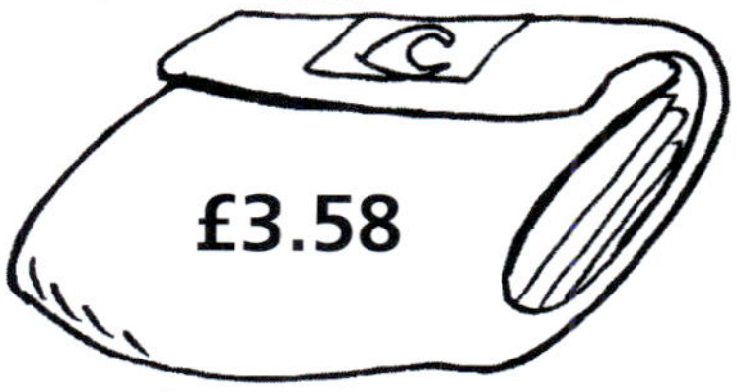

______ ______ ______

______ ______ ______

______ ______ ______

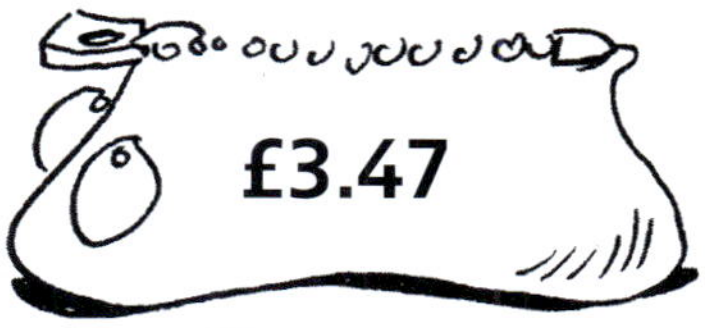

______ ______ ______

______ ______ ______

Name ______________________________

Adding two 2-digit numbers

Choose balls from the table that add to give these scores.

1. 46 + 35 — score 81
2. ◯ ◯ — score 62
3. ◯ ◯ — score 65
4. ◯ ◯ — score 73
5. ◯ ◯ — score 77
6. ◯ ◯ — score 45
7. ◯ ◯ — score 94
8. ◯ ◯ — score 56
9. ◯ ◯ — score 105
10. ◯ ◯ — score 84
11. ◯ ◯ — score 86

Name ____________________

Adding 9, 19, 29 ...

1. 43 + 19 = ☐
2. 54 + 9 = ☐
3. 72 + 29 = ☐
4. 81 + 19 = ☐
5. 68 + 29 = ☐
6. 29 + 19 = ☐
7. 37 + 9 = ☐
8. 46 + 19 = ☐
9. 28 + 29 = ☐
10. 37 + 29 = ☐
11. 46 + 9 = ☐
12. 55 + 19 = ☐
13. 87 + 19 = ☐
14. 64 + 19 = ☐
15. 82 + 29 = ☐
16. 75 + 29 = ☐
17. 63 + 19 = ☐
18. 52 + 9 = ☐
19. 14 + 39 = ☐
20. 42 + 39 = ☐

Name ______________________________

Adding 9, 19, 29 ...

Teacher's instructions
A game for two players.
Take turns to throw the dice and move your counter around the track.
Add the numbers you land on, keeping a running total. Stop when someone's total goes over 100.
Find 5 numbers on the track that make 65.

Materials
A dice
Counters

Name ______________________________

Taking away 19

All these toys have gone down by 19p.

Write the new prices.

1.

46p – 19p =

2.

3.

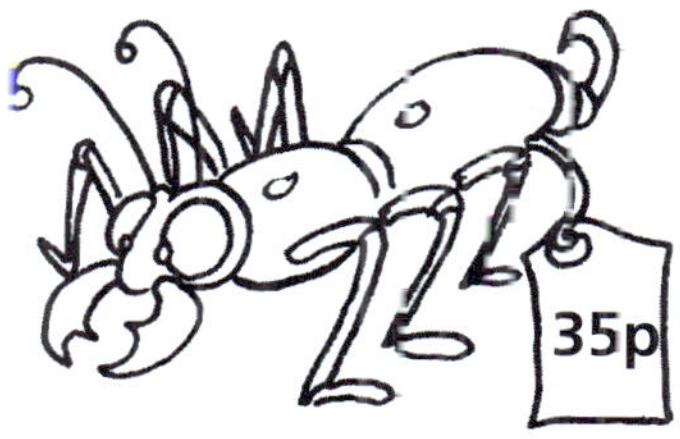

4.

5.

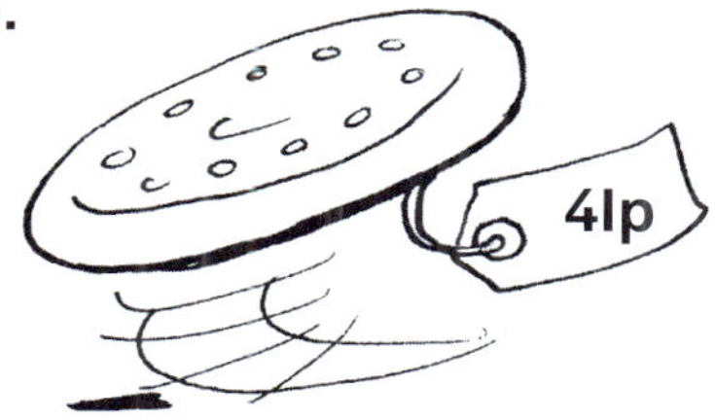

6.

7.

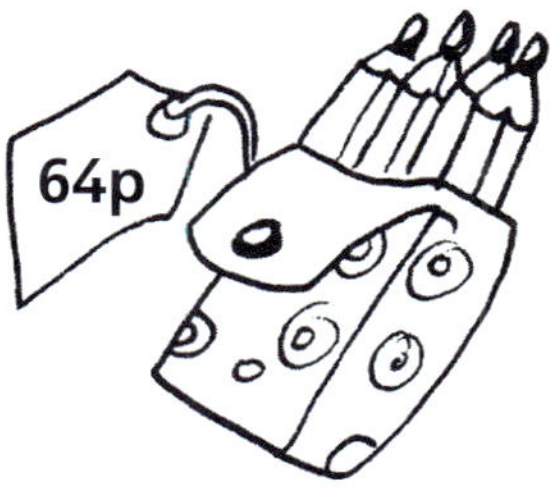

8.

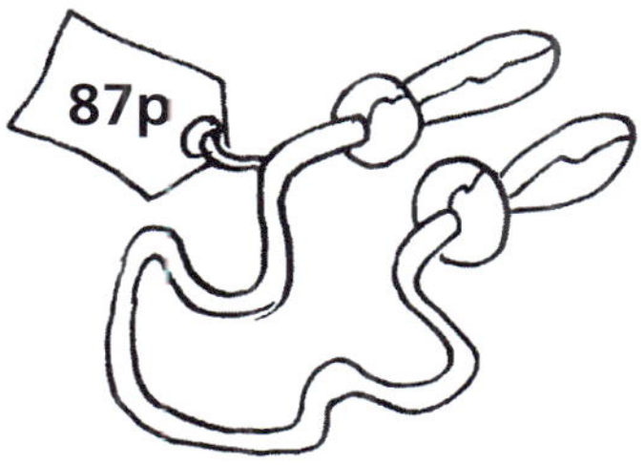

9.

10.

11.

12.

Name ___________________________

Multiples

Complete the table with ticks and crosses.

	Multiple of 10	Multiple of 50	Multiple of 100	Multiple of 2	Multiple of 5
630					
950					
35					
180					
220					
95					
20					
46					
17					
100					

Name ______________________________

Odd and even

Complete these. Colour the odd answers green. Colour the even answers yellow.

1. 15 + 5 =

2. 16 + 3 =

3. 17 + 5 =

4. 8 + 8 =

5. 13 + 7 =

6. 12 + 3 =

7. 21 + 3 =

8. 21 + 2 =

9. 16 + 5 =

10. 17 + 4 =

11. 11 + 4 =

12. 12 + 2 =

13. 16 + 2 =

14. 17 + 1 =

Name ______________________

Missing numbers

Write the missing numbers.

1. 30 + ___ = 100
2. ___ + 40 = 100
3. 80 + ___ = 100
4. 10 + ___ = 100
5. ___ + 50 = 100
6. ___ + 60 = 100
7. 70 + ___ = 100
8. 20 + ___ = 100
9. 90 + ___ = 100
10. ___ + 65 = 100
11. ___ + 75 = 100
12. 85 + ___ = 100
13. 45 + ___ = 100
14. ___ + 35 = 100
15. 15 + ___ = 100
16. ___ + 25 = 100
17. ___ + 95 = 100
18. 55 + ___ = 100

Name ______________________________

Adding to 100

Loop pairs that add to 100.

The numbers must be next to each other.

52	43	11	89	44	25
36	65	27	18	46	75
31	35	49	26	54	19
69	33	72	28	10	30
72	45	55	43	90	20
8	92	16	59	27	80

Write your own numbers (up to 100) in the grid, so that pairs can be looped.

Loop pairs that add to 100.

Name ______________________

Adding

Complete these additions.

1. 69 + 30 = ______
2. 61 + 41 = ______
3. 78 + 20 = ______
4. 34 + 65 = ______
5. 25 + 74 = ______
6. 85 + 16 = ______
7. 44 + 54 = ______
8. 66 + 35 = ______
9. 16 + 85 = ______
10. 76 + 26 = ______
11. 96 + 5 = ______
12. 56 + 45 = ______
13. 35 + 75 = ______
14. 65 + 45 = ______
15. 18 + 90 = ______
16. 32 + 73 = ______
17. 41 + 62 = ______
18. 23 + 81 = ______
19. 72 + 31 = ______
20. 82 + 21 = ______

Name ______________________________

Doubling machine

Complete these doubling tables.

in	21	24	32	23	14	41	31	42
out								

in	11	34	22	12	44	33	13	43
out								

in	25	5	45	75	15	65	35	55
out								

Name ______________________

Adding near doubles

Add by doubling first.

1. 25 + 26 = ______

2. 14 + 15 = ______

3. 35 + 37 = ______

4. 11 + 12 = ______

5. 13 + 14 = ______

6. 22 + 23 = ______

7. 33 + 34 = ______

8. 44 + 45 = ______

9. 15 + 16 = ______

10. 23 + 24 = ______

11. 41 + 42 = ______

12. 35 + 36 = ______

13. 12 + 14 = ______

14. 24 + 26 = ______

15. 36 + 37 = ______

16. 45 + 46 = ______

17. 42 + 44 = ______

18. 31 + 33 = ______

Name ______________________

Tens

Colour each bee and the hive that is × 10.

Use one colour for each pair.

Name ______________________

Fives

Write the missing numbers.

1. 3 × 5 = 15

2. ___ × 5 = 20

3. ___ × 5 = 30

4. 4 × 5 = ___

5. ___ × 5 = 25

6. ___ × 5 = 10

7. 2 × 5 = ___

8. ___ × 5 = 45

9. ___ × 5 = 50

10. 8 × 5 = ___

11. ___ × 5 = 60

12. ___ × 5 = 40

13. 6 × 5 = ___

14. 10 × 5 = ___

15. ___ × 5 = 5

Name ______________________________

Multiplying

1. 3 × [5] = [15]

2. 3 × [ ] = [ ]

3. 5 × [ ] = [ ]

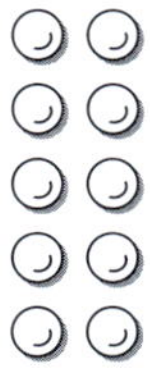

4. 3 × [ ] = [ ]

5. 5 × [ ] = [ ]

6. 6 × [ ] = [ ]

7. 2 × [ ] = [ ]

8. 4 × [ ] = [ ]

9. 4 × [ ] = [ ]

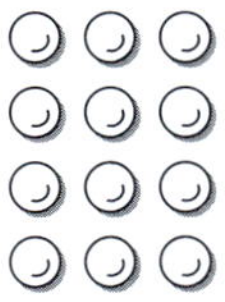

10. 6 × [ ] = [ ]

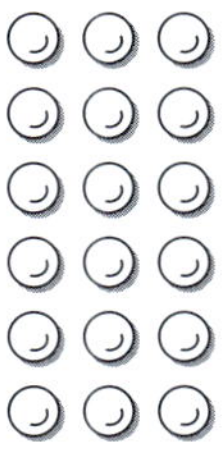

Name ____________________

Multiplying

A 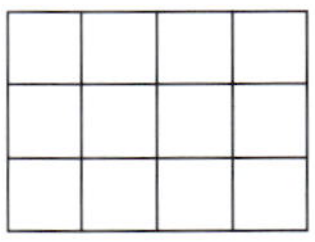

B 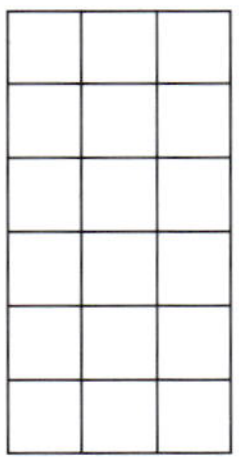

C 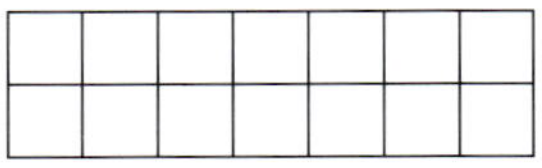

D 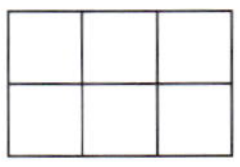

E 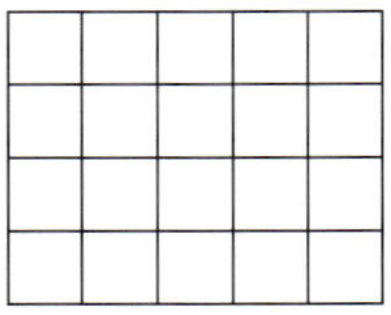

F 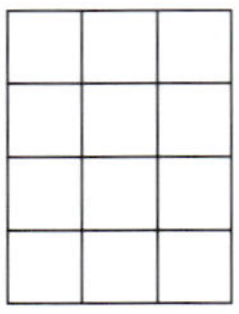

G 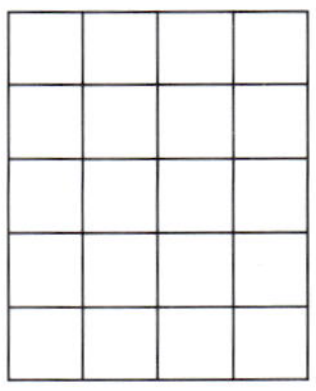

H 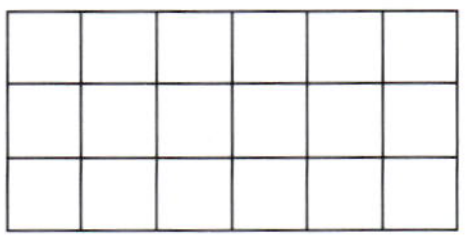

I 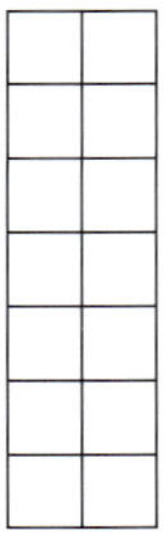

J 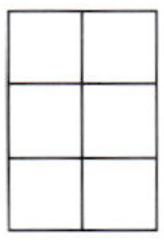

Write pairs that have the same number of squares.

1. [A] and [F] 3×4 = 4×3
2. [ ] and [ ]   ______ = ______
3. [ ] and [ ]   ______ = ______
4. [ ] and [ ]   ______ = ______
5. [ ] and [ ]   ______ = ______

Name ______________________

Twos and threes

Complete the grids.

1	2
3	4
5	

1	2	3
4	5	6
7		

Colour the twos and threes.

Threes

Write numbers in the windows on the right.

4	8	2
1	5	7
6	9	3

× 3 →

12		
	15	

3	7	5
6	8	2
10	4	9

× 3 →

12	8	4
9	3	11
5	10	7

× 3 →

Colour the odd numbers.

Name ______________________

Fractions

Colour the fraction of each shape.

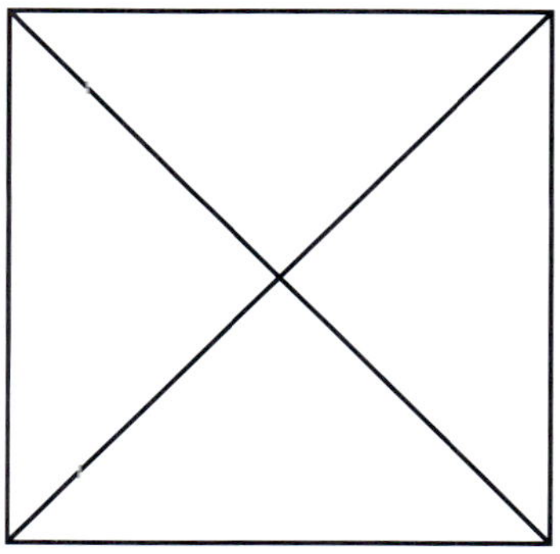

$\frac{3}{4}$

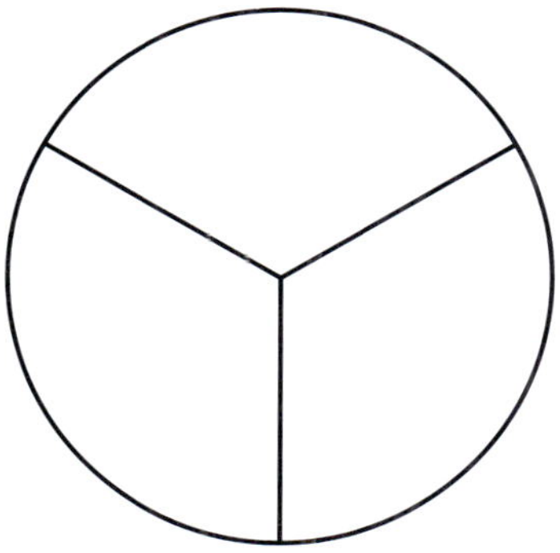

$\frac{2}{3}$

$\frac{7}{8}$

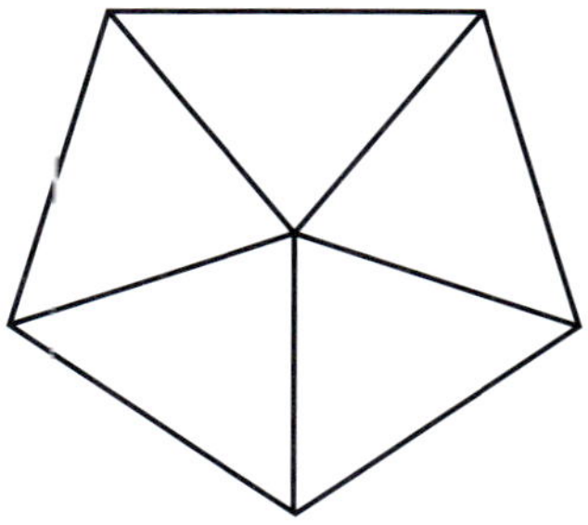

$\frac{2}{5}$

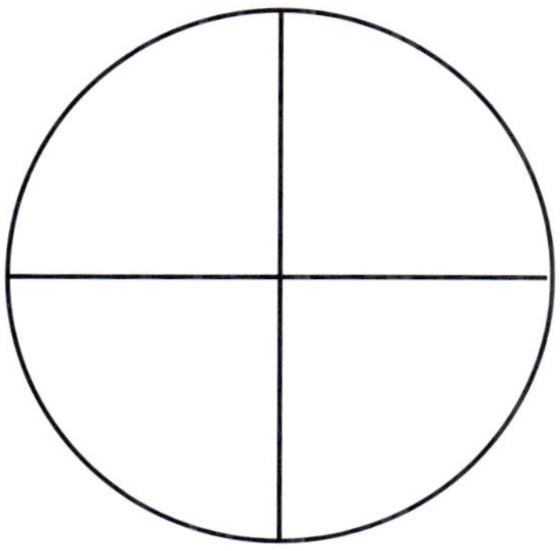

$\frac{2}{4}$

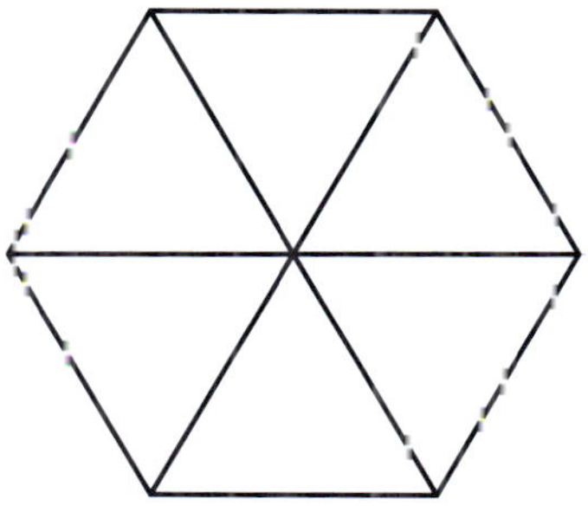

$\frac{4}{6}$

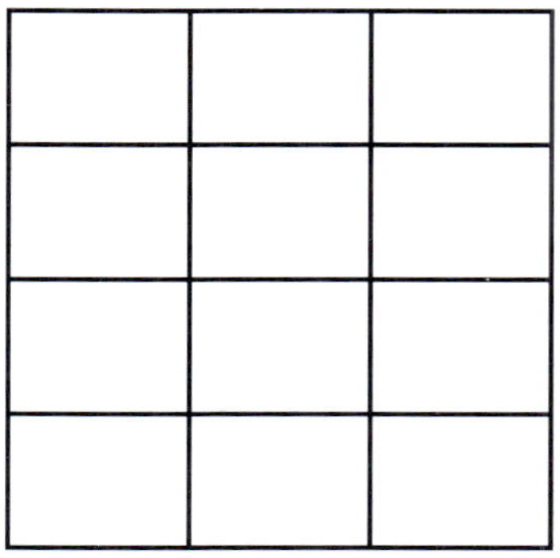

$\frac{7}{12}$

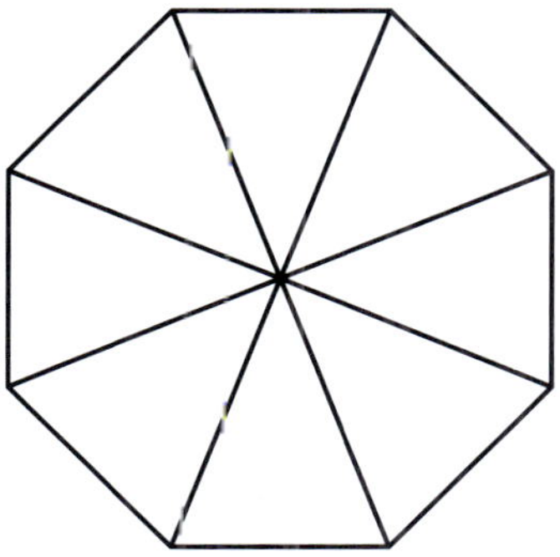

$\frac{3}{8}$

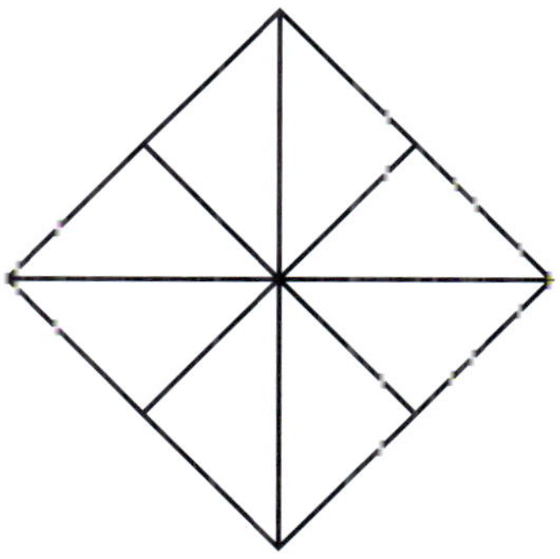

$\frac{5}{8}$

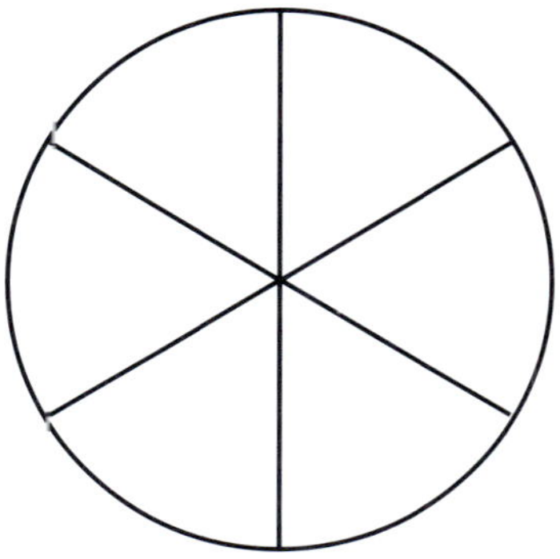

$\frac{5}{6}$

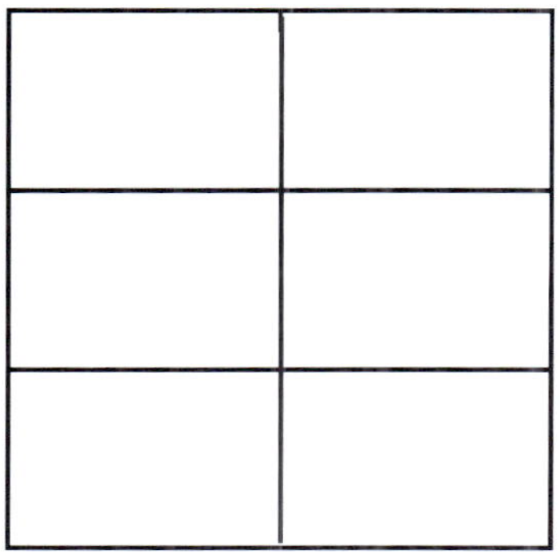

$\frac{2}{6}$

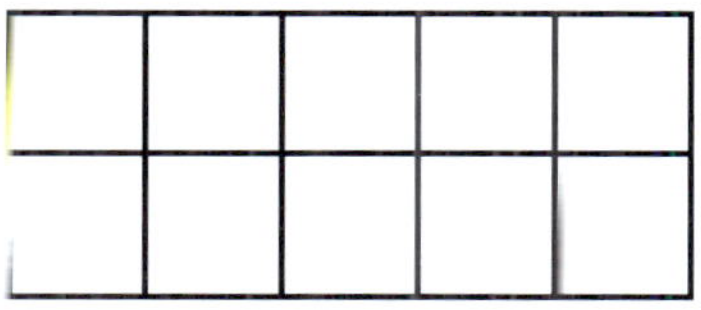

$\frac{7}{10}$

Name ______________________

Fractions

Complete these.

1. 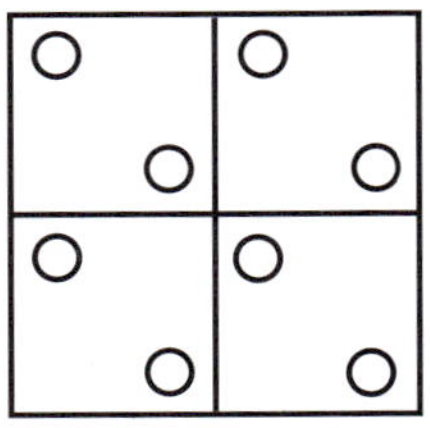 $\frac{3}{4}$ of $\square$ = $\square$

2. 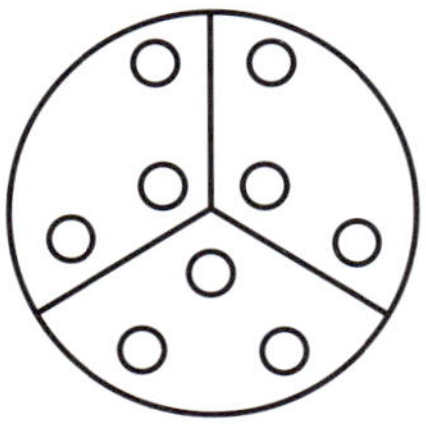 $\frac{2}{3}$ of $\square$ = $\square$

3. 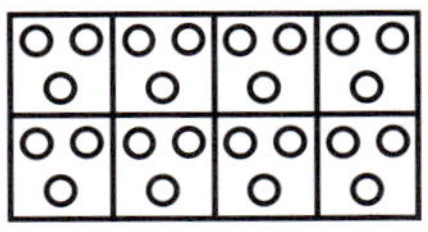 $\frac{7}{8}$ of $\square$ = $\square$

4. 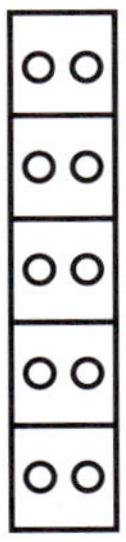 $\frac{3}{5}$ of $\square$ = $\square$

5. 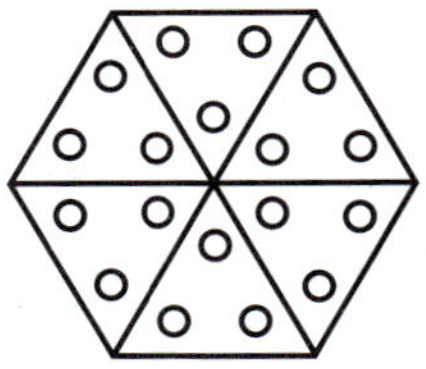 $\frac{5}{6}$ of $\square$ = $\square$

6. 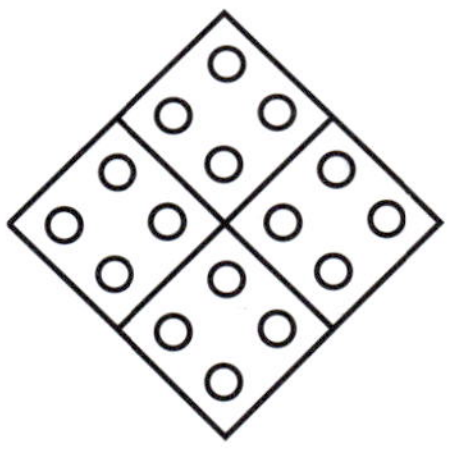 $\frac{1}{4}$ of $\square$ = $\square$

7. 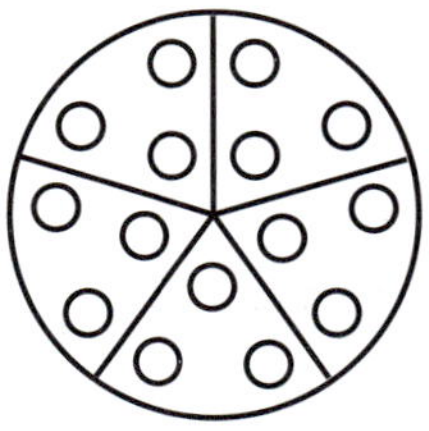 $\frac{2}{5}$ of $\square$ = $\square$

8. 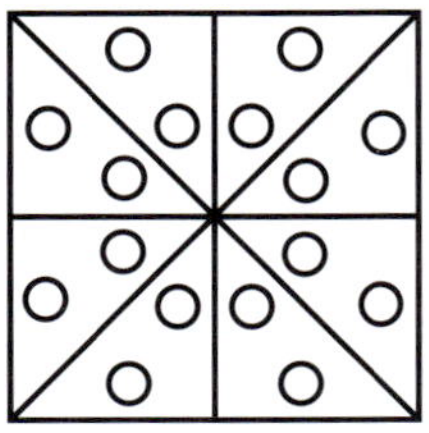 $\frac{1}{8}$ of $\square$ = $\square$

Name ______________________________

Nearest ten

For the blue garage, colour blue the cars that have 60 as their nearest ten.

Do the same for the green, orange and yellow garages.

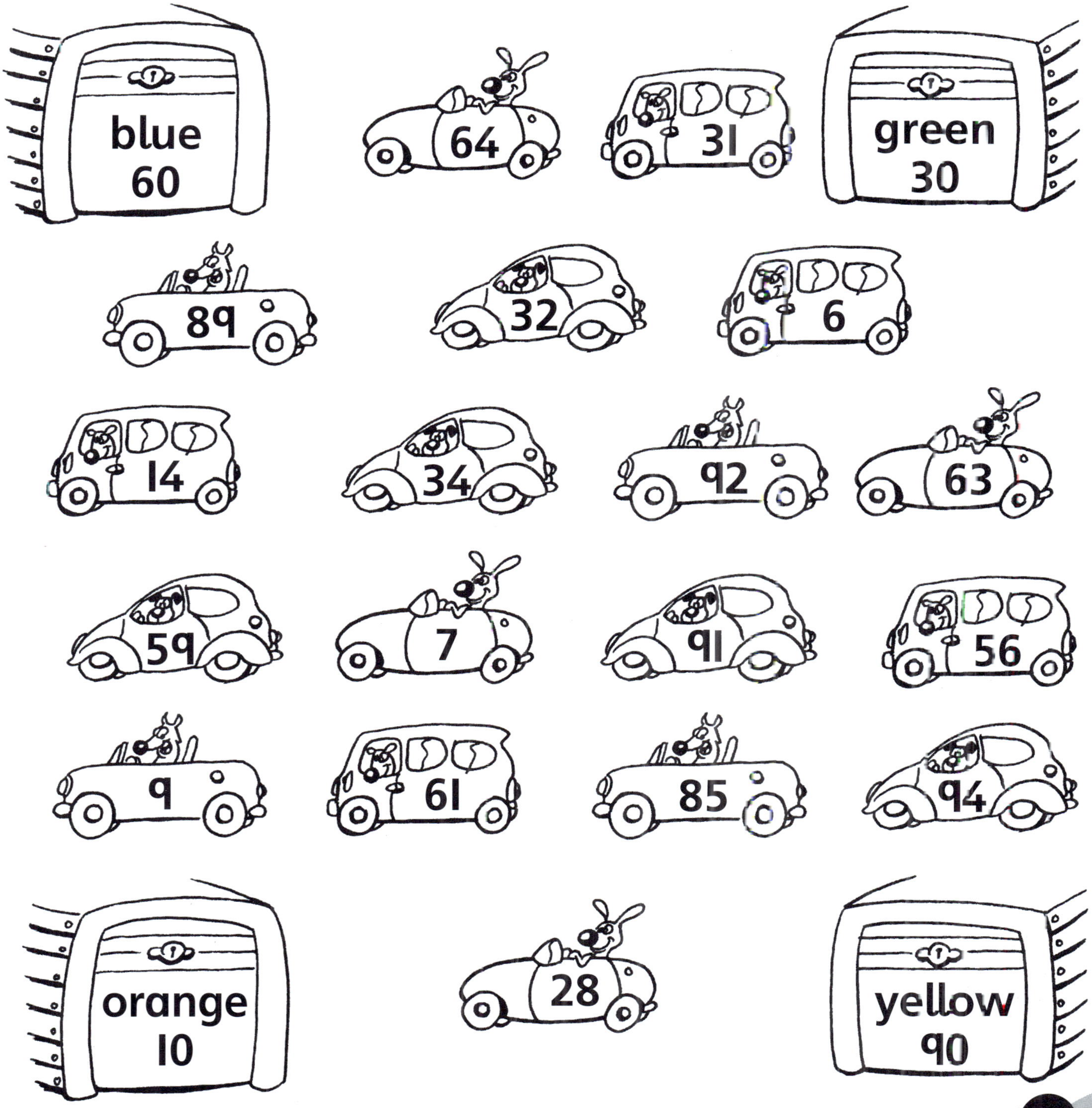

Name ______________________________

Nearest ten

Write 8 numbers that have the middle number as their nearest ten.

1.

558	561	562
557	**560**	563
556	555	564

2.

	480	

3.

	330	

4.

	210	

5.

	800	

6.

	950	

7.

	690	

Name ______________________________

Nearest hundred

Use number cards 2, 7, 9, 4 to make 3-digit numbers.

Find the nearest hundred to each.

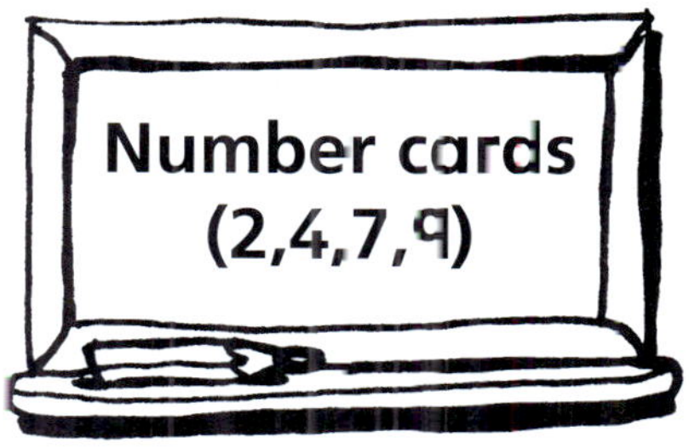

1. | 2 | 9 | 4 | → nearest hundred → 300

2. | | | | → nearest hundred → ____

3. | | | | → ____

4. | | | | → ____

5. | | | | → ____

6. | | | | → ____

7. | | | | → ____

8. | | | | → ____

9. | | | | → ____

10. | | | | → ____

11. | | | | → ____

12. | | | | → ____

Name ______________________

Addition tables

Complete these addition tables.

+	10	60	30	50
50				
20				
40				
30				

+	15	35	5	25
20				
30				
10				
40				

+	45	35	5	25
15				
35				
25				
55				

+	25	20	40	45
45				
30				
35				
50				

Name ______________________

Problem page

1. When Geri last measured her flower it was 30 cm tall. It then grew another 25 cm. How tall is it now?

2. Renee has saved 15p towards buying a magazine which costs 45p. How much more does she need?

3. 50 children sang in the concert. 35 were girls. How many boys were there?

4. Two coaches took children on a day out. There were 35 children on the first coach and 25 on the second. How many children altogether?

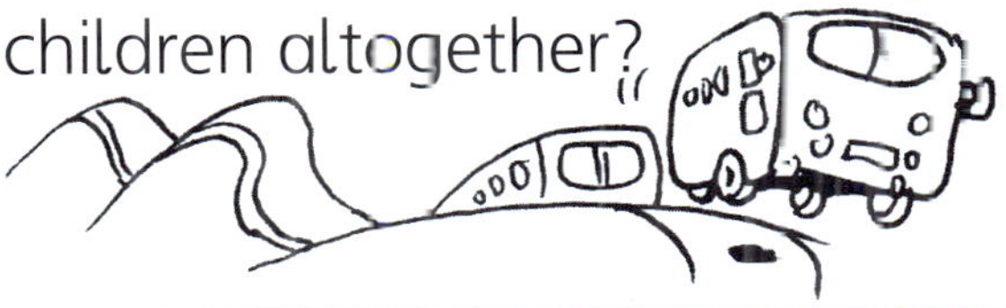

5. Grandad lives 85 miles away. After 60 miles we stop for a rest. How much further to go?

6. Barry collects football stickers. There are 70 different ones, and he has collected 45 so far. How many more does he need?

7. On our team, Jason scored 20 points, Abdul scored 30 points, and Dan scored 15 points. What is our team's total score?

8. Sara has 35p, Patti has 25p and Rosa has 20p. How much more do they need between them to buy a ball which costs £1?

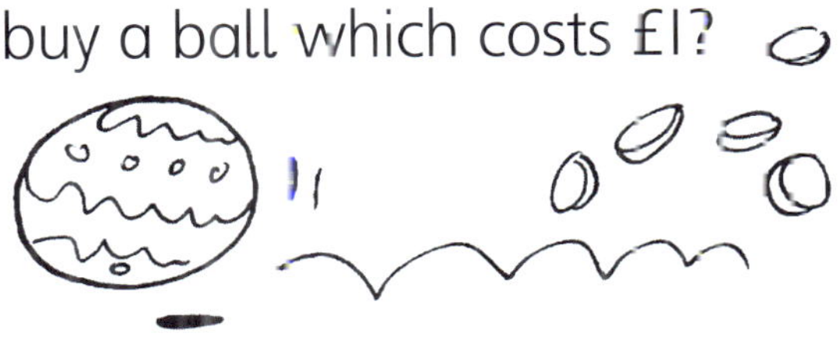

Name ________________________________

Subtracting 20, 30, 50

Complete these grids.

31	25	46
29	63	34
52	27	75

Subtract 20

39	91	56
82	48	51
64	70	73

Subtract 30

63	89	92
72	80	75
57	84	93

Subtract 50

Name ____________________

Taking away 30

Each item goes down by 30p.

Write the new prices.

1.

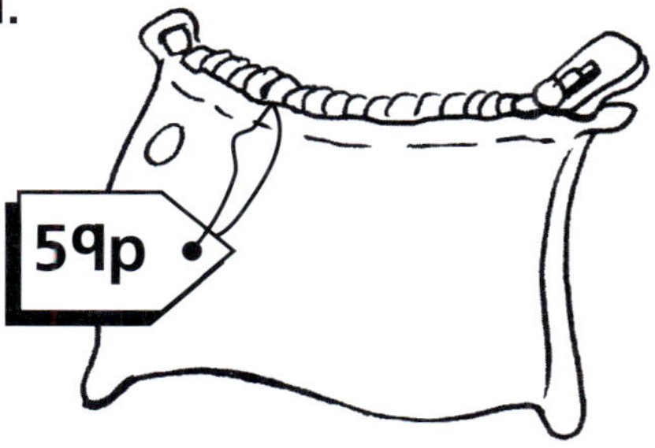

59p – 30p = 29p

2.

3.

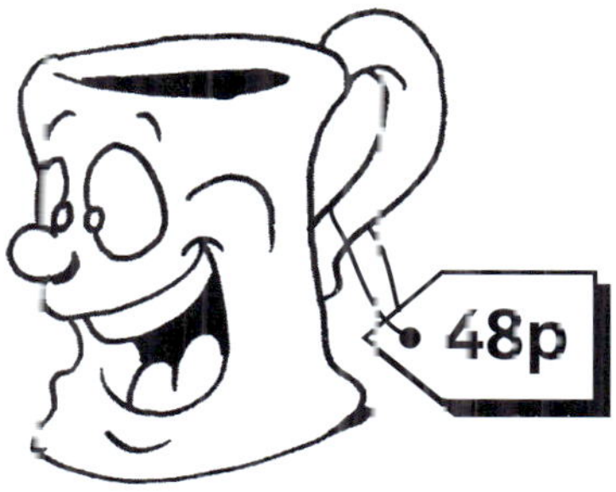

4.

5.

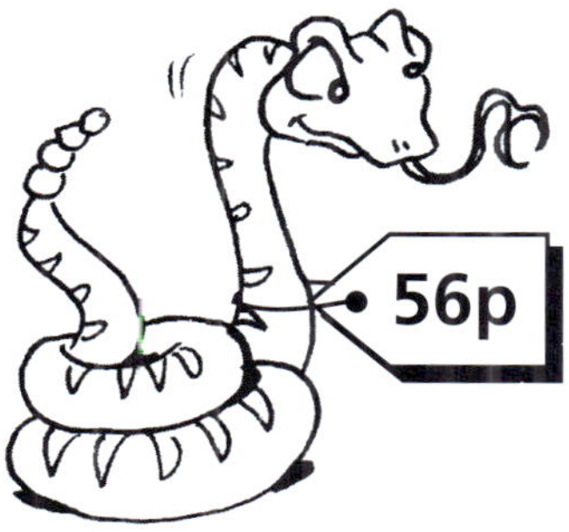

6.

7.

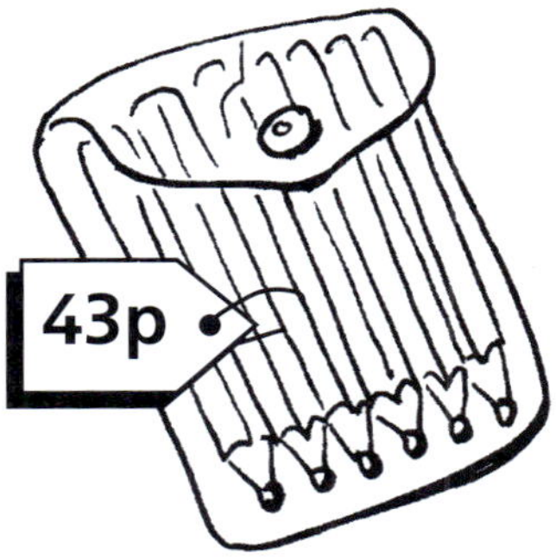

8.

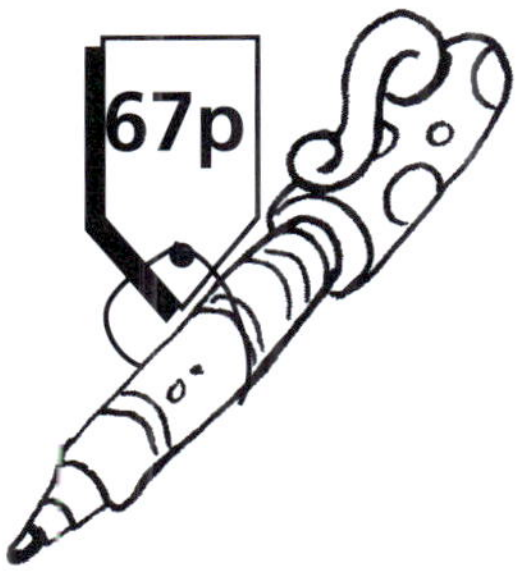

9.

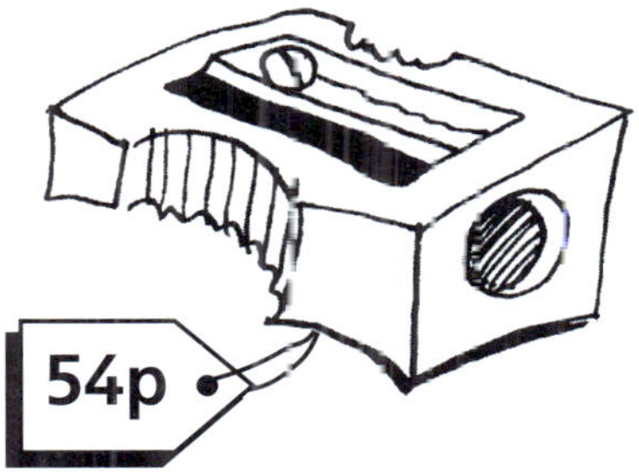

Name ______________________________________

Problem page

1. Selo had 45p, but lost 20p. How much has he left?

2. Toni had 76p, then bought an ice-cream for 35p and a chew for 5p. How much has she left?

3. Phil is playing his computer game. He had 38 points, but then lost 21 points. How many points does he have now?

4. Mary has a piece of string 65 cm long. She cut it in two. One piece is 31 cm long. How long is the other?

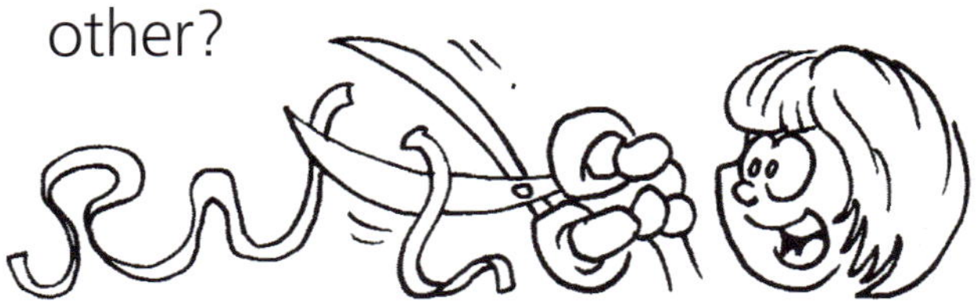

5. Gita has 54 Christmas cards to write. She has written 33. How many more need to be written?

6. The bus is taking 48 children home. At the first stop, 13 children get off. How many are left?

7. Patrick has 67p left after buying a comic which cost 22p. How much did he have before he bought the comic?

8. Lassie the sheepdog has 76 sheep to round up. She has 42 sheep in the pen. How many more still to go?

Name ______________________

Difference tables

Complete these difference tables.

d	17	23	19	22
16				
18				
25				
21				

d	31	34	27	30
28				
33				
29				
32				

d	42	39	44	37
36				
43				
38				
46				

d	62	58	65	55
59				
63				
57				
64				

Name ____________________

Problem page

1. John is 13 years old, and Adrian is 9 years old. What is the age difference?

2. In the school play there are 23 girls and 17 boys. What is the difference between the number of boys and girls?

3. Corkie bars are 29p at one supermarket and 32p at another. What is the price difference?

4. The difference in length between two sticks is 5 cm. The longer one is 43 cm. How long is the shorter stick?

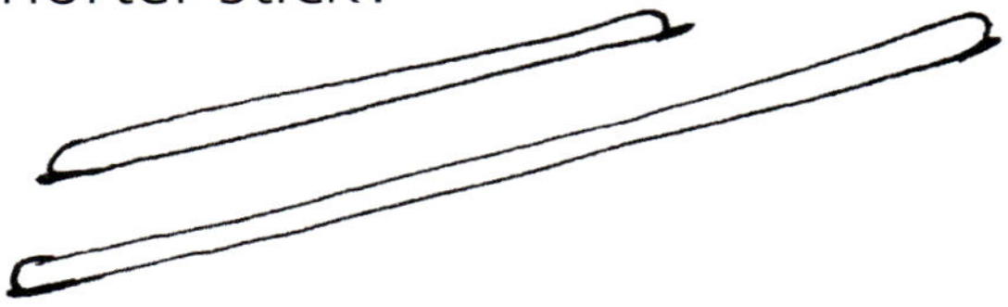

5. Ben can jump 19 cm off the ground, and Dan can jump 26 cm. What is the difference in the heights they can jump?

6. Abdul takes 48 paces to reach the wall, Arran takes 54 paces. What is the difference between them?

7. The coat cost £73, but was reduced in the sale to £65. What is the price difference?

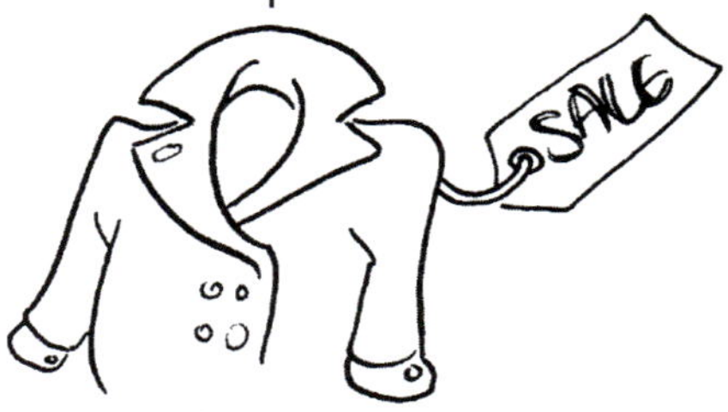

8. Two numbers have a difference of 4. The larger number is 23. What is the smaller number?

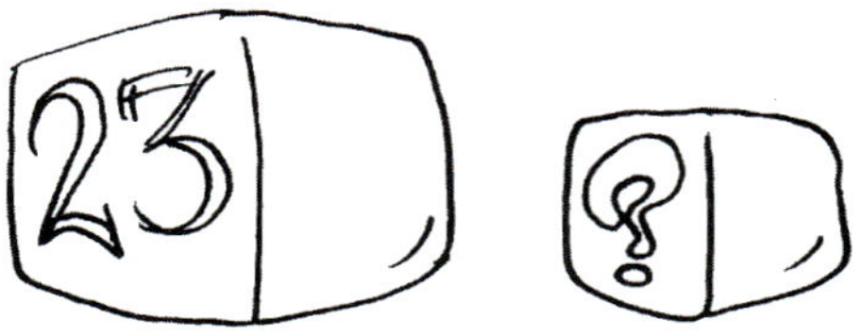

Name ____________________

Adding three 2-digit numbers

											Score
round 1	☐	☐	+	☐	☐	+	☐	☐	=	☐	☐
round 2	☐	☐	+	☐	☐	+	☐	☐	=	☐	☐
round 3	☐	☐	+	☐	☐	+	☐	☐	=	☐	☐
round 4	☐	☐	+	☐	☐	+	☐	☐	=	☐	☐
round 5	☐	☐	+	☐	☐	+	☐	☐	=	☐	☐
round 6	☐	☐	+	☐	☐	+	☐	☐	=	☐	☐

Teacher's instructions
A game for two or more players, each with a copy of this scoresheet.
Throw the dice six times in each round. After each throw, all the players write the number in one of their boxes. After the sixth throw the players add their numbers (checking each other's work).
The player closest to 100 scores 5 points, the next closest 4 points and so on.
The winner is the one with the most points after six rounds.

Materials
A dice

Name ______________________________

Adding

Complete these.

1. $35 + 15 + 7 =$ ______
2. $25 + 25 + 12 =$ ______
3. $45 + 25 + 14 =$ ______
4. $35 + 35 + 13 =$ ______
5. $5 + 45 + 16 =$ ______
6. $35 + 5 + 17 =$ ______
7. $65 + 15 + 13 =$ ______
8. $25 + 75 + 15 =$ ______
9. $35 + 5 + 21 =$ ______
10. $25 + 15 + 22 =$ ______
11. $45 + 35 + 23 =$ ______
12. $75 + 15 + 11 =$ ______
13. $25 + 35 + 32 =$ ______
14. $65 + 25 + 14 =$ ______
15. $35 + 45 + 15 =$ ______
16. $85 + 5 + 16 =$ ______

Name ______________________________

Adding three 2-digit numbers

All 3 balls must be in a line.

There are 8 different totals.

Find them, and write them in order.

Name ______________________________

Missing numbers

Write the missing numbers.

1. 135 + 5 = ___

2. 127 + 3 = ___

3. 156 + 4 = ___

4. 238 + 2 = ___

5. 327 + ___ = 330

6. 514 + ___ = 520

7. 626 + ___ = 630

8. 329 + ___ = 330

9. ___ + 8 = 260

10. ___ + 2 = 150

11. ___ + 7 = 530

12. ___ + 5 = 490

13. 277 + 3 = ___

14. 191 + 9 = ___

15. 138 + ___ = 140

16. ___ + 6 = 280

Name ______________________

Adding

Complete these additions.

1. 126 + 13 = ________
2. 361 + 14 = ________
3. 235 + 21 = ________
4. 182 + 16 = ________
5. 424 + 31 = ________
6. 423 + 22 = ________
7. 313 + 43 = ________
8. 215 + 51 = ________
9. 506 + 42 = ________
10. 374 + 13 = ________
11. 532 + 46 = ________
12. 651 + 24 = ________
13. 443 + 25 = ________
14. 264 + 14 = ________
15. 125 + 64 = ________
16. 376 + 22 = ________

Name ______________________________

Problem page

1. Kim reached page 135 in her book, then read another 20 pages. What page is she on now?

2. Beni had 216 marbles, and was given another 7. How many has he now?

3. 8 days ago, Fabio the cat was 325 days old. How old is he now?

4. Jenny had 135 points, and then scored 14 points in the next round. What is her new total score?

5. Tom was given £1 for his birthday to add to his 56p savings. How much does he need to buy a game which costs £1.62?

6. There were 128 children in the hall, then another class of 30 children came in. How many are there in the hall now?

7. Layla's savings were £4.32 last week and £4.58 this week. How much has she saved in the last week?

8. Beka has collected 547 stamps. She was given a packet of new stamps. She now has 579 stamps. How many stamps were in the packet?

Name ______________________

Adding multiples of 100

Throw a dice each time to add a matching multiple of 100,
e.g.  means add 400.

1. 230 + □ = □

2. 340 + □ = □

3. 120 + □ = □

4. 130 + □ = □

5. 324 + □ = □

6. 132 + □ = □

7. 154 + □ = □

8. 289 + □ = □

9. 176 + □ = □

10. 231 + □ = □

11. 97 + □ = □

12. 385 + □ = □

13. 276 + □ = □

14. 177 + □ = □

15. 85 + □ = □

16. 209 + □ = □

Name ______________________

Adding 3-digit numbers

Throw three dice and make a 3-digit number. Write it in the cloud. Complete the addition.

1. + 210 = ______

2. + 130 = ______

3. + 230 = ______

4. + 340 = ______

5. + 140 = ______

6. + 220 = ______

7. + 320 = ______

8. + 120 = ______

9. + 240 = ______

10. + 310 = ______

11. + 110 = ______

12. + 350 = ______

13. + 330 = ______

14. + 420 = ______

Name ______________________________

Subtracting 3-digit numbers

Write the missing numbers.

1. 354 − 110 = ___

2. 426 − 220 = ___

3. 473 − 150 = ___

4. 158 − 140 = ___

5. 274 − ___ = 144

6. 229 − ___ = 119

7. 634 − ___ = 414

8. 748 − ___ = 418

9. ___ − 410 = 127

10. ___ − 220 = 266

11. 194 − ___ = 44

12. 288 − ___ = 128

13. ___ − 230 = 135

14. 644 − ___ = 224

Name ______________________________

Odd and even

Write the missing numbers.

Colour the odd numbers red.

Colour the even numbers blue.

1	2	3	4	5	6	7	8	9	10
11	12						18		20
21		23		25		27			30
31		33	34		36		38		40
41	42					47			50
51		53		55				59	60
61			64		66		68		70
71									80
81	82				86			89	90
91	92	93	94	95	96	97	98	99	100

Name ______________________________

Money

Write how many pennies match each amount:

1.

2

3.

4.

5.

6.
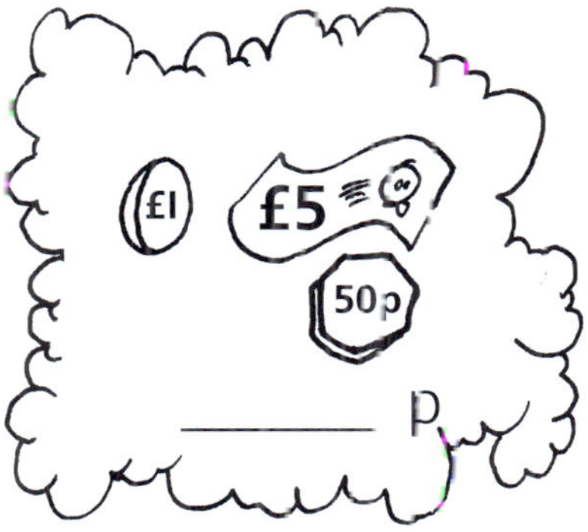

7.

8.
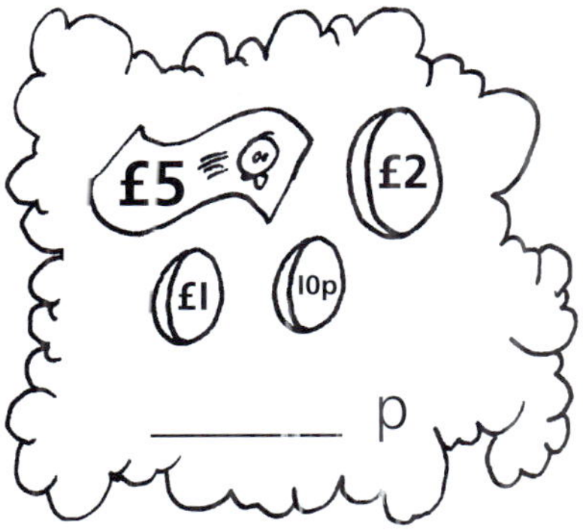

9.

10.

11.
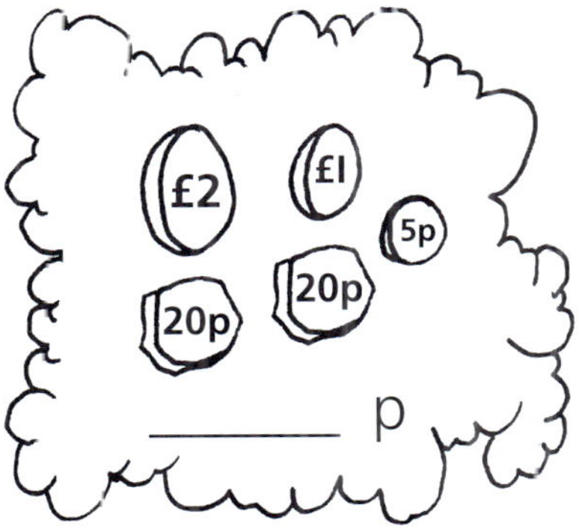

12.

Name ______________________

Tens

Complete these.

1. 9 × 10 = ☐
2. 7 × 10 = ☐
3. 3 × 10 = ☐
4. 18 × 10 = ☐
5. 16 × 10 = ☐
6. 12 × 10 = ☐
7. 240 ÷ 10 = ☐
8. 360 ÷ 10 = ☐
9. 910 ÷ 10 = ☐

Now complete these.

10. 56 × 10 = ☐
11. 8 × 10 = ☐
12. 2 × 10 = ☐
13. 430 ÷ 10 = ☐
14. 290 ÷ 10 = ☐
15. 31 × 10 = ☐
16. 100 ÷ 10 = ☐
17. 15 × 10 = ☐
18. 380 ÷ 10 = ☐

Multiplying

Complete these.

1. $2 \times 30 =$ ______
2. $3 \times 20 =$ ______
3. $4 \times 20 =$ ______
4. $2 \times 40 =$ ______
5. $5 \times 40 =$ ______
6. $3 \times 40 =$ ______
7. $6 \times 30 =$ ______
8. $4 \times 30 =$ ______
9. $7 \times 30 =$ ______
10. $8 \times 20 =$ ______
11. $2 \times 50 =$ ______
12. $3 \times 60 =$ ______
13. $5 \times 30 =$ ______
14. $6 \times 20 =$ ______
15. $9 \times 20 =$ ______
16. $4 \times 40 =$ ______
17. $7 \times 40 =$ ______
18. $5 \times 70 =$ ______
19. $3 \times 50 =$ ______
20. $4 \times 60 =$ ______

Multiplying

Roll a dice to find the multiplying number each time, then multiply.

1. □ × 30 = ______

2. □ × 20 = ______

3. □ × 40 = ______

4. □ × 70 = ______

5. □ × 50 = ______

6. □ × 90 = ______

7. □ × 60 = ______

8. □ × 80 = ______

9. □ × 30 = ______

10. □ × 20 = ______

11. □ × 40 = ______

12. □ × 70 = ______

13. □ × 50 = ______

14. □ × 90 = ______

15. □ × 60 = ______

16. □ × 80 = ______

Name ______________________________

Threes and fours

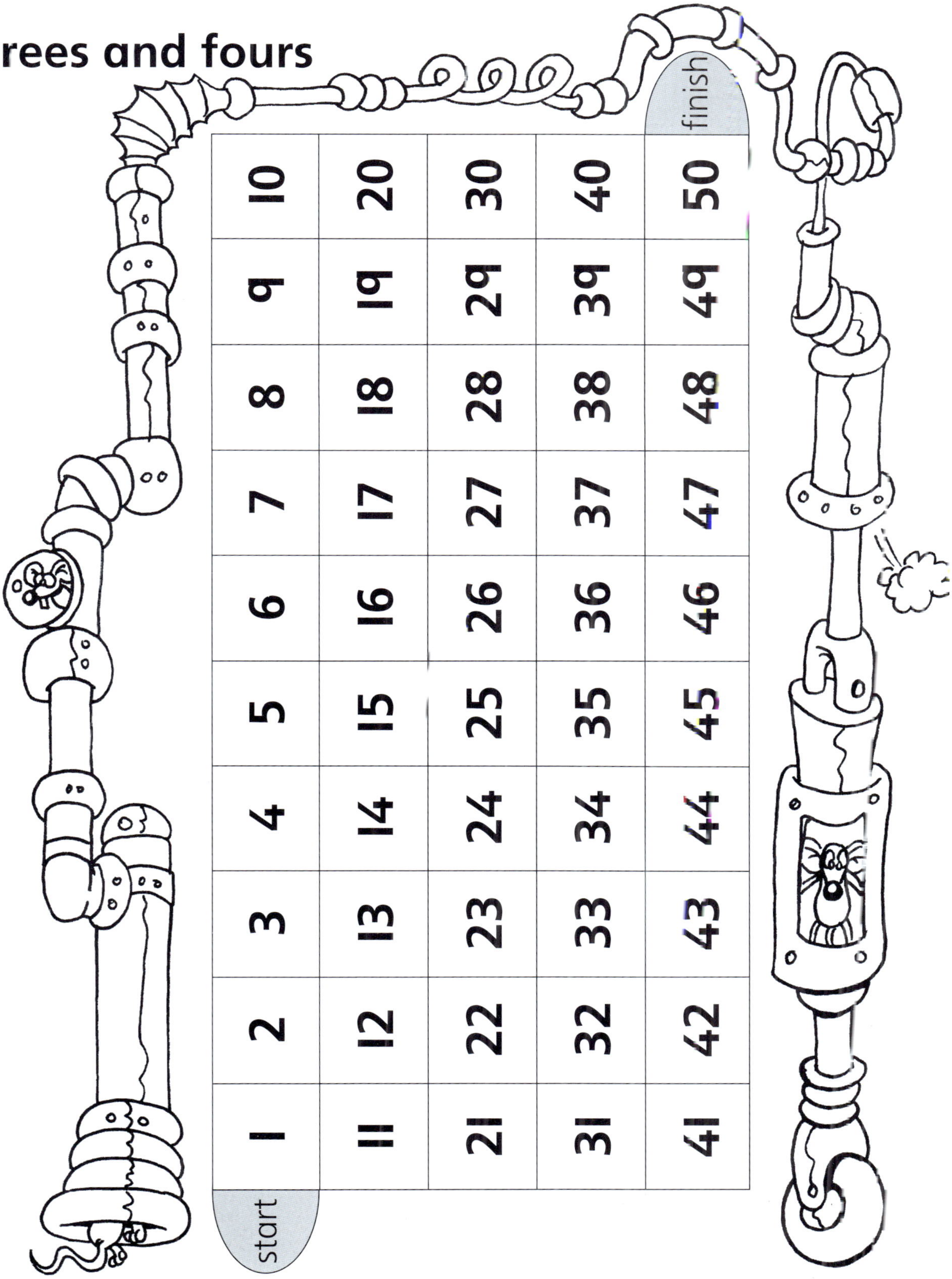

start										finish
	1	2	3	4	5	6	7	8	9	10
	11	12	13	14	15	16	17	18	19	20
	21	22	23	24	25	26	27	28	29	30
	31	32	33	34	35	36	37	38	39	40
	41	42	43	44	45	46	47	48	49	50

Teacher's instructions

A game for two or more players. Each place a counter at 'start'.
Take turns to throw the dice, and move your counter a matching number of spaces.
If you land on a number in the ×4 table, jump forwards to the next number in the ×4 table.
If you land on a number in the ×3 table, jump backwards to the previous number in the ×3 table.
The winner is the first to reach 'finish'.

Colour the threes and the fours in different colours. (Some numbers will be more than one colour.)

Materials
A dice
Counters

Name ______________________________

Fours

Write numbers in the window on the right.

4	2	6
3	8	1
7	5	9

× 4 →

16		

2	9	4
8	5	10
6	3	7

× 4 →

6	10	3
4	8	7
9	11	5

× 4 →

Name ________________________________

Dividing

Write how the cubes have been divided.

1.

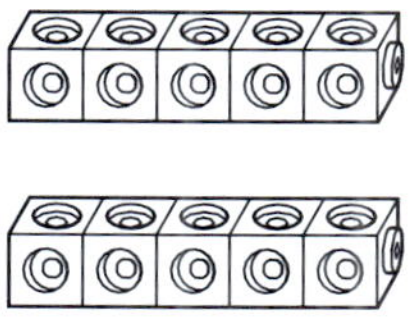

10 ÷ 2 = 5

2.

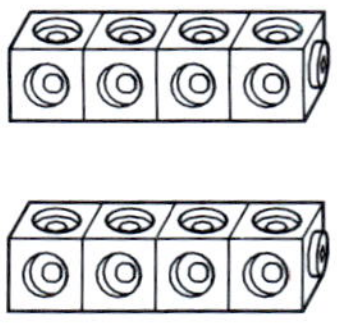

3.

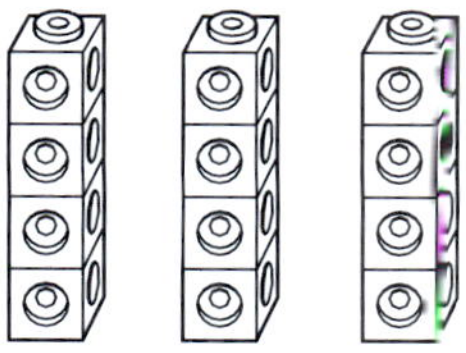

4.

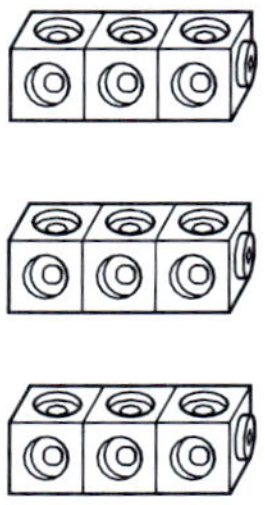

5.

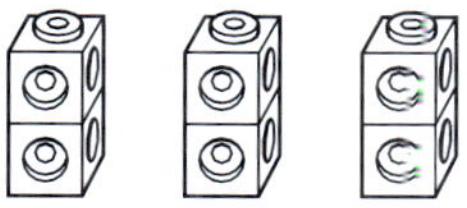

6.

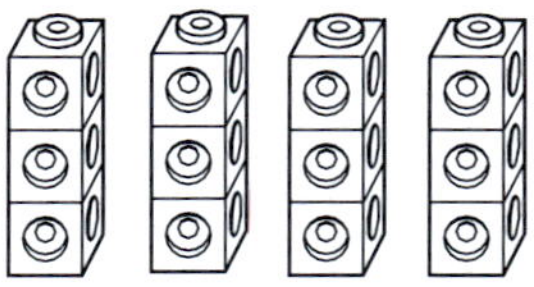

7.

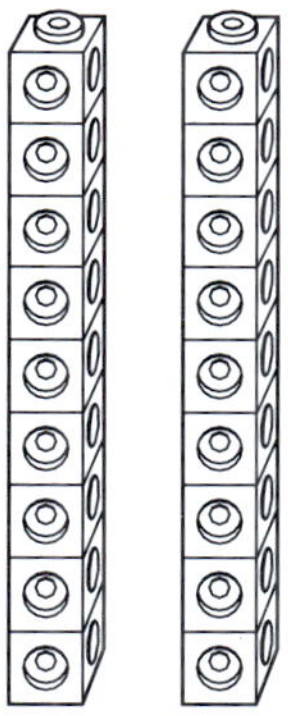

8.

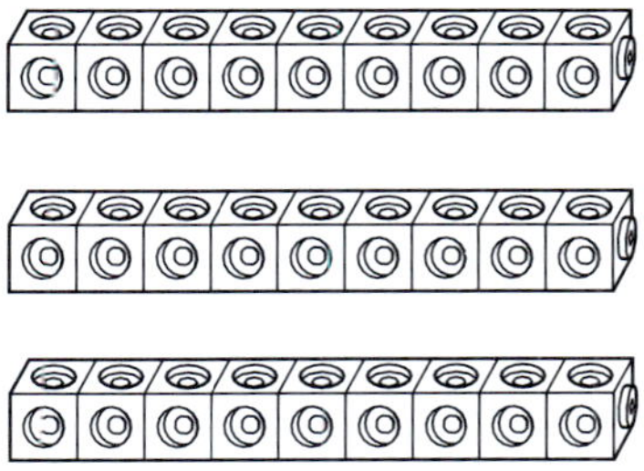

9.

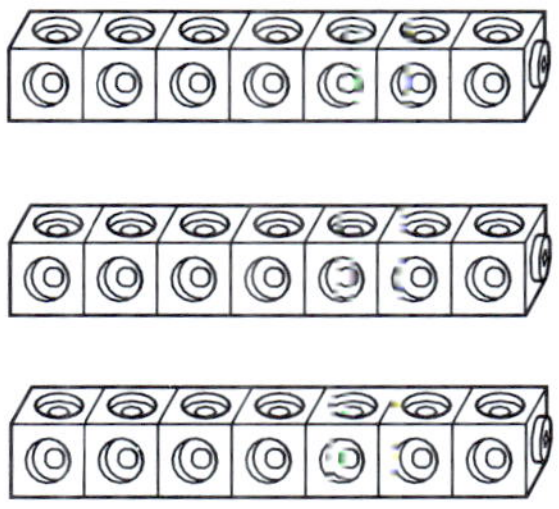

Name ______________________________

Remainders

Complete these divisions, writing the remainders.

1. 9 ÷ 4 = ________ r ________

2. 7 ÷ 2 = ________ r ________

3. 4 ÷ 3 = ________ r ________

4. 11 ÷ 4 = ________ r ________

5. 11 ÷ 3 = ________ r ________

6. 19 ÷ 2 = ________ r ________

7. 17 ÷ 5 = ________ r ________

8. 47 ÷ 10 = ________ r ________

9. 8 ÷ 3 = ________ r ________

10. 17 ÷ 4 = ________ r ________

11. 13 ÷ 2 = ________ r ________

12. 38 ÷ 5 = ________ r ________

13. 33 ÷ 10 = ________ r ________

14. 26 ÷ 4 = ________ r ________

15. 17 ÷ 3 = ________ r ________

16. 46 ÷ 5 = ________ r ________

Name ______________________

Fractions

Write the fraction of people that:

1. are happy [___]
2. are wearing a hat [___]
3. have a bow-tie [___]
4. have a scarf [___]
5. are happy and have pointed ears [___]
6. are sad [___]
7. have round ears [___]
8. are not wearing a hat [___]
9. have pointed ears [___]
10. are sad and wearing a hat [___]

Name ______________________

Fractions

Write the matching fractions for each pair.

1. 

$\frac{1}{2} = \frac{3}{6}$

2. 

— = —

3. 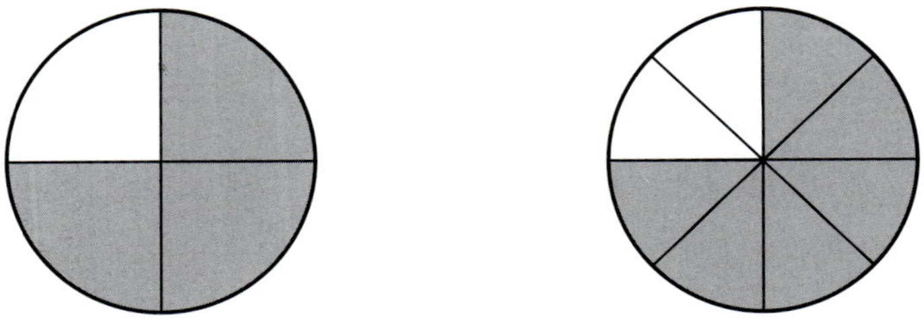

— = —

4. 

— = —

5. 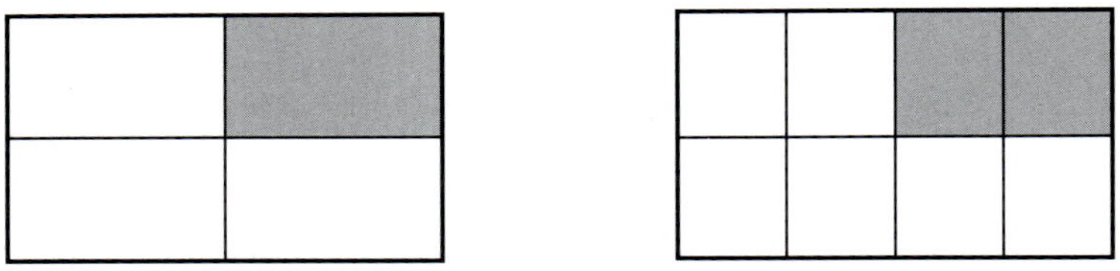

— = —

6. 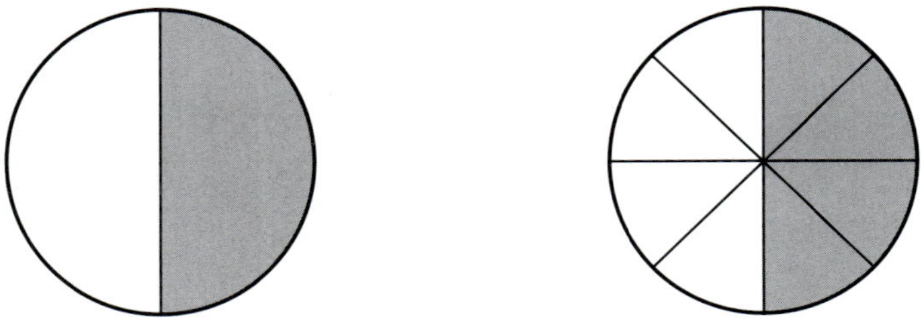

— = —

7. 

— = —

Name ______________________________

Fractions

I whole											
$\frac{1}{2}$	$\frac{1}{2}$										
$\frac{1}{3}$	$\frac{1}{3}$	$\frac{1}{3}$									
$\frac{1}{4}$	$\frac{1}{4}$	$\frac{1}{4}$	$\frac{1}{4}$								
$\frac{1}{6}$	$\frac{1}{6}$	$\frac{1}{6}$	$\frac{1}{6}$	$\frac{1}{6}$	$\frac{1}{6}$						
$\frac{1}{12}$	$\frac{1}{12}$	$\frac{1}{12}$	$\frac{1}{12}$	$\frac{1}{12}$	$\frac{1}{12}$	$\frac{1}{12}$	$\frac{1}{12}$	$\frac{1}{12}$	$\frac{1}{12}$	$\frac{1}{12}$	$\frac{1}{12}$

Write the missing numbers to make pairs of matching fractions.

1. $\frac{1}{3} = \frac{\square}{6}$

2. $\frac{\square}{4} = \frac{3}{6}$

3. $\frac{2}{3} = \frac{\square}{6}$

4. $\frac{3}{6} = \frac{\square}{12}$

5. $\frac{\square}{4} = \frac{9}{12}$

6. $\frac{1}{2} = \frac{\square}{4}$

7. $\frac{\square}{2} = \frac{3}{6}$

8. $\frac{5}{6} = \frac{\square}{12}$

9. $\frac{\square}{4} = \frac{3}{12}$

10. $\frac{1}{3} = \frac{\square}{12}$

11. $\frac{1}{2} = \frac{\square}{12}$

12. $1 = \frac{\square}{6}$

Name ______________________

Adding

335 426 107 104

534 625 303 205

Write the numbers in the shapes, then add them together.

1. ○ + ⬠ = ______

2. ⏢ + ⬡ = ______

3. ▭ + ⬡ = ______

4. ◠ + ⬭ = ______

5. ○ + ⬭ = ______

6. ▱ + ⏢ = ______

7. ◠ + ⬡ = ______

8. ⬭ + ⏢ = ______

9. ▭ + ▱ = ______

10. ⬠ + ◠ = ______

11. ○ + ▱ = ______

12. ▭ + ⬭ = ______

Name ______________________________

Adding

Throw a dice 6 times, and write the numbers to make two 3-digit numbers.

Add them together.

	4	3	2
+	2	1	5
	6	0	0
		4	0
			7
	6	4	7

1.

+

2.

+

3

+

4.

+

5.

+

6.

+

Name ________________________________

Adding three 3-digit numbers

1.

	H	T	U
	2	3	4
	1	5	2
+	3	2	1

2.

	H	T	U
	3	2	5
	2	3	6
+	1	2	7

3.

	H	T	U
	2	4	1
	3	2	5
+	1	1	7

4.

	H	T	U
	3	2	8
	1	3	7
+	2	2	6

5.

	H	T	U
	1	4	1
	2	2	5
+	3	1	6

6.

	H	T	U
	1	2	8
	3	3	2
+	2	4	1

7.

	H	T	U
	4	1	6
	1	2	3
+	2	3	9

8.

	H	T	U
	1	2	4
	2	3	2
+	4	4	8

9.

	H	T	U
	2	4	5
	4	2	1
+	1	1	7

10.

	H	T	U
	4	5	8
	2	1	9
+	1	4	2

11.

	H	T	U
	2	2	7
	1	3	1
+	4	6	9

12.

	H	T	U
	1	4	5
	4	1	2
+	2	3	8

Name ______________________________

Adding three 3-digit numbers

round 1

	H	T	U
+			

score

round 2

	H	T	U
+			

score

round 3

	H	T	U
+			

score

round 4

	H	T	U
+			

score

round 5

	H	T	U
+			

score

round 6

	H	T	U
+			

score

Total

Teacher's instructions
A game for two or more players, each with a copy of this scoresheet.
Throw the dice nine times in each round. After each throw, all the players write the number in one of their boxes. After the ninth throw the players add their numbers (checking each other's work).
The player with the largest total scores 5 points, the next largest 4 points, and so on. The winner is the one with the most points after six rounds.

Materials
A dice

Name ____________________________

Centimetres (cm)

Find one of each object.

Measure its length in centimetres.

1.

☐ cm

2.

☐ cm

3.
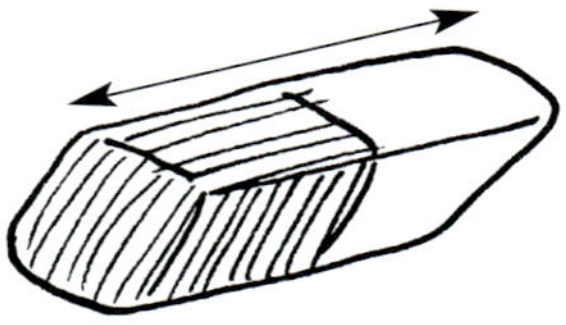

☐ cm

4.
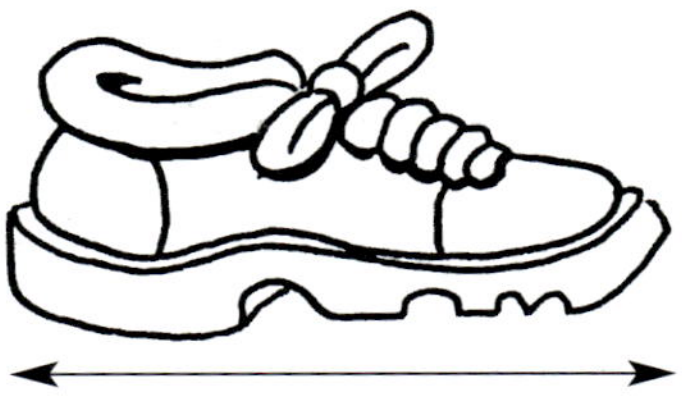

☐ cm

5.
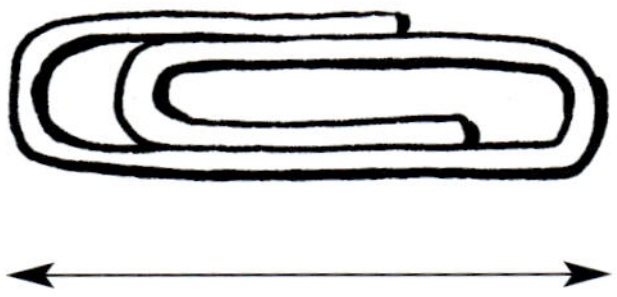

☐ cm

6.

☐ cm

7.
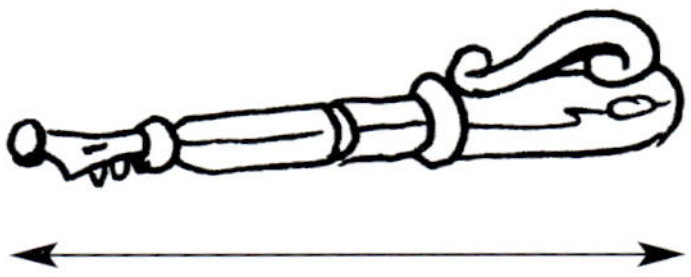

☐ cm

8.

☐ cm

9.

☐ cm

10.

☐ cm

11.

☐ cm

12.
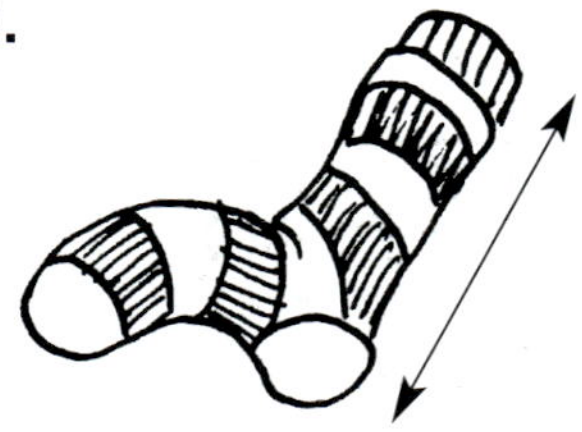

☐ cm

Name ______________________________

Metres

Put a ring round the length you think is nearest.

1. your height

1 m

2 m

3 m

2. teacher's height

1 m

2 m

3 m

3. classroom length

4 m 6 m 8 m

4. classroom height

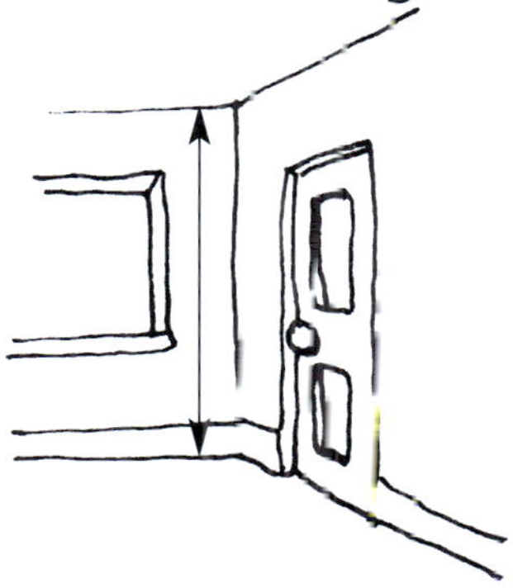

2 m 3 m 4 m

Write your own estimates for these lengths.

5. height of a room

☐ m

6. height of school

☐ m

7. width of playground

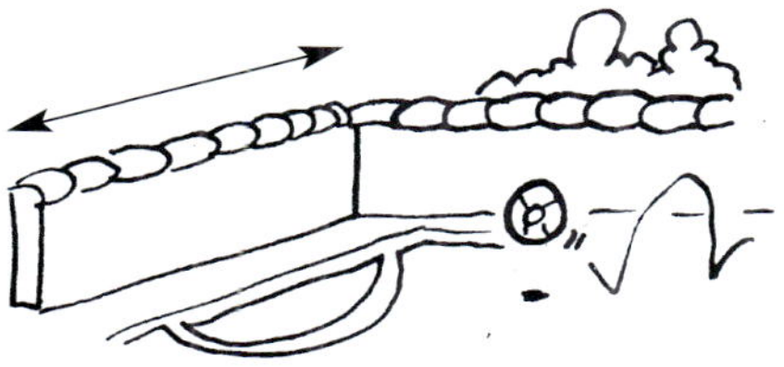

☐ m

8. length of hall

☐ m

Name ______________________________

Metres and centimetres

Write these lengths in centimetres (cm).

1. 1 m 35 cm = ________ cm

2. 2 m 10 cm = ________ cm

3. 3 m = ________ cm

4. $1\frac{1}{2}$ m = ________ cm

5. $2\frac{1}{4}$ m = ________ cm

6. 4 m 58 cm = ________ cm

7. 6 m 7 cm = ________ cm

8. 9 m 20 cm = ________ cm

Write these lengths in metres (m) and centimetres (cm).

9. 245 cm = _______ m _______ cm

10. 325 cm = _______ m _______ cm

11. 400 cm = _______ m _______ cm

12. 150 cm = _______ m _______ cm

13. 208 cm = _______ m _______ cm

14. 306 cm = _______ m _______ cm

15. 65 cm = _______ m _______ cm

16. $2\frac{1}{2}$ m = _______ m _______ cm

Name ______________________________

Quarter past, half past, quarter to

Write or draw the matching times.

1.

2 : 15

2.

:

3.

:

4.

:

5.

:

6.

:

7.

1 : 15

8.

4 : 45

9.

5 : 15

10.

6 : 30

11.

7 : 00

12.

10 : 45

Name ______________________________

Timing

Write how many minutes are shaded.

1.

☐ minutes

2.

☐ minutes

3.

☐ minutes

4.

☐ minutes

5.

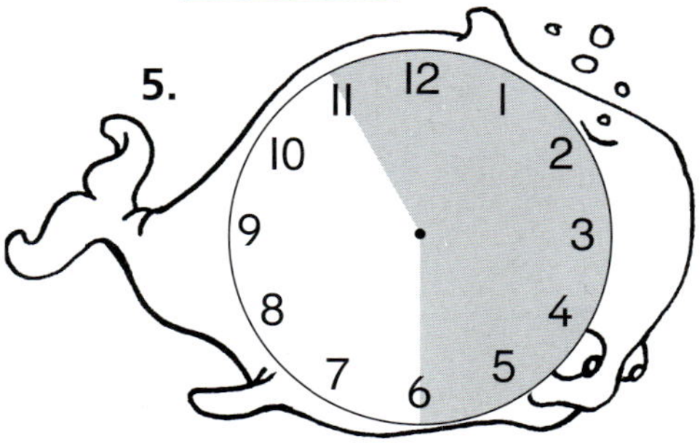

☐ minutes

6.

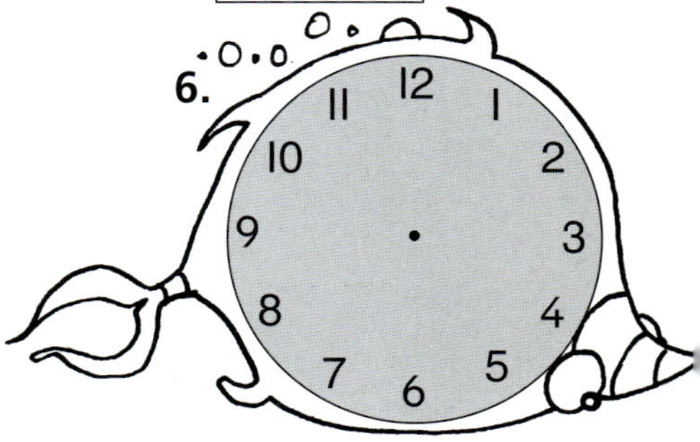

☐ minutes

7.

☐ minutes

8.

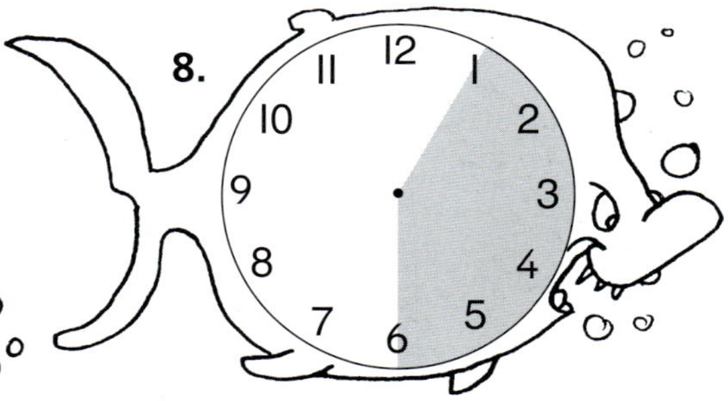

☐ minutes

9.

☐ minutes

10.

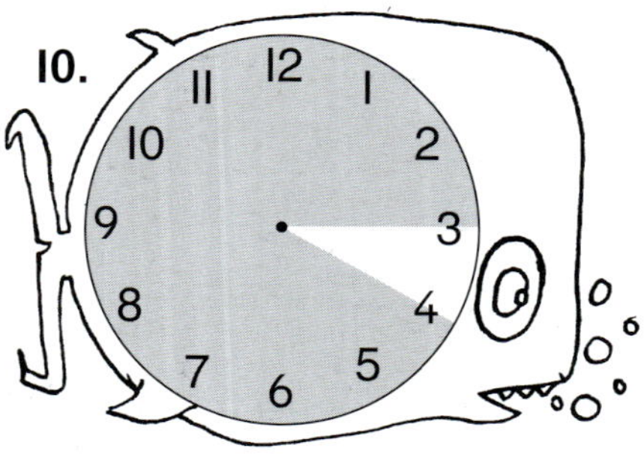

☐ minutes

11.

☐ minutes

12.

☐ minutes

Name ______________________________

5 minutes

Write the matching times.

1.
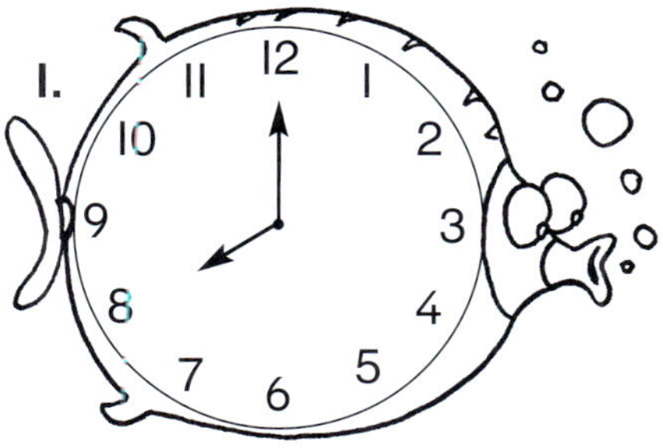

:

2.

:

3.
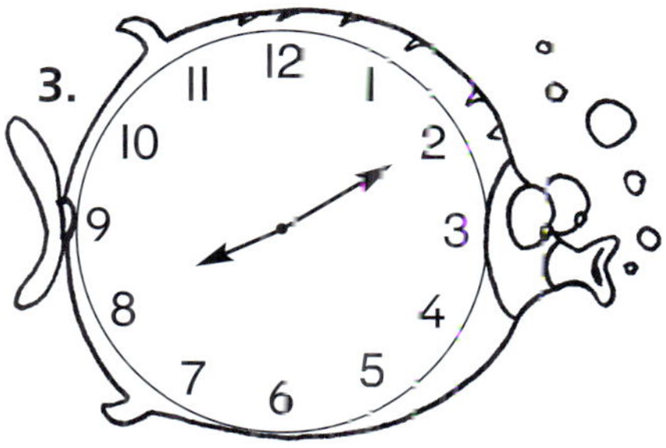

:

4.

:

5.

:

6.

:

7.

:

8.

:

9.
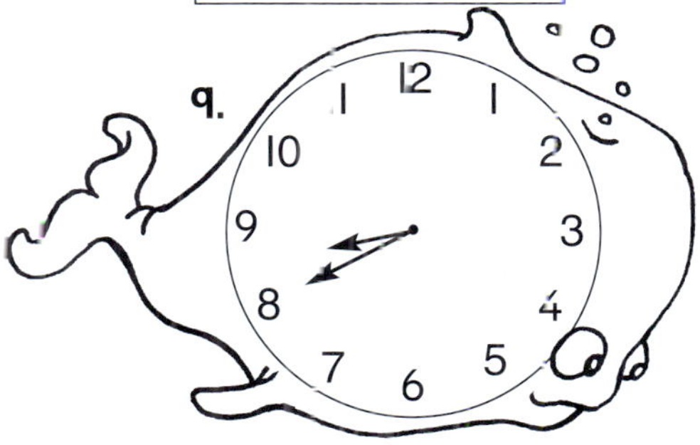

:

10.

:

11.

:

12.

:

Name ______________________________

5 minutes

Write and draw the matching times.

1. 3 : 20

twenty past 3

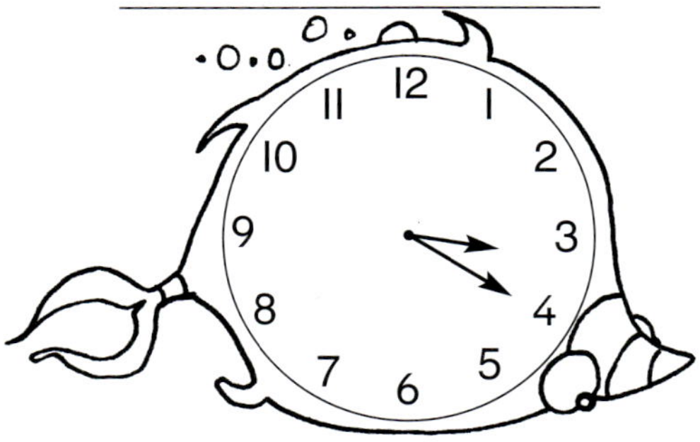

2. 5 : 40

____

3. 7 : 05

____

4. 1 : 35

____

5. 6 : 10

____

6. 2 : 50

____

7. 9 : 25

____

8. 4 : 55

____

9. 8 : 45

____

Name ______________________________

Litres and millilitres

Write these capacities in millilitres (ml).

1. 1 l 200 ml = _______ ml

2. 2 l 400 ml = _______ ml

3. 5 l = _______ ml

4. $3\frac{1}{2}$ l = _______ ml

5. 1 l 700 ml = _______ ml

6. 4 l 600 ml = _______ ml

7. $2\frac{1}{2}$ l = _______ ml

8. $1\frac{1}{2}$ l = _______ ml

Write these capacities in litres (l) and millilitres (ml).

9. 1500 ml = _______ l _______ ml

10. 2300 ml = _______ l _______ ml

11. 700 ml = _______ l _______ ml

12. 3000 ml = _______ l _______ ml

13. $1\frac{1}{2}$ l = _______ l _______ ml

14. 5600 ml = _______ l _______ ml

15. 1100 ml = _______ l _______ ml

16. $4\frac{1}{2}$ l = _______ l _______ ml

Name ______________________________

Hours and minutes

Write these times in minutes.

1. 1 hr 10 mins = _______ mins

2. 2 hrs 30 mins = _______ mins

3. 1 hr 55 mins = _______ mins

4. 2 hrs 5 mins = _______ mins

5. $1\frac{1}{2}$ hrs = _______ mins

6. $2\frac{1}{4}$ hrs = _______ mins

7. $3\frac{1}{2}$ hrs = _______ mins

8. 4 hrs = _______ mins

Write these times in hours and minutes.

9. 90 mins = _____ hrs _____ mins

10. 130 mins = _____ hrs _____ mins

11. 65 mins = _____ hrs _____ mins

12. 200 mins = _____ hrs _____ mins

13. 100 mins = _____ hrs _____ mins

14. 50 mins = _____ hrs _____ mins

15. $1\frac{1}{2}$ hrs = _____ hrs _____ mins

16. $3\frac{1}{4}$ hrs = _____ hrs _____ mins

Name ______________________________

Grams (g)

Find one of each object.

Weigh it in grams.

1.

☐ g

2.

☐ g

3.

☐ g

4.

☐ g

5.

☐ g

6.

☐ g

7.

☐ g

8.

☐ g

9.

☐ g

Name ______________________________

Grams (g) and kilograms (kg)

Put a ring around the weight you think is nearest.

1. 
1 g   10 g   100 g

2. 
12 g
120 g
500 g

3. 

500 g
500 kg
50 g

4. 
30 kg
1500 kg
50 g

5. 
1 kg
100 kg
100 g

Which weights match the totals?

1 kg	500 g	200 g	100 g	50 g	20 g	totals
	✓		✓	✓		650 g
						270 g
						850 g
						1520 g
						1870 g

Name ______________________________

Months

Complete each sentence.

1. The first month of the year is:
2. The last month of the year is:
3. The fourth month is:
4. The tenth month is:
5. The month before May is:
6. The month after July is:
7. The month before March is:
8. The month after September is:
9. The month between March and May is:
10. The month between October and December is:
11. The summer months are:
12. The winter months are:
13. The autumn months are:
14. The spring months are:
15. My birthmonth is:

Name ______________________________

2-d shape

Complete each pattern.

Colour: squares red, rectangles pink, triangles yellow, hexagons blue, octagons green.

Make up one of your own.

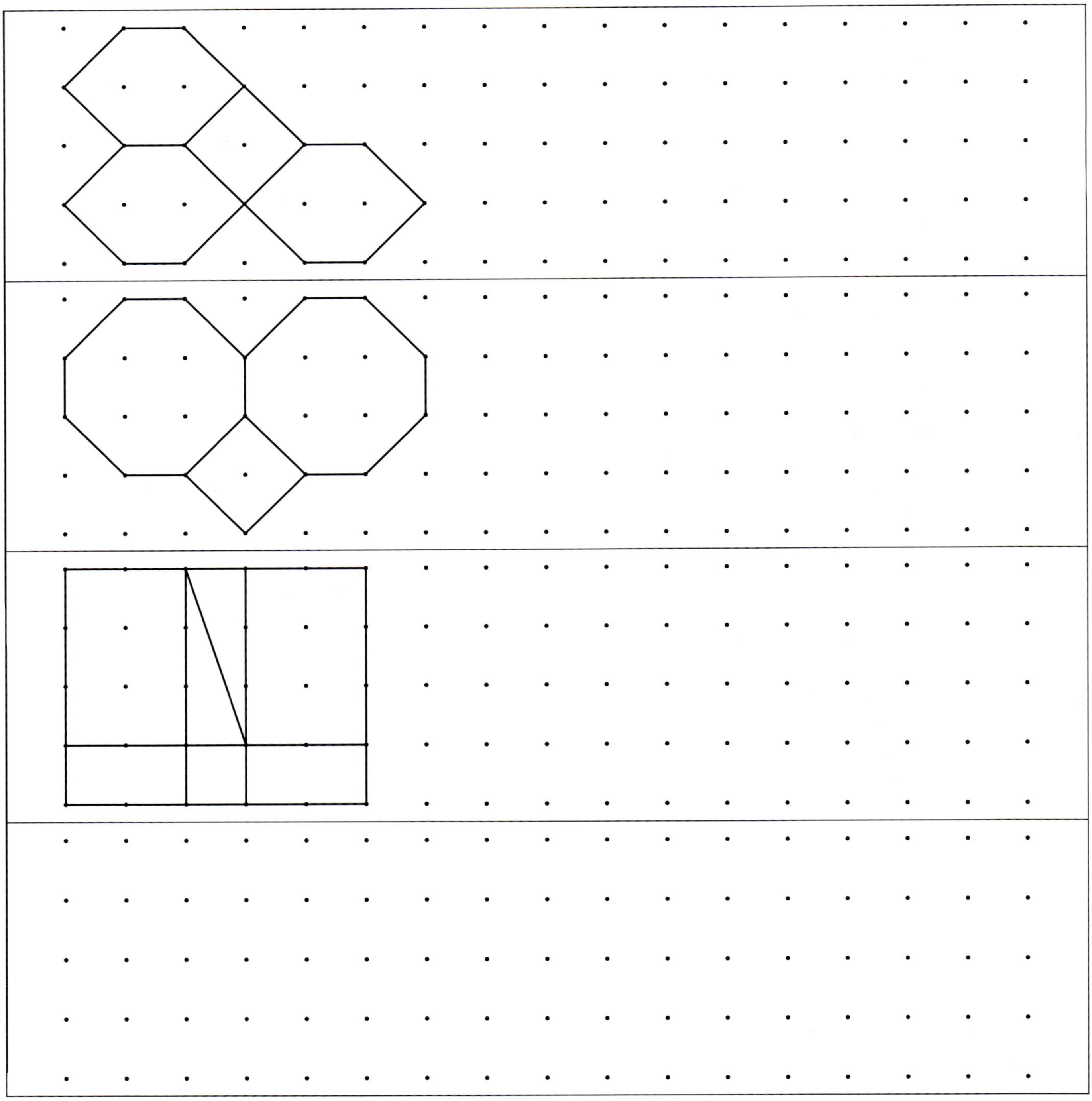

Name ______________________

2-d shape

Write the name of each shape.

1. 

rectangle

2. 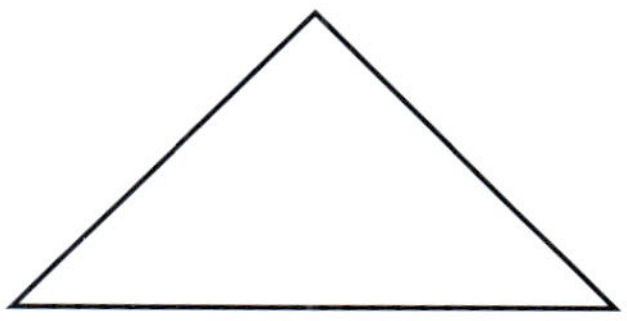

____

3. 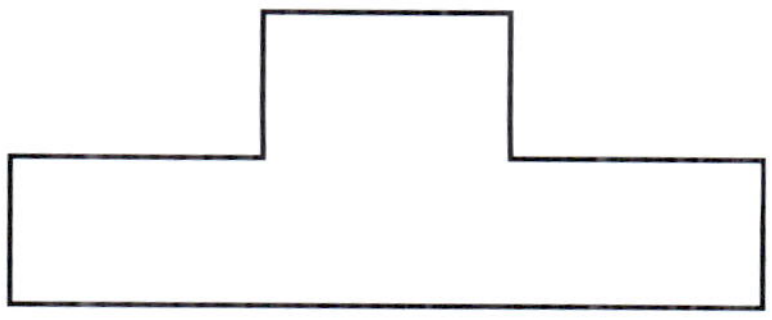

____

4. 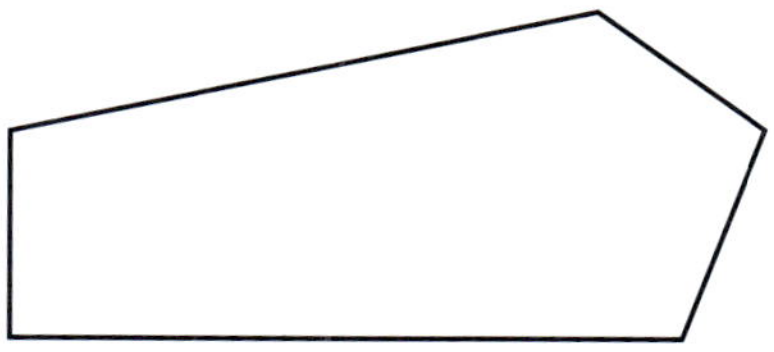

____

5. 

____

6. 

____

7. 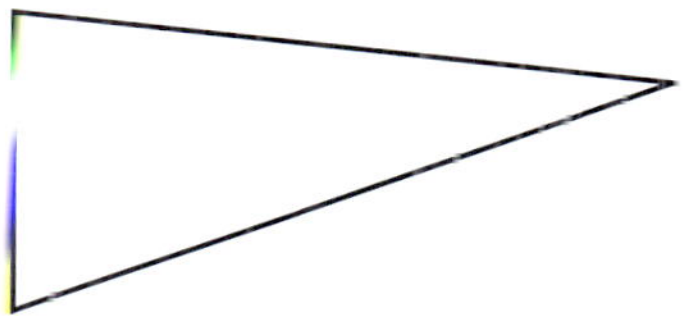

____

8. 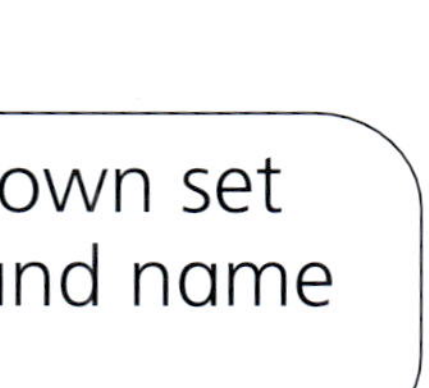

____

9. 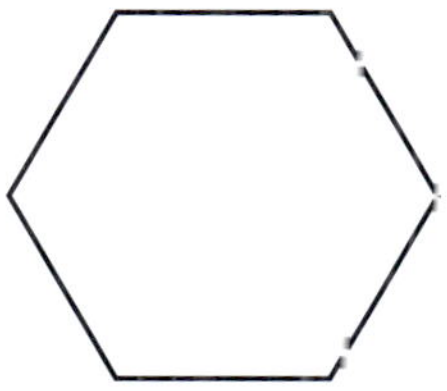

____

Draw your own set of shapes and name them.

Name ______________________

Symmetry

Draw the lines of symmetry on these shapes.

1.

2.

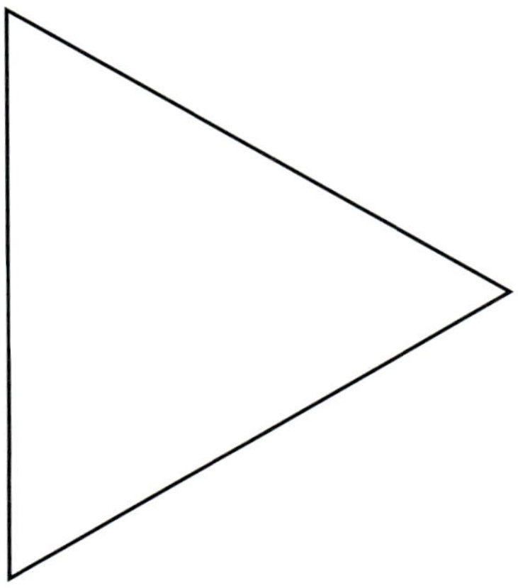

3.

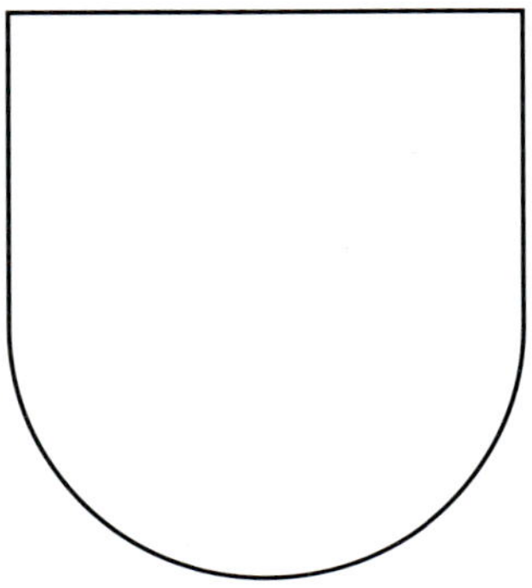

4.

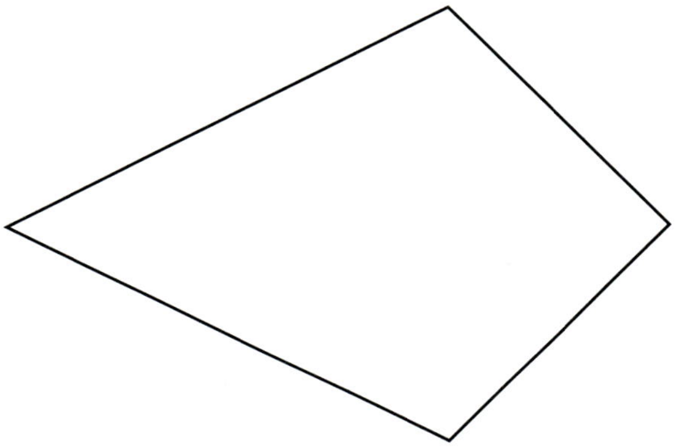

5.

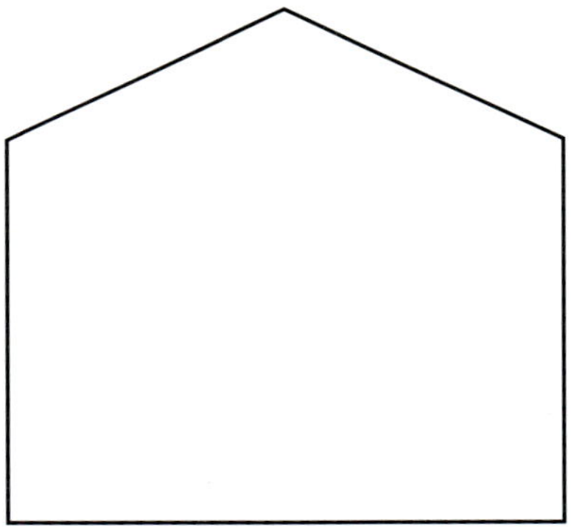

6.

Which shapes have more than one line of symmetry?

____

Name ____________________

Symmetry

Draw the other side of the fold-line on each shape.

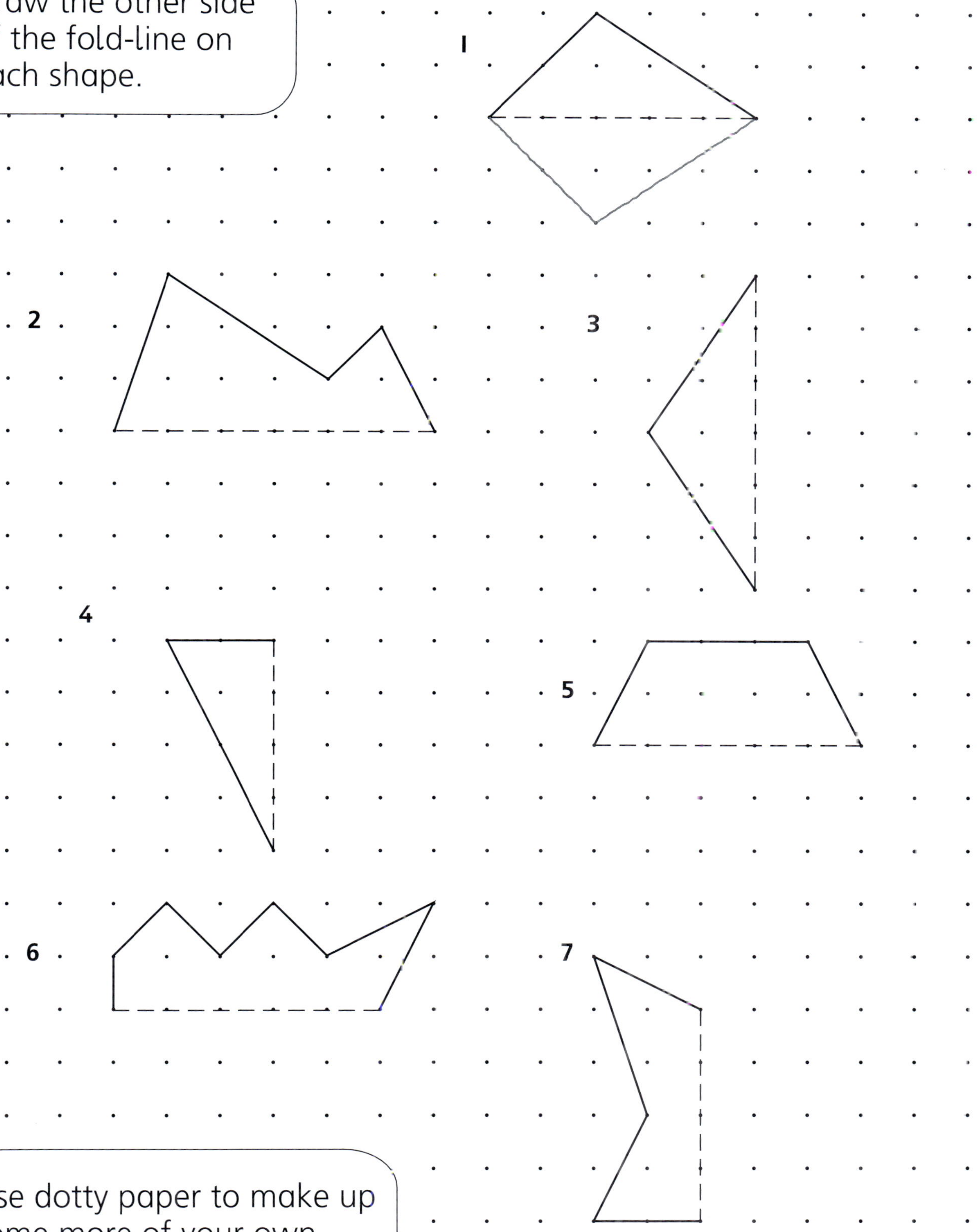

Use dotty paper to make up some more of your own.

Name ____________________

North, east, south, west

Describe these paths. Start at the spot each time.

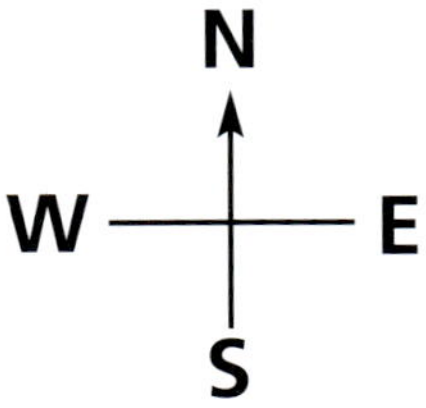

1.

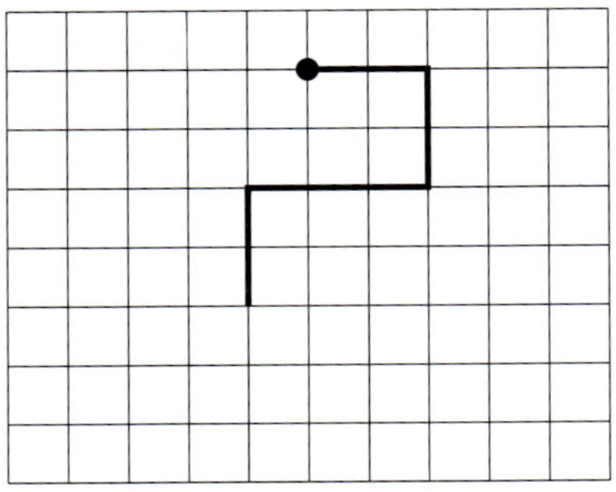

east 2
south 2
west 3
south 2

2.

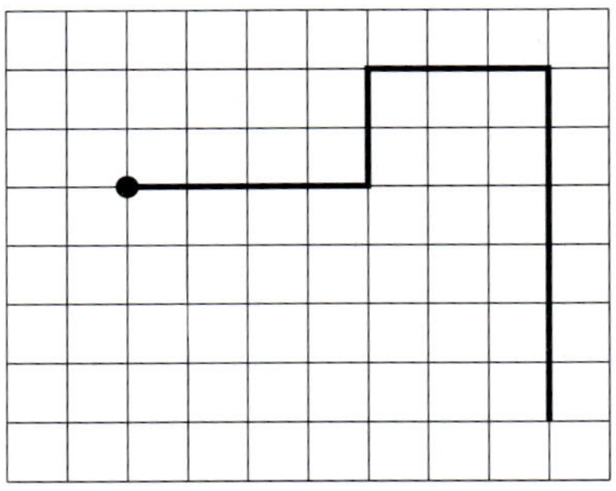

3.

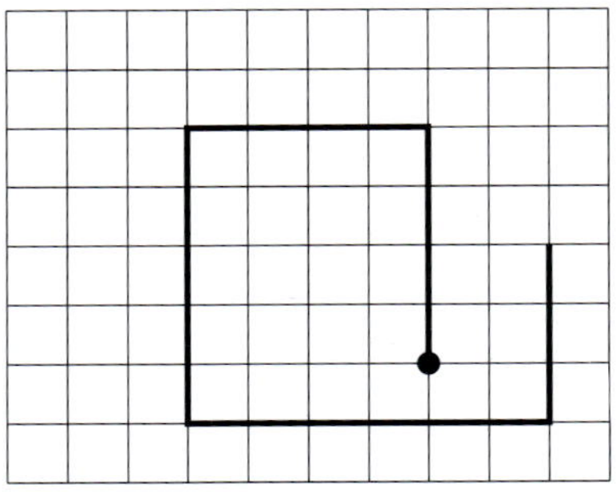

4.

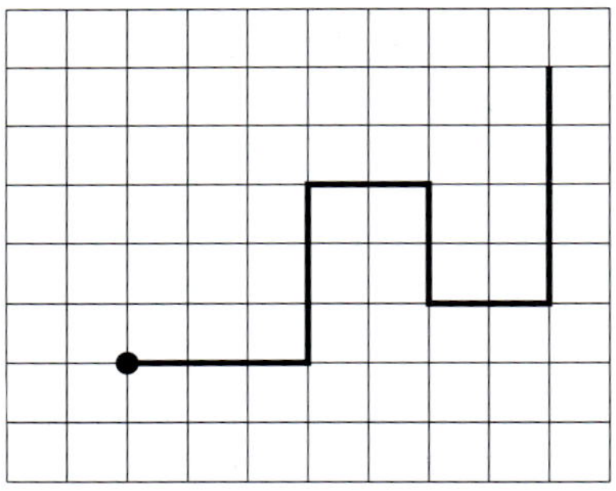

5.

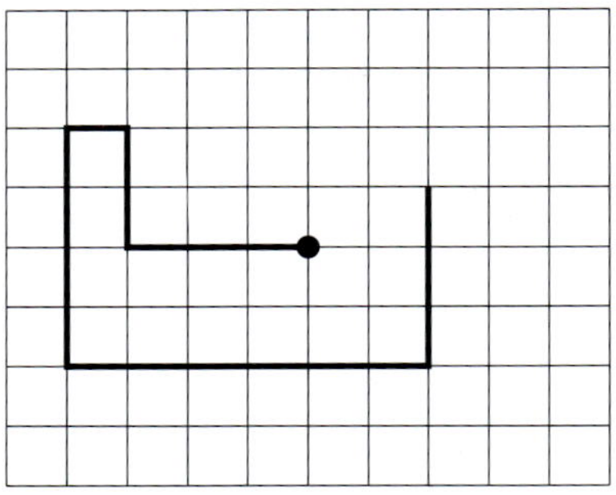

Describe each path from the end back to the spot.

Name ______________________________

North, east, south, west

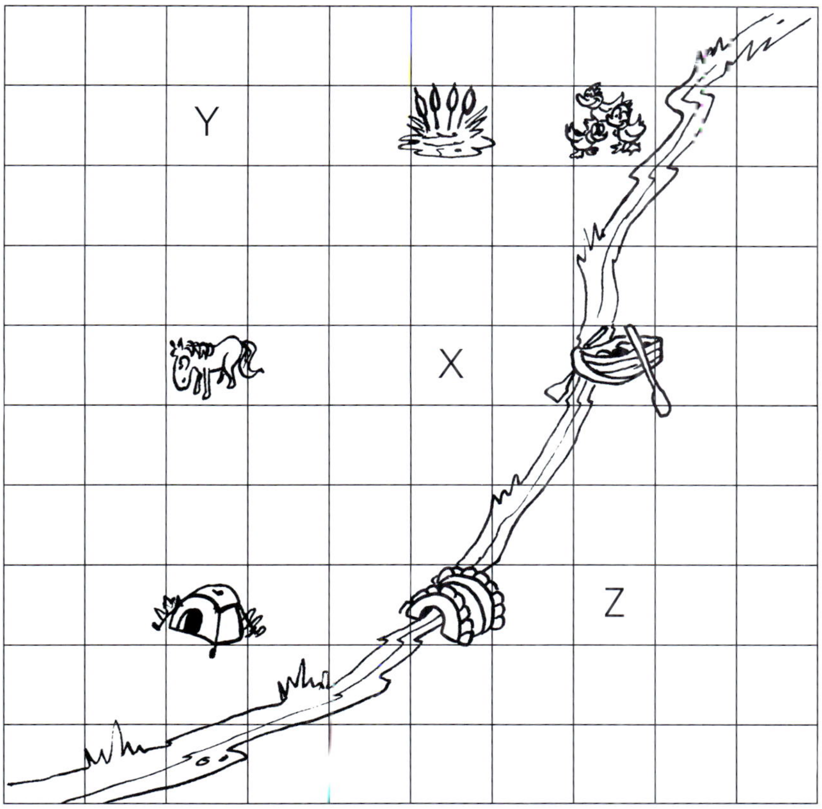

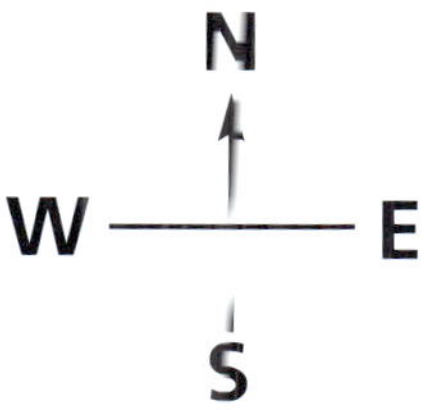

From X, what direction is:

1.  S

2.  ☐

3.  ☐

4.  ☐

From Y, what direction is:

5.  ☐

6.  ☐

7.  ☐

8.  ☐

From Z, what direction is:

9.  ☐

10.  ☐

11.  ☐

12.  ☐

Name ______________________________

Right-angles

Fold a piece of paper once to make a straight line.

Fold it again to make a right-angle.

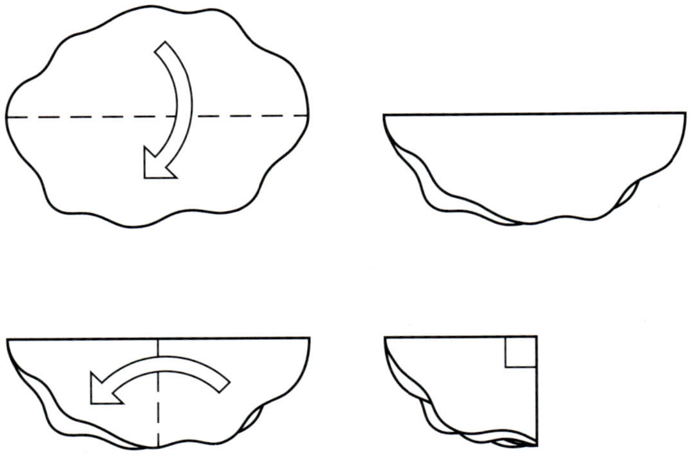

Use your right-angle measure to check these.

Colour the right-angles blue. Colour the smaller angles yellow and the larger angles green.

1.

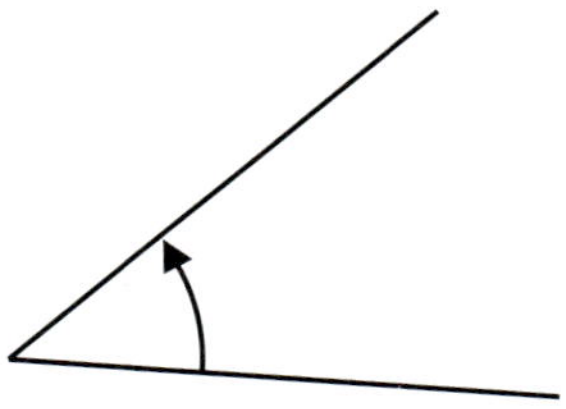

2.

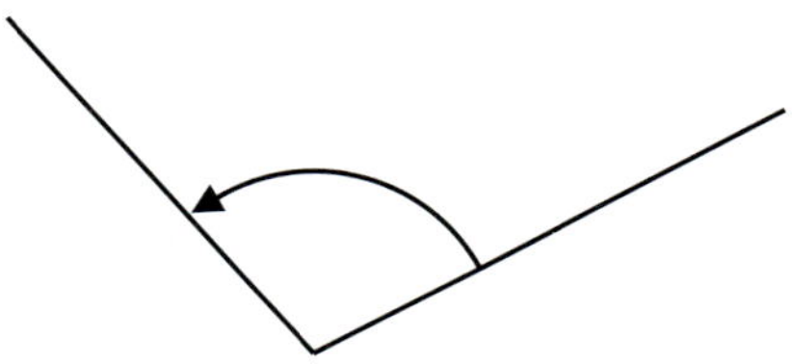

3.

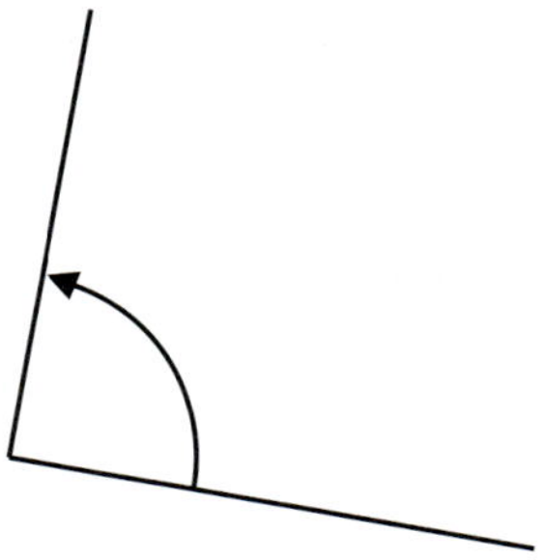

4.

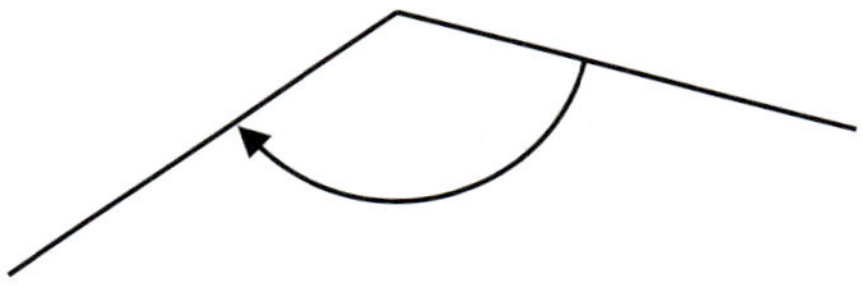

5.

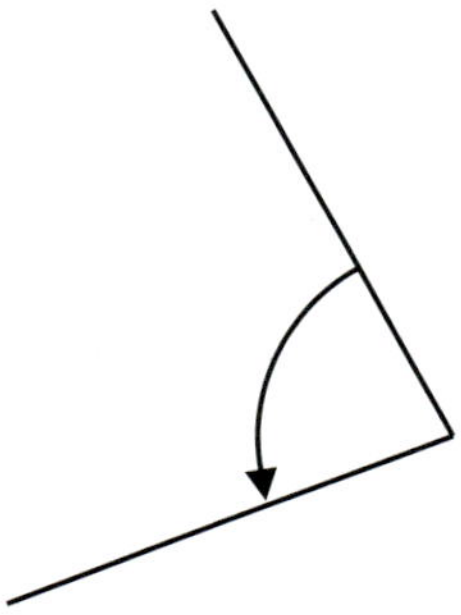

6.

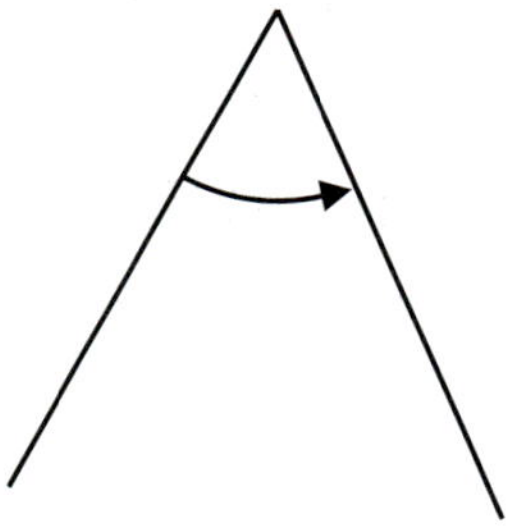

7.

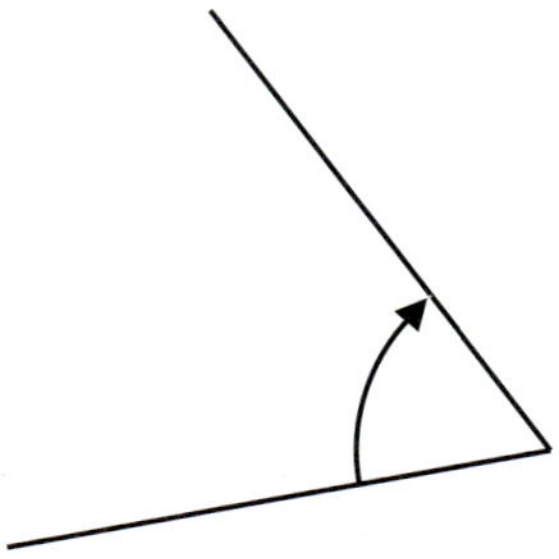

8.

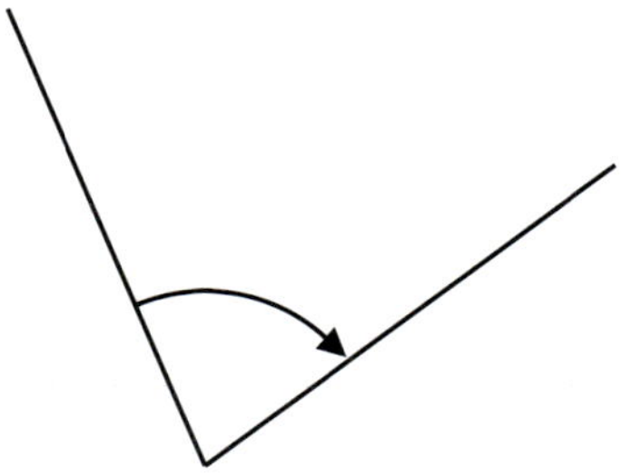

9.

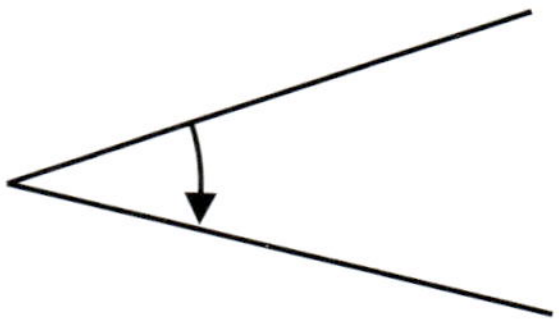

Name ______________________________

Turning north, east, south, west

Face north. Turn clockwise 2 right angles.	Face south. Turn clockwise 1 right angle.	Face east. Turn clockwise 3 right angles.	Face west. Turn clockwise 4 right angles.
Face north. Turn clockwise 1 right angle.	Face south. Turn clockwise 3 right angles.	Face north. Turn anticlockwise 2 right angles.	Face south. Turn anticlockwise 1 right angle.
Face east. Turn anticlockwise 3 right angles.	Face west. Turn anticlockwise 3 right angles.	Face east. Turn anticlockwise 2 right angles.	Face west. Turn anticlockwise 1 right angle.

Teacher's instructions
A game for four players.
Cut out these cards, shuffle them and place them face down in a pile. Each player chooses a direction (N, E, S, W), and sits round a table to match.
Take turns to pick a card, decide the final direction, and give the card to the player sitting in that direction. Check each other's moves.
The winner is the first one to collect three cards.

Materials
Scissors

Name ______________________

Position

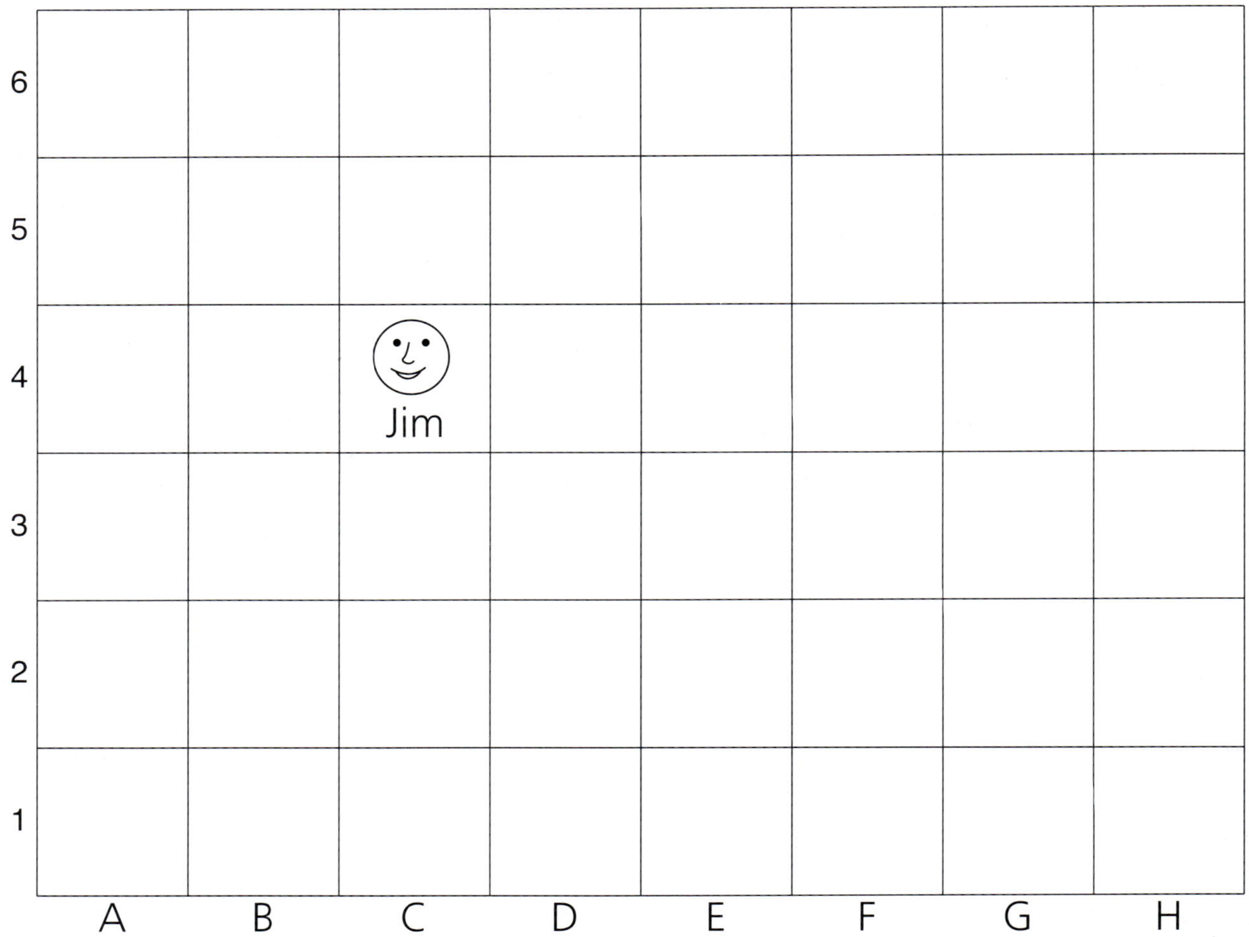

Show on the diagram where these people will sit.

1. 

Tom, A2

2. 

Clare, E6

3. 

Mark, H5

4. 

Ann, D4

5. 

Joe, B1

6. 

Lisa, C2

7. 

Dev, F3

8. 

Helen, G4

Who is:

9. nearest the front? ______________________

10. nearest Jim? ______________________

11. in the same row as Jim? ______________________

Name ______________________________

Tally charts

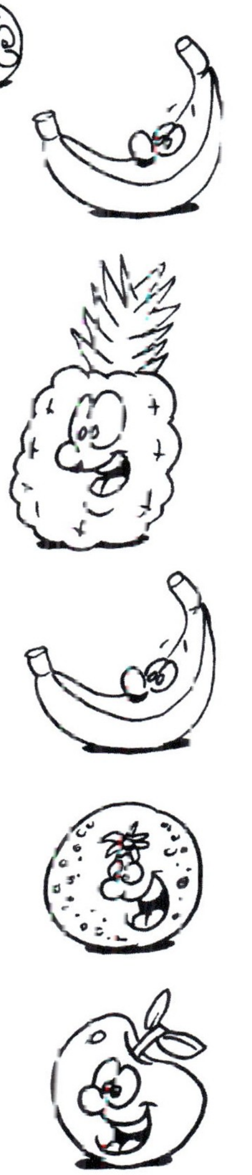

Fruits in the picture

fruit	tallies	total
apple		
orange		
banana		
plum		
pineapple		

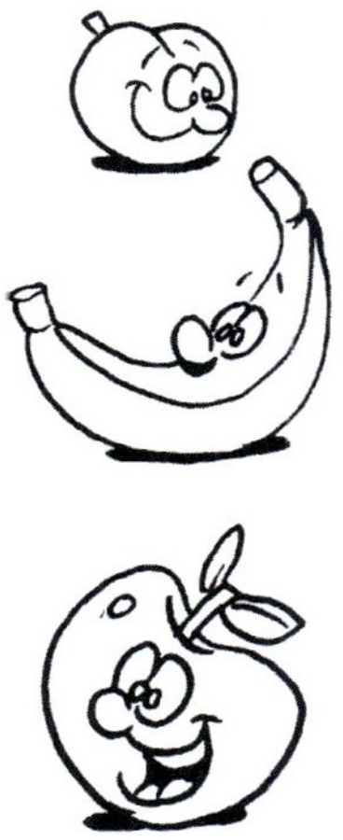

Complete the tally chart to show how many there are of each fruit.

How many pieces of fruit are there in total?

Write which fruit:

1. appeared most ______________________

2. appeared least ______________________

Name ______________________________

Frequency table

Vegetables:

pea	swede	cabbage	parsnip
bean	turnip	pepper	mushroom
cauliflower	courgette	yam	leek
potato	marrow	beetroot	fennel
carrot	squash	sprout	pumpkin
spinach	okra	brocolli	lettuce

Complete a frequency table to show how many times the vowels a, e, i, o and u appear in the vegetables.

Number of vowels in vegetable names

Vowel	Frequency
a	
e	
i	
o	
u	

Write which vowel appears:

1. most often ______________________

2. least often ______________________

Name ______________________

Bar graph

The bar graph shows the number of books borrowed from the library each day of last week.

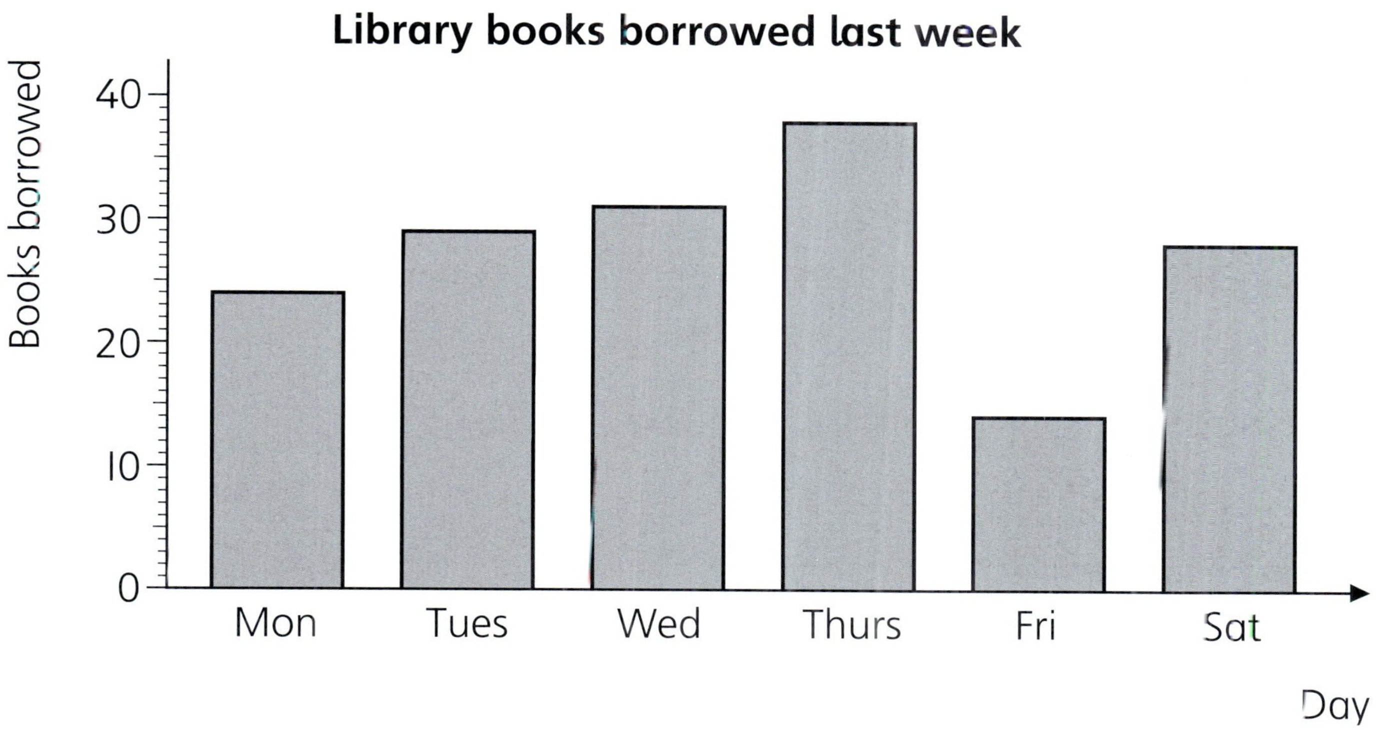

1. How many books were borrowed on:
   - **(a)** Monday? ☐
   - **(b)** Saturday? ☐
2. On which day were:
   - **(a)** 31 books borrowed? ☐
   - **(b)** 29 books borrowed? ☐
   - **(c)** the most books borrowed? ☐
   - **(d)** the fewest books borrowed? ☐
   - **(e)** twice as many books borrowed as on Friday? ☐
3. On how many days were:
   - **(a)** more than 30 books borrowed? ☐
   - **(b)** fewer than 28 books borrowed? ☐
4. How many books were borrowed in the week? ☐

Name ______________________________

Pictograph

Some children were asked for their favourite season.
The results are shown in the pictograph.

Our favourite season

Write which season:

1. has 5 votes ☐
2. has 7 votes ☐
3. is the most popular ☐
4. is the least popular ☐
5. has 3 more votes than winter ☐
6. has 3 less votes than summer ☐
7. has twice as many votes as autumn ☐
8. has 2 votes more than autumn ☐
9. is the second most popular ☐
10. has 5 votes less than summer ☐
11. How many children voted altogether? ☐

CW01670044

RHYME WORLD
Teacher's Guide
Stages 2 and 3

Rea Reason
Jo Wilson
Laura Huxford

Heinemann

Heinemann Educational Publishers
Halley Court, Jordan Hill, Oxford OX2 8EJ
a division of Reed Educational & Professional Publishing Ltd
Heinemann is a registered trademark of Reed Educational & Professional Publishing Limited.

OXFORD FLORENCE PRAGUE MADRID ATHENS
MELBOURNE AUCKLAND KUALA LUMPUR SINGAPORE TOKYO
IBADAN NAIROBI KAMPALA JOHANNESBURG GABORONE
PORTSMOUTH NH (USA) CHICAGO MEXICO CITY SAO PAULO

First published 1998

02 01 00 99 98
10 9 8 7 6 5 4 3 2

British Library Cataloguing in Publication Data
A catalogue record for this book is available from the British Library.

Rhyme World Teacher's Guide (Stages 2 and 3): ISBN 0 435 09528 5

Photocopy masters illustrated by Shelagh McNicholas
Cover designed by Gecko Limited
Printed in the UK by Heanor Gate Printing Limited

Contents

Welcome to Rhyme World!

What is Rhyme World?

Rhyme World is a systematic programme of early phonics taught through rhyming stories and accompanying activities. The phonic structure of the programme is clear and easy to follow and is based on up-to-date research about the role of phonics in teaching children to read.

Rhyme World is ideal for use during the Literacy Hour. The programme has been designed specifically to fulfil the requirements and objectives of the National Literacy Strategy. Rhyme World includes big books to be used during whole class sessions, a variety of pupil books, ideal for group reading, and follow-up activities in the form of games, workbooks and photocopiable materials designed to help children to consolidate their skills during independent group work.

Rhyme World ensures children's active participation in an investigative approach to phonics, includes information for parents and carers, and contains built-in opportunities for assessing progress.

Links with other literacy programmes

Rhyme World can be used alongside any other literacy programme. However, special attention has been given to links with its two 'sister' programmes, Storyworlds and Discovery World.

These three programmes offer distinct skills while complementing each other in developing a balanced approach to literacy. Each 'world':

- is carefully graded;
- has exceptional support for the beginning reader;
- covers a particular form of text: rhyme, fiction or non-fiction;
- has large format Literacy Lesson books, big books for shared reading, small books for group reading, and a range of support material for use during the Literacy Hour.

The chart opposite has been designed to help you run all three programmes together.

The role of phonics in reading

Children's ability to communicate and construct meaning through written language is central to the development of literacy. The ability to communicate through reading and writing is dependent on three main areas of literacy learning: the text (comprehension and composition); the sentence (grammar and punctuation) and the word (phonics, spelling and vocabulary). Learning at the word level requires planned activities that are supported by children's developing knowledge at the text and sentence levels. By teaching phonics in the context of meaningful and enjoyable texts, Rhyme World enables children to draw on all three areas of literacy learning.

<table>
<tr><th>AGE</th><th>RHYME WORLD STAGES</th><th>STORYWORLDS STAGES</th><th>DISCOVERY WORLD STAGES</th></tr>
<tr><td>4</td><td rowspan="2">1</td><td>1</td><td>A</td></tr>
<tr><td></td><td>2</td><td rowspan="2">B</td></tr>
<tr><td>5</td><td>2</td><td>3</td></tr>
<tr><td></td><td rowspan="3">3</td><td>4</td><td>C</td></tr>
<tr><td></td><td>5</td><td rowspan="2">D</td></tr>
<tr><td>6</td><td>6</td></tr>
<tr><td></td><td rowspan="3">4</td><td>7</td><td>E</td></tr>
<tr><td></td><td>8</td><td rowspan="2">F</td></tr>
<tr><td>7</td><td>9</td></tr>
</table>

Stages of phonic development

Current research suggests that there is a predictable order in which children develop their phonological competencies. This can be expressed as a series of stages:

Stage 1: Phonological awareness

Children's ability to hear and discriminate sounds in words is the basis for success in working with print. An ideal preparation for literacy starts with the spoken word. Through nursery rhymes, poems and alliterative jingles, children learn to appreciate the rhythm of language, and to recognize rhyme and alliteration in order to link it with print.

Stages 2 and 3: Onset and rime

Single syllable words can be broken up into two units: the onset and the rime. The onset is the initial sound of a word, i.e. the letters that appear before the first vowel; the rime is the part of the word that makes it rhyme with others. For example:

dog	'd' is the onset and 'og' is the rime
stroke	'str' is the onset and 'oke' is the rime

As they see the shared spelling patterns of words ending with the same rime, children learn to generalise by analogy. For example:

dog		joke
fog	*or*	broke
log		stroke
frog		

Rimes and rhymes are not identical. Rhymes have word endings which sound the same but are not necessarily spelled in the same way (e.g. rain/plane). In contrast, rimes are word endings which always retain the same spelling pattern (e.g. rain/Spain).

By increasing the complexity of the onsets (from single consonants to consonant blends, e.g. from 'f' to 'fr') and the rimes (e.g. from 'og' to 'ake' to 'all' to 'ight') children build up an extensive reading vocabulary which incorporates letter patterns included in traditional phonic teaching sequences.

Stage 4: Recognition of phonemes

The rhyme books at Stage 4 have been specially written to offer the teacher opportunities to focus on phonemes. Children following the Rhyme World programme from Stage 1 will have acquired the prerequisite phonological skills and knowledge to enable them to deal effectively with phonemic work at Stage 4.

Phonic development in Rhyme World

Rhyme World has been carefully designed to support these four stages of phonic development. The format and style of the Rhyme World books are designed to emphasise sounds in words and the way that these sounds are translated into print.

The model of progression adopted by Rhyme World is shown below.

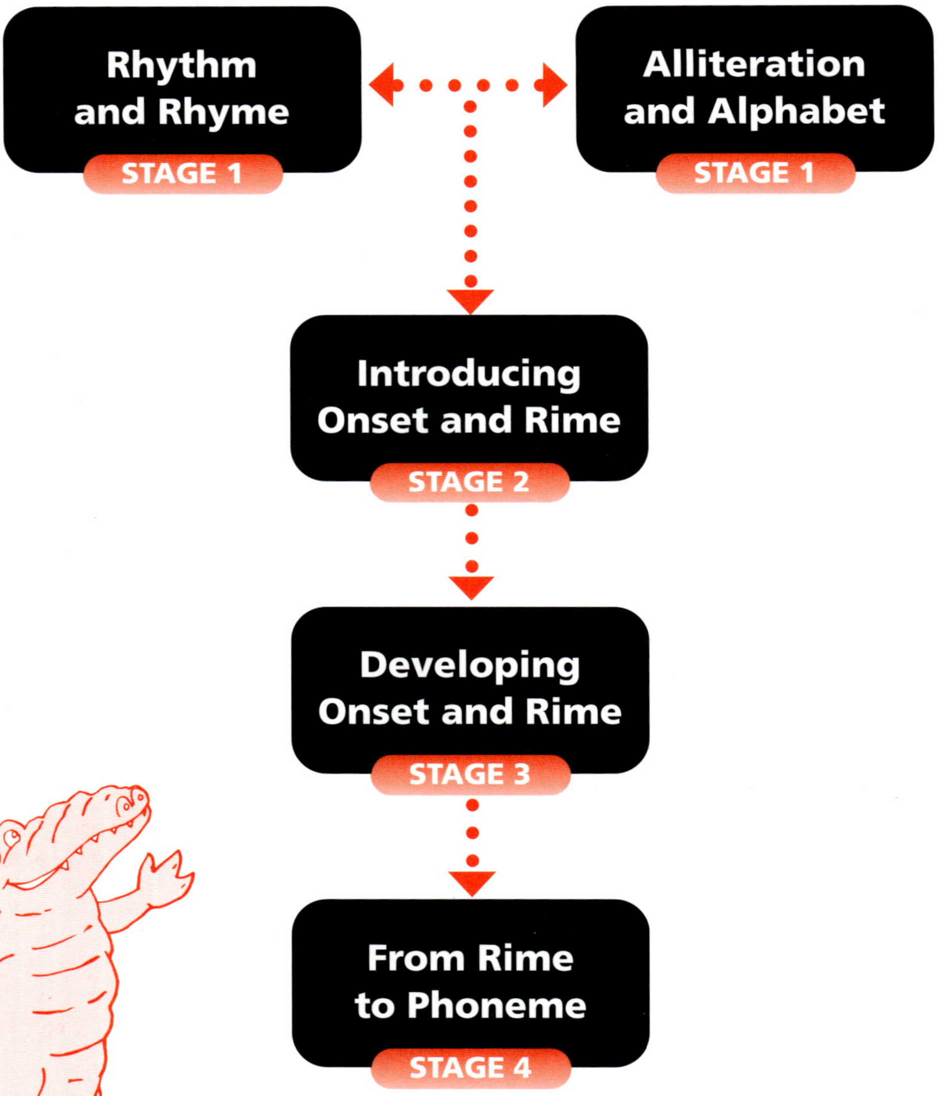

Rhyme World Stages

Stage 1

Stage 1 is primarily an auditory stage designed to help children to tune in to the rhythms and rhymes in language.

The Rhythm and Rhyme Literacy Lesson Book contains a collection of specially chosen new and traditional rhymes, together with full teaching notes, which help children to appreciate rhythm and rhyme, to learn about words and syllables, to notice similarities and differences in the sounds of words and to recognize when words rhyme.

The Alliteration and Alphabet Literacy Lesson Book contains activities and full teaching notes to help children to isolate initial sounds in words. This book, together with the individual ABC books, helps children to make the connection between sound and print.

Stage 2

Stage 2 consists of big and small books of rhyming stories. These are designed to introduce children to the concept of onset and rime. The two Literacy Skills Big Books contain eight rhyming stories, each of which focuses on one rime. By adding a variety of onsets as the story progresses, children learn to notice the similarities between words. The small books concentrate on one story each, and their split-page design physically divides words into two components to reinforce the children's understanding of onset and rime.

Stage 3

Stage 3 also contains big and small books. The two Literacy Skills Big Books contain ten stories written in rhyming couplets, which develop the principle of onset and rime with a variety of onset and rime combinations. By seeing words on the page which sound the same and have the same spelling pattern, children make the connection between sound and spelling patterns. As at Stage 2, each of the stories is available as an individual small book.

Stage 4

The big book and the small books at Stage 4 teach children to begin to recognize phonemes within the rimes (e.g. rain/rail; sleep/sleet; bike/stile/kite). Through word patterns and word play children learn to recognize medial, beginning and end phonemes in words.

Assessment

Finding out what children have learned and need to learn next is central to planning the activities in Rhyme World. Built into the programme are opportunities for checking which children are moving through quite quickly and which children require further practice. The assessments can be undertaken in the course of interactive whole class or group teaching by noting individual progress through focused observations of particular children. In this Teacher's Guide, photocopiable whole class record sheets and assessment sheets are provided as Photocopy Masters 22-30 (Stage 2) and 57-62 (Stage 3).

Further activities

This Teacher's Guide contains a bank of further activities and games which provide extra reinforcement. They are designed to be easy to use by children in the independent group work part of the Literacy Hour. It is important to recognize, however, that many children come to school with good phonological skills and learn very quickly. We recommend, therefore, that the further activities and games described in this Teacher's Guide are used selectively with those children who need extra practice.

Children with special educational needs

The research basis of Rhyme World implies that children with learning difficulties, particularly in the area of phonology, do not need to follow a different programme from the rest of the class. Individual educational plans based on Rhyme World make the teaching more deliberate, repetitive and carefully monitored. In the context of interactive whole class teaching the children making slower progess have opportunities to learn from models provided by the rest of the class. By preparing these children in a separate session beforehand, you will enable them to participate fully in interactive whole class teaching and even to 'shine' in front of the rest of the class.

Children with English as an additional language

Many children from minority linguistic and cultural backgrounds come to school unable to speak English and are developing their understanding of English at the same time as learning to read and write in English. For these children the understanding of content is paramount. Regardless of linguistic background, children must develop the phonological skills and understandings needed for reading in an alphabetic script. Rhyme World offers all children the opportunity to develop these important and fundamental skills and understandings.

Home-school links

Photocopiable take-home letters are provided which give full instructions to parents and carers on how to help their child to read the rhyme books at Stage 2 (Photocopy Master 21) and Stage 3 (Photocopy Master 56).

How Rhyme World teaches phonics

Rhyme World teaches phonics within the context of stimulating and enjoyable text and illustrations. Children acquire initial phonic skills and learn to apply them to continuous text.

At Stage 1 of Rhyme World children are given plenty of opportunity to explore and experience rhymes and short verses on a sound only basis. The transition to print is made through shared reading of simple, easily remembered rhyming couplets, which help children to learn to make the links between what they hear (i.e. the rhyming words) and what they see (i.e. the words in print on the page).

At Stages 2 and 3, each story rhyme contains words made up of focus onsets and rimes and it is these, through detailed word and phonic teaching, that the child learns to read out of context. Guidance on specific teaching is given which helps you to focus on particular onsets and rimes in the text.

The repetition and predictable content enable children to read all the story rhyme words in context but children are not expected to read every word on the page independently or out of context. The purpose of Rhyme World Stages 2 and 3 is to enable children to read and spell fluently and automatically the onset and rime units introduced in particular books.

Rhyme World provides big books designed to be used for whole class reading and teaching of phonics. The Rhyme World small books are an ideal resource for use in group work to consolidate and practise the language in the rhyming texts introduced in the big books.

Rhyme World Stages 2 and 3

Components of Stages 2 and 3

The chart below shows how the big books in each stage link with the small books, the Photocopy Masters for further activities, and the workbooks.

	Big books	Small books	Photocopy Masters		Workbook
STAGE 2				8 × text level 8 × word level 4 × composite 8 × assessment	
STAGE 3	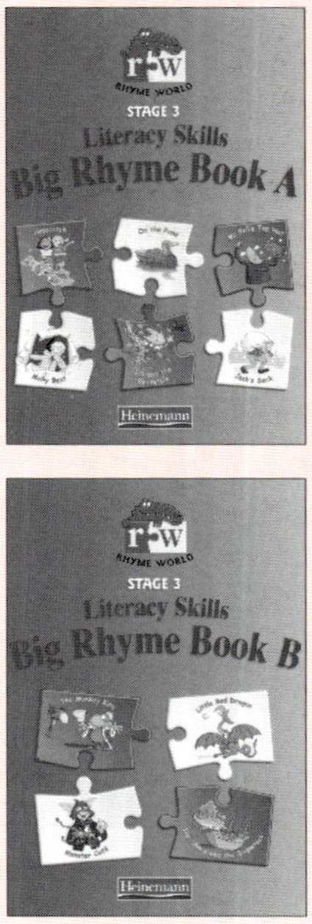			10 × text level 10 × word level 5 × composite 5 × assessment	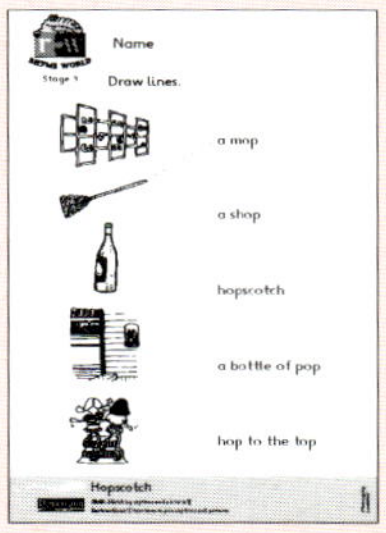

The Literacy Hour and Rhyme World

The National Literacy Strategy places great importance on the teaching of phonics within the Literacy Hour.

The Literacy Hour is divided into four sections:

1 shared reading and writing
2 word or sentence work
3 work done independently of you while you work with a group
4 the plenary session.

The first fifteen minutes of the Literacy Hour is for whole class work involving shared reading of a big book. The second fifteen minutes is the time when you can engage in concentrated interactive teaching of phonics, spelling and sentence work with the whole class. For a number of children this will be all the specific phonics work that they need. Others will need reinforcement or even further specific teaching. This can be achieved in a group reading session. Children carry out reinforcement activities in pairs, groups or individually. If a classroom assistant is available, further word level teaching could take place at this time.

The diagram below shows the four sections of the Literacy Hour.

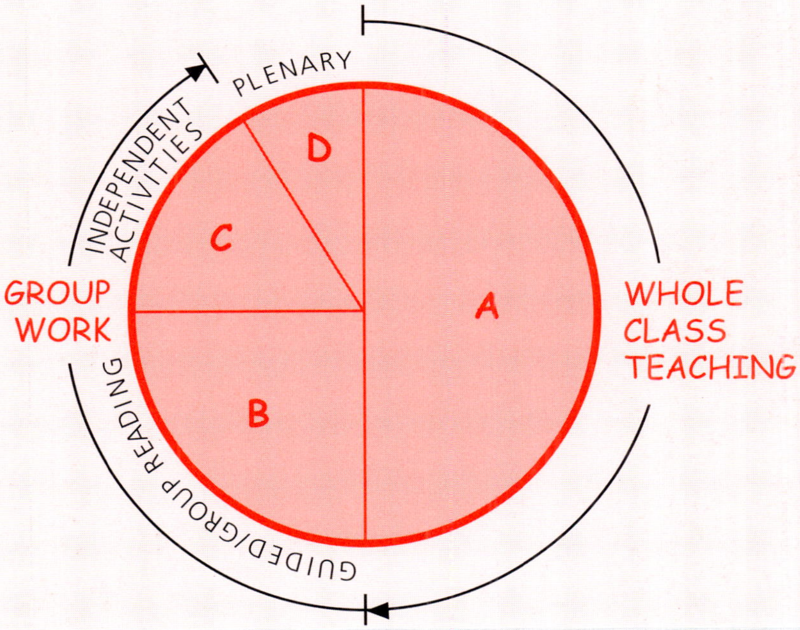

A The whole class shares a big book. Phonic patterns are pointed out, leading to detailed word work.

B The groups take it in turns to use small books for group reading.

C Other groups do independent work.

D Everyone meets up for the plenary session to talk about what they have done.

Stages 2 and 3 of Rhyme World provide big books, small books, and support material for teaching phonics in the context of the Literacy Hour. The chart opposite shows how the books can be used in:

- interactive whole class teaching
- group reading
- independent work (group or individual)
- the plenary session.

Using a big book, share the reading of a story rhyme with the whole class. Point out particular phonic patterns and use the story rhyme as a basis for detailed phonic teaching. Many children can then go on to read the small books for independent practice and reinforcement.

There will be groups of children who need further explicit teaching and the small books may be used by you or the classroom assistant for group teaching sessions on word level work. Other groups of children may undertake independent reinforcement activities and games provided in the workbooks or Photocopy Masters in this Teacher's Guide.

At the end of the Literacy Hour the plenary session gives groups or individuals an opportunity to report on and talk about the activities they have completed. This enables them to reinforce their learning and also provides you with an informal opportunity to assess progress.

An alternative model, which is particularly effective with children making slower progress, is to prepare the these children to participate fully in the whole class interactive session by reading the small version of the book with them in a group session beforehand.

Rhyme World Stages 2 and 3 within the Literacy Hour

Interactive whole class teaching

Big books

Shared reading of a chosen story rhyme with an emphasis on the onset and rime units. The text enables children to generate lists of words illustrating particular phonic patterns.

See page 16 for a sample lesson at Stage 2 and page 26 for a sample lesson at Stage 3.

Group reading

Small books

The small books are designed for group reading. Children can read the text for themselves after the shared reading session with the big book. The small books can also be used by you for small group teaching sessions and by the classroom assistant to prepare the groups making slower progress for the whole class teaching sessions.

See page 18 for a sample lesson at Stage 2 and page 28 for a sample lesson at Stage 3.

Independent activities

Continued use of small books

The rhyming books are supported by worksheets in the form of Photocopy Masters and workbooks. The worksheets contain reinforcement activities and games. The instructions and rules are generic but the content varies. This provides the children with clear, predictable routines and enables them to work independently.

See pages 19-20 for a description of the activities and games at Stage 2, and pages 29-30 for Stage 3.

Plenary session

Groups or individual children tell the class what they have achieved. The session might then finish with a 'fun phrase finale' where the children clap the phrases and words from a text. Alternatively, the children re-read the text together once more at a brisk and confident pace.

How to use Rhyme World Stage 2

Big books and small books

Stage 2 consists of big and small books of rhyming stories which introduce children to the concept of onset and rime. Each rhyming story focuses on one rime. As the story progresses, a variety of onsets are added to the rime. This enables children to notice similarities between words.

Big books

- Het the Vet
- Billy Bop's Magic Mop
- The Bin Twins
- Leggy Lug

- Ben and the Hen
- Mr Clog and the Log
- Zap!
- Minnie May and the Jay

There are two big books at Stage 2. Each big book is an anthology of four rhyming stories designed for shared reading during the whole class part of the Literacy Hour. Each story is accompanied by a 'word work' page designed for use during the word level work part of whole class teaching. Organising the big books in this way means that a complete rhyming story can be introduced to the whole class as a stimulus for focused phonic work.

Small books

There are eight small books at Stage 2. Each book has one story focusing on one rime. The small books have a split-page design which physically divides words into their two component parts to reinforce children's understanding of onset and rime.

The Stage 2 small books are ideal for group reading within or outside the Literacy Hour. The chart on the next page outlines the onsets and rimes at Stage 2.

Focus onsets and rimes at Stage 2

Book title	Learning outcome: to read and spell words ending in:	Onsets in the text	Rhyming words in the text	Photocopy Masters (text level)	Photocopy Masters (word level)
Het the Vet	et	g, H, j, m, n, p, v, w, y	met, Het, vet, jet, pet, wet, net, get, yet	1	2 and 5
Billy Bop's Magic Mop	op	B, m, p, dr, fl, sh, sl, st	Bop, shop, pop, drop, slop, mop, flop, stop	3	4 and 5
The Bin Twins	in	b, d, M, N, t, sk, th, tw	Min, thin, Nin, twin, bin, tin, din, in, skin	6	7 and 10
Leggy Lug	ug	b, h, j, L, m, r, sl, sn	Lug, bug, mug, jug, slug, rug, hug, snug	8	9 and 10
Ben and the Hen	en	B, d, h, m, p, th	Ben, pen, hen, then, men, den	11	12 and 15
Mr Clog and the Log	og	c, d, f, j, l, Cl, fr	Clog, log, dog, cog, jog, fog, frog	13	14 and 15
Zap!	ap	l, m, n, t, y, z, fl, sl, sn	map, nap, lap, flap, yap, snap, zap, tap, slap	16	17 and 20
Minnie May and the Jay	ay	d, j, M, p, pl, tr	May, tray, day, play, jay, (away), pay, (okay)	18	19 and 20

Interactive whole class teaching at Stage 2

Interactive whole class teaching is based on the rhyming stories in the big books. Below is a suggested sample lesson relating to the story rhyme, *Het the Vet* in Literacy Skills Big Rhyme Book A. This sequence can be followed with any of the story rhymes at Stage 2.

1 Look through *Het the Vet* in the big book and talk about the content and the illustrations.

2 Read the whole story rhyme to the children running your finger along the text as you read.

3 Re-read the story rhyme and ask the children to supply the rhyming word at the end of each line. The children need not learn to read all the other words independently.

4 Ask the children to read the story with you.

Word work

Each story rhyme is accompanied by a 'read the words' page in the big book (see above). The 'read the words' page can be used for a number of activities such as:

1 You read a word and choose a child to point to it.

2 A child reads a word and chooses another child to come and point to it.

3 The whole class reads together words selected (pointed to) by you or one of the children.

4 Writing down words which share the same ending. This requires a whiteboard or large sheets of paper together with magnetic plastic letters or marker pens. The chart on page 15 lists the onsets and rimes covered by each book. Children may take it in turns to write a word on the whiteboard or sheet of paper.

A suggested weekly plan using the Stage 2 Literacy Skills Big Rhyme Books

As each big book at Stage 2 contains four stories, it is helpful to think of a weekly plan that reinforces the learning of the first story while introducing the second story. We have illustrated this below with reference to Literacy Skills Big Rhyme Book A. The same sequence can also be followed with Literacy Skills Big Rhyme Book B. The amount of repetition depends on the rate of progress of the children.

Week 1

MONDAY *Het the Vet* and 'et' word building

TUESDAY *Billy Bop's Magic Mop* and 'op' word building

WEDNESDAY *Het the Vet* and 'et' word building

THURSDAY *Billy Bop's Magic Mop* and 'op' word building

FRIDAY Word building with 'et' and 'op' from the two books. Finish the session by re-reading the two stories with the children.

Week 2

MONDAY *The Bin Twins* and 'in' word building

TUESDAY *Leggy Lug* and 'ug' word building

WEDNESDAY *The Bin Twins* and 'in' word building

THURSDAY *Leggy Lug* and 'ug' word building

FRIDAY Word work with 'in' and 'ug'. Finish the session by re-reading the two stories with the children.

Week 3

- Reinforce all the rimes in Literacy Skills Big Rhyme Book A.
- Practise word building with 'et', 'op', 'in' and 'ug' as illustrated below.
- Re-read stories chosen by the children with the children sharing the reading with you.

Word building from Literacy Skills Big Rhyme Book A

et	op	in	ug
met	mop	bin	mug
set	top	pin	bug
net	hop	thin	rug
get	drop	win	slug

Group reading at Stage 2

After the children have participated in a whole class shared reading of a big book, they can then read the sets of small books in groups. For children making good progress this can be done for reinforcement and extra practice. You may find it useful to do a small group teaching session with the children making slower progress using the small books. This can be particularly effective for these children as it prepares them beforehand for participation during whole class sessions. Below is a suggested sequence of activities for small group teaching relating to *Het the Vet*. This sequence can be followed with any of the eight small books.

1 Talk about the illustrations and characters.

2 Read the book to the group. Ask the children to follow the lines with their fingers.

3 Read the book together – you and the children. The children follow each line with their fingers.

4 Ask the children what sound they can hear at the end when you say, "Het", "vet", "pet", "jet", etc. Ask the children to point to 'et'.

5 Say, "Let's read all these 'et' words". Starting with the first page say, "Listen … vvv…et – vet. Let's say it together: vvv…et – vet". Continue with the other pages, emphasising the first sound before reading the word.

6 Now say, "Let's read these 'et' words quickly". Let the children flip through the pages as fast as they can turn them while they say together, "vet", "pet", "yet", etc. Give individual children the opportunity to take turns to read the words quickly.

7 Say, "I'm going to say a sound and I want you to guess which 'et' word I'm going to write". Say, "vvv". The children respond, "vet". Write 'vet' on a whiteboard or large sheet of paper. Repeat with more 'et' words. Ask the children if they can think of more 'et' words.

8 Ask the children to volunteer to read the 'et' words listed.

9 This sequence can be followed with activities where the children write the 'et' words from dictation. However, if time is limited, the writing can be done during independent work using the Photocopy Masters and workbooks provided.

10 Read the story again with the children taking turns to read each page.

Independent activities at Stage 2

In order to enable you to work without interruption with a group, it is important to make the independent individual or group activities as routine and easily understood as possible. Consequently, this Teacher's Guide includes a variety of phonic activities, supported by Photocopy Masters, which are available for each of the eight small books at Stage 2. While the content of the activity varies according to the chosen book, the format and instructions stay the same for each book. These activities reinforce the learning that has taken place during teacher directed whole class and group work.

1 Text level work

Purpose
To reinforce children's understanding and comprehension of a particular rhyming story book.

Materials
There is one Photocopy Master on text level work for each book (see the chart on page 15).

The Photocopy Masters comprising pictures to match to captions provide a focus for recalling the story. They may also include some rhyming words which help children to make predictions about the text in the story rhyme. Whilst not essential, it is recommended that children complete the pictures and captions matching activity before moving on to the word level work described below.

2 Word level work

Purpose
To reinforce children's ability to make up and spell words ending with a particular rime.

Materials
There is one Photocopy Master on word level work for each book (see page 15).

Ask the children to "use the letters at the top of the sheet to make and write words ending in …". The line illustrations act as visual prompts but the children should be encouraged to focus on the sounds of the words, rather than pictures or meaning, in order to gain maximum benefit from the activity.

There are also four composite pages each containing word level work on two of the Stage 2 rhyming stories (see page 15).

3 Card games

Purpose
To provide further practice in making up, reading and writing words ending with the rimes covered at Stage 2.

Materials
No Photocopy Masters are required for these games, just the following:

- Two packs of blank playing cards, made up from large sheets of card; 42 cards will be needed for the first game described on the next page.
- A thick felt pen.

Instructions
These instructions apply to Literacy Skills Big Rhyme Book A, which contains the following stories: *Het the Vet*; *Billy Bop's Magic Mop*; *The Bin Twins*; *Leggy Lug*.

1 Make up one pack of cards with one of the following onsets on each card: b, d, g, h, j, l, m, n, p, r, t, v, w, dr, fl, sh, sk, sl, sn, st, th, tw.

2 Make up the other pack of cards with five cards each for the following rimes: et, op, in, ug.

3 Shuffle each pack of cards and place them face down in front of the children.

4 The children turn over the top card from each pack and place them side by side.

5 The children read the 'word' made by combining the onset and rime. If it is a 'real' word, i.e. if it 'makes sense', they write it down on a sheet of paper. Even when the word does not 'make sense', the blending of the onsets and rimes provides valuable practice in the phonological skills involved.

6 When all the cards have been used up in any one of the packs, the children can shuffle the cards and start the game again.

An easier version
To make the game easier, use only two rimes and the onsets that go with these rimes (see the chart on page 15). You will need two cards for each onset and five cards for each rime.

An even easier version
Place one rime card face up on the table. Then put the onset cards from two stories face down near it. The children take turns to pick one onset card and place it in front of the rime card; they decide whether the cards make a 'real' word. If they decide yes, they write the word down.

Similar games can be constructed with onsets and rimes taken from the stories in Literacy Skills Big Rhyme Book B. Refer to the chart on page 15 for the lists of onsets and rimes covered in *Ben and the Hen*; *Mr Clog and the Log*; *Zap!*; *Minnie May and the Jay*.

4 Track game

The games are best managed when children work co-operatively in pairs and take turns to try to make up a word and write it down on a shared list. However, a competitive element can be added by introducing a simple track game.

To play the track game
You will need:
- the baseboard made up from Photocopy Masters 63 and 64
- a die
- two counters.

Each child takes it in turn to throw the die, moves their counter along the appropriate number of blocks and then turns over the top cards from each pack (see above). If the resultant word 'makes sense', the child gets another turn. In order to make sure that one child does not get too many turns, it is important to include a larger selection of different onsets in the first pack.

The Stage 2 workbook

The Stage 2 workbook provides opportunities for further reinforcement. It is designed for independent work and contains instructions that remain the same across all stories. The workbook consists of two kinds of activity for each of the eight story books. In the first, children match captions and pictures. In the second, children identify words ending with a particular rime and then write down the words ending with that rime.

Assessing progress

While many children learn to read and write the onsets and rimes at Stage 2 remarkably easily, others need more practice. It is important, therefore, to notice differential progress in order to plan teaching arrangements accordingly.

The interactive whole class teaching based on the big books and the group reading of the small books provides ideal opportunities for informal assessment of progress. In the course of these activities, you can 'keep an eye on' targeted children and invite them to participate individually whenever possible. If different children or groups of children are targeted over the sessions, you will be able to notice to what extent each child or group has acquired the onset and rime skills covered at Stage 2.

In order to enable you to record these observations as easily as possible at Stage 2, this Teacher's Guide provides a photocopiable class record sheet (Photocopy Master 22), and photocopiable assessment sheets (Photocopy Masters 23–30). If children can read and write a selection of words ending in a particular rime, you may assume that they have learned that rime.

Home-school links

As discussed earlier, parents and carers play a vital role in reinforcing their children's learning at home. In order to provide information about the purposes and teaching methods of Stage 2 in Rhyme World, a photocopiable letter is included in this Teacher's Guide (Photocopy Master 21).

How to use Rhyme World Stage 3

Stage 2 of Rhyme World shows children that short simple words can be 'broken up' into two component parts, i.e. the onset and the rime. The split-page small books demonstrate this in a concrete way by physically separating the initial sounds from the common rime unit each time a page is turned. The story books at Stage 3 are designed to move on from this type of text to provide a variety of increasingly complex stories within the framework of rhyming texts based largely on couplets.

This arrangement is of great benefit for early readers for the following reasons:

1 Rhyming text is easy to remember, making it simpler for children to learn the words and phrases within the story.

2 The repetition and consolidation of some of the onsets and rimes which are featured in the Stage 2 stories will help children to transfer and generalise skills from one context to another.

3 The gradual introduction of new onsets and rimes will help children to build up their ability to recognize a wide range of rimes through both listening to text and seeing the rimes in the text as parts of words.

4 The introduction of a number of new onsets and rimes means that children can develop skills in the use of analogies. They can then use a 'mix and match' strategy for generating new words, by analogy, for reading and spelling.

5 Stories written in rhyming text are often predictable in terms of language. Through working with whole rhyming stories, children develop strategies such as using the context to anticipate and predict events in addition to using phonic strategies for decoding print.

How to use Rhyme World Stage 3

Stage 3 consists of big and small books of rhyming stories which develop the concept of onset and rime. Each rhyming story features a variety of onsets and rimes.

Big books

- Hopscotch
- On the Pond
- Mr Bell's Top Hat
- Molly Best
- Jill and the Beanstalk
- Jack's Sack

- The Monkey King
- Little Red Dragon
- Monster Café
- The Shark and the Shipwreck

There are two big books at Stage 3. Each big book is an anthology of rhyming stories. There are six stories in Literacy Skills Big Rhyme Book A and four in Literacy Skills Big Rhyme Book B. These are designed for shared reading during the whole class part of the Literacy Hour. Organising the big books in this way means that a complete rhyming story can be introduced to the whole class as a stimulus for focused phonic work.

Small books

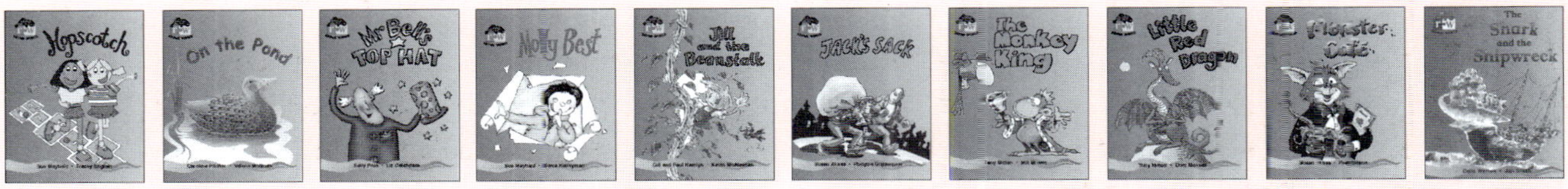

There are ten small books. Each book has one story written in rhyming couplets and featuring a variety of onset and rime combinations. By seeing words on the page which sound the same and have the same spelling pattern, children make the connection between sound and spelling patterns.

These books are ideal for group reading within or outside the Literacy Hour.

The onsets and rimes at Stage 3

In each Stage 3 storybook particular onsets and rimes are selected for attention during the interactive whole class and group sessions. In this way it is possible for children gradually to build up a useful bank of rime knowledge, without becoming overwhelmed by the introduction of too many new rimes at any one time.

In addition to focusing on new rimes, attention is also given to the introduction of new and more complex onsets to enable children to learn and use initial consonant blends.

The recommended onsets and rimes have been carefully selected to provide the best balance between consolidating existing skills and knowledge and extending and developing phonic awareness through onsets and rimes across all of the stories featuring at Stage 3.

The following chart lists the story books at Stage 3 together with the onsets and rimes covered by each book.

Focus onsets and rimes at Stage 3

Book title	Learning outcome: to read and spell words ending in:	Onsets in the text	Rhyming words in the text	Photocopy Masters (text level)	Photocopy Masters (word level)
Hopscotch	op	h, m, p, t, dr, sh, st	hop, shop, pop, stop, top, drop, mop	31	32 and 35
On the Pond	ill, eed, all, est, ond	b, f, h, n, p, r	pond, (beyond), hill, bill, reeds, needs, all, fall, rest, best	33	34 and 35
Mr Bell's Top Hat	at, ell, ot, it, own	B, f, h, l, M, s, t, w, cl, fl, th	hat, flat, that, Bell, well, Mot, hot, lot, sit, fit, clown, town	36	37 and 40
Molly Best	est, ug, own	B, g, j, m, n, p, r, v, w, fr, sl	Best, pest, jest, vest, nest, west, rug, slug, mug, frown, gown	38	39 and 40
Jill and the Beanstalk	y, op, eep	t, ch, cr, sk, st, tr	try, sky, stop, top, chop (asleep), creep	41	42 and 45
Jack's Sack	ack	b, J, s, bl, cr, sh, wh	black, shack, Jack, sack, crack, back whack, (attack)	43	44 and 45
The Monkey King	ing, ell	b, k, p, s, t, w, y, z, br, dr, fl, st, sw, th	king, thing, boing, dring, ping, ting, zing, wing, sing, swing, bring, fling, sting, tell, bell, yell	46	47 and 50
Little Red Dragon	est, op, et, og	b, h, l, n, p, r, t, v, w, ch, cr, fr, pl	chest, nest, test, west, rest, vest, crest, pest, best, hop, plop, net, pet, log, frog	48	49 and 50
Monster Café	ay, ake, ine, ice, ush	c, h, m, n, r, w, fl, pl, sl, sn, sp	play, (today) snake, cake, flake, wine, spine, (porcupine), nice, mice, spice, rice, hush, slush, mush	51	52 and 55
The Shark and the Shipwreck	atch, ump, old, ight	c, g, h, j, l, n, p, s, br, fr, sn, th, scr	patch, latch, hatch, catch, scratch, thump, jump, hold, old, gold, sight, fright, night, light, bright	53	54 and 55

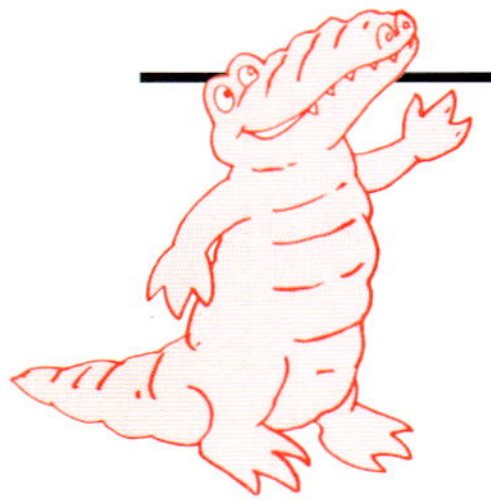

Interactive whole class teaching at Stage 3

Interactive whole class teaching is based on the rhyming stories in the big books. Below is a suggested sequence of activities relating to the story rhyme, *Mr Bell's Top Hat* in Literacy Skills Big Rhyme Book A. This sequence can be followed with any of the story rhymes at Stage 3.

Mr Bell's TOP HAT

Mr Bell has a big top hat
That pops up tall or squashes flat.

Here's a boat for Mr Bell.
Here's a tray for tea as well.

When Miss Mot
got very hot,
it cooled her down
an awful lot.

6

Here's a nest for a hen to sit.
Here's a snug and comfy fit.

A bed for a pet, a fishing net.
Even a place for a jelly to set.

Here's a bucket for a clown.
Here's a bag to take to town.

Fancy that! A fancy hat!
Oh what a hat that does all that!

7

1 You and the children look at the pictures together. Ask the children to say what is happening in each picture and guide them to notice that it is always about a top hat, e.g. "What is happening to the hat now?"

2 Read the whole story to the children, running your finger along the text as you read.

3 Re-read the story up to the rhyming words, asking the children to supply the word, e.g., "When I stop I want you to say the next word." At the end of each line the children then say, "hat", "flat", "Bell", "well", "Mot", "hot", "lot", "sit", "fit", "net", "set", etc.

4 Together with a group of children, read the first two lines of the story. A second group reads the third and fourth lines, a third group the fifth to eighth lines, etc. (Reading in small groups rather than as a whole class gives you a better chance to notice individual participation and progress.)

5 Return to the first two lines of the story. Say, "Listen. Mr Bell has a big top hat, that pops up tall and squashes flat" (emphasising the 'at' part of the word). Then write the letters 'at' on a flipchart or whiteboard saying, "These letters say at". Pointing to the first line of the book say, "Can you find the at words?" The children find 'hat' and 'flat' and you write these words on the chart or board underneath the letters 'at'. Then ask, "Can you tell me any more words which end with at?" Write these down too. Four or five words are quite enough. (This is not too difficult if children have completed successfully Stages 1 and 2 of Rhyme World.)

6 Then go to the third and fourth lines. Repeat the sequence described in point 5, i.e. you read, "Here's a boat for Mr Bell, here's a tray for tea as well" (emphasising 'ell'). You then write the letters 'ell' on a flipchart or whiteboard saying, "These letters say ell" and, pointing to the second page of the book, then ask, "Can you find the ell words?". The children find 'Bell' and 'well' and you write these words on the chart or board underneath the letters 'ell'. Then ask, "Can you tell me any more words which end with ell?" You write these down. Again, four or five words are enough.

7 Repeat this sequence for the other lines of the story, e.g. for 'ot', 'it' and 'own'. The completed flipchart or whiteboard page is illustrated below.

Word building from Literacy Skills Big Rhyme Book A

at	ell	ot	it	own
hat	Bell	hot	sit	town
flat	well	lot	fit	clown
mat	sell	pot	pit	down
pat	tell	cot	hit	brown
cat				

8 Individual children or pairs of children may choose which list to read out to the rest of the class. If they get stuck, read with them or involve the whole class in reading the list together. (This is a useful activity for assessing progress.)

9 Finish the session by asking the whole class to read the story again with you.

10 The whole class session is followed by group work in which the children use the sets of individual books to re-read the story and to stimulate writing that supports and reinforces the reading. (See the Photocopy Masters described in the section on independent activities on page 29.)

Group reading at Stage 3

After the children have participated in a whole class shared reading of a big book, they can then read the sets of small books in groups. For children making good progress this can be done for reinforcement and extra practice. You may find it useful to do a small group teaching session with the children making slower progress using the small books. This can be particularly effective for these children as it prepares them beforehand for participation during whole class sessions. Below is a suggested sequence of activities relating to the story rhyme *Jill and the Beanstalk*. This sequence can be followed with any of the ten Stage 3 small books.

1 Remind the children of the story if it has already been read in the big book as part of a whole class session. If not, look at the cover and title of the book and discuss with the children what the story might be about. Do they know of any other stories about beanstalks (i.e. make the link with *Jack and the Beanstalk* if possible)?

2 Look through the book page by page discussing the events in the story as shown in the illustrations. Encourage the children to make predictions about what may happen next before you turn to the next illustration.

3 Write the word 'beanstalk' on the whiteboard or flipchart and tell the children what the word says.

4 Read through the whole story at a fairly brisk pace so that children are aware of the rhythm and rhyme of the story.

5 Go back to the beginning again and read each page with the children, running your finger along the lines of print. Pause before saying the final rhyming word on each page to give the children the opportunity to say the word before you.

6 Read the whole story again together with the children. Ask the children to point along the line of print while they read.

7 Use the whiteboard or flipchart to list words sharing rimes, e.g. write 'try' on the board and then ask the children to think of another word in the story with the same end sound (e.g. sky). Suggest and write some other words from this family, e.g. cry, fly, my. Repeat for 'op' and 'eep' words. It is not necessary to make long lists of words – 5 or 6 are sufficient.

8 Invite volunteers to identify (point to) the written word as you say the word. This may lead to further activities where a child chooses a word from the list and reads it, and another child identifies (points to) the word that the first child has read.

9 Given time, this can be followed by written activities involving the children in writing the words. If time is limited, the writing can be undertaken in pairs during independent work. (See the Photocopy Masters described in the section on independent activities on page 29.)

Independent activities at Stage 3

In order to enable you to work without interruption with a group, it is important to make the independent individual or group activities as routine and easily understood as possible. Consequently, this Teacher's Guide includes a variety of phonic activities, supported by Photocopy Masters, which are available for each of the ten small books at Stage 3. While the content of the activity varies according to the chosen book, the format and instructions stay the same for each book. These activities reinforce the learning that has taken place during teacher directed whole class and group work.

1 Text level work

Purpose
To reinforce children's understanding and comprehension of a particular rhyming story book.

Materials
There is one Photocopy Master on text level work for each book (see page 25).

The Photocopy Masters comprising pictures to match to captions provide a focus for recalling the story. They may also include some rhyming words which help children to make predictions about the text in the story rhyme. Whilst not essential, it is recommended that children complete the pictures and captions matching activity before moving on to the word level work described below.

2 Word level work

Purpose
To reinforce children's ability to make up and spell words ending with a particular rime.

Materials
There is one Photocopy Master on word level work for each book (see page 25).

Ask the children to "use some of the letters at the top of the sheet to make and write words ending in …". The line illustrations act as visual prompts but the children should be encouraged to focus on the sounds of the words, rather than pictures or meaning, in order to gain maximum benefit from the activity.

There are also five composite pages each containing word level work on two of the Stage 3 rhyming stories (see page 25).

3 Card games

Purpose
To provide further practice in making up, reading and writing words ending with the rimes covered at Stage 3.

Materials
No Photocopy Masters are required for these games, just the following:

- Two packs of blank cards which can be made up from sheets of card; 46 cards will be needed in all for the first game described on the next page.
- A thick felt pen.

Instructions

The following instructions apply to the small books *Hopscotch*; *Mr Bell's Top Hat*; *Molly Best*.

1 Make up one pack of cards with one of the following onsets on each card: b, f, g, h, j, l, m, n, p, r, s, t, v, w, cl, dr, fl, fr, sh, sl, st, th.

2 Make up the other pack of cards with three cards each for the following rimes: op, at, ell, ot, it, own, est, ug.

3 Shuffle each pack of cards and place them face down in front of the children.

4 The children turn over a card from each pack and place them side by side.

5 The children read the 'word' made from combining the onset and rime. If it is a 'real' word, i.e. if it 'makes sense', they write it down on a sheet of paper. Even when the word does not 'make sense', the blending of the onsets and rimes provides valuable practice in the phonological skills involved.

6 When all the cards have been used up in any one pack, the children can shuffle the cards and start the game again.

An easier version

To make the game easier, use only two rimes and the onsets that go with these rimes (see the chart on page 25). You will need two cards for each onset and four cards for each rime to make up sufficiently large packs of cards.

An even easier version

Place one rime card face up on the table. Then put a selection of onset cards face down near it. The children take turns to pick one onset card and place it in front of the rime card; they decide whether the cards make a 'real' word. If they decide yes, they write the word down.

Similar games can be constructed with onsets and rimes taken from the other stories. See the chart on page 25 for the lists of onsets and rimes covered in each book.

4 Track game

The games are best managed when children work co-operatively in pairs and take turns to try to make up a word and write it down on a shared list. However, a competitive element can be added by introducing a simple track game.

To play the track game

You will need:

- the baseboard made up from Photocopy Masters 63 and 64
- a die
- two counters.

Each child takes it in turn to throw the die, moves their counter along the appropriate number of blocks and then turns over the top cards from each pack (see above). If the resultant word 'makes sense', the child gets another turn. In order to make sure that one child does not get too many turns, it is important to include a larger selection of different onsets in the first pack.

The Stage 3 workbook

The Stage 3 workbook provides opportunities for further reinforcement. It is designed for independent work and contains instructions that remain the same across all stories. The workbook consists of three kinds of activity for each of the ten story books. In the first, children match captions and pictures. In the second, children identify words ending with a particular rime and then write down the words ending with that rime. The third activity consists of composite pages containing work on a selection of the story books.

Assessing progress

While many children learn to read and write the onsets and rimes at Stage 3 remarkably easily, others need more practice. It is important, therefore, to notice differential progress in order to plan teaching arrangements accordingly.

The interactive whole class teaching based on the big books and the group reading of the small books provides ideal opportunities for informal assessment of progress. In the course of these activities, you can 'keep an eye on' targeted children and invite them to participate individually whenever possible. If different children or groups of children are targeted over the sessions, you will be able to notice to what extent each child or group has acquired the onset and rime skills covered at Stage 3.

In order to enable you to record these observations as easily as possible at Stage 3, this Teacher's Guide provides a photocopiable class record sheet (Photocopy Master 57), and photocopiable assessment sheets (Photocopy Masters 58–62). If children can read and write a selection of words ending in a particular rime, you may assume that they have learned that rime.

Home-school links

As discussed earlier, parents and carers play a vital role in reinforcing their children's learning at home. In order to provide information about the purposes and teaching methods of Stage 3 in Rhyme World, a photocopiable letter is included in this Teacher's Guide (Photocopy Master 56).

Photocopy Masters

The following Photocopy Masters are designed to support the activities described in this guide. They are cleared for copying by the purchasing school only.

Stage 2

Assessment sheets

Stage 3

Assessment sheets

Name ______________________________

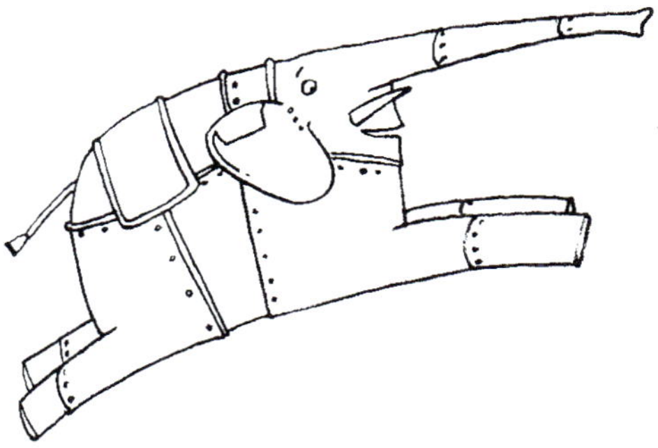

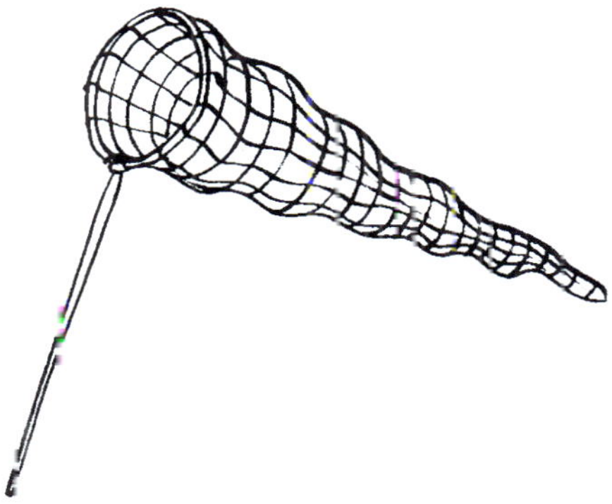

a jumbo jet	Het the vet	a net
Het's pet	a wet pet	

Het the Vet

Skill: Matching captions and pictures

Instructions: Cut out the captions and paste them below the matching picture.

RHYME WORLD

Name ______________________________

Het

et

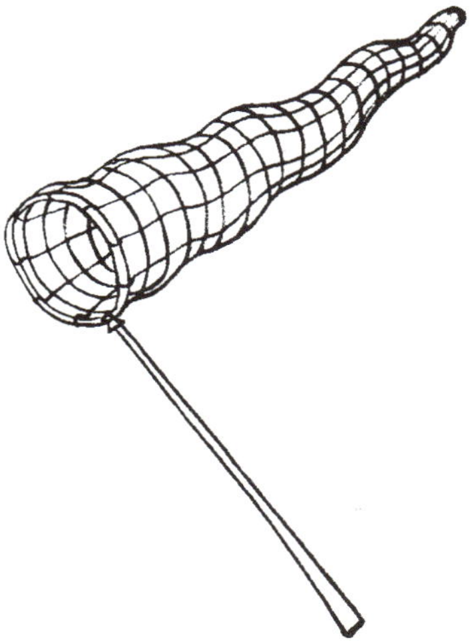

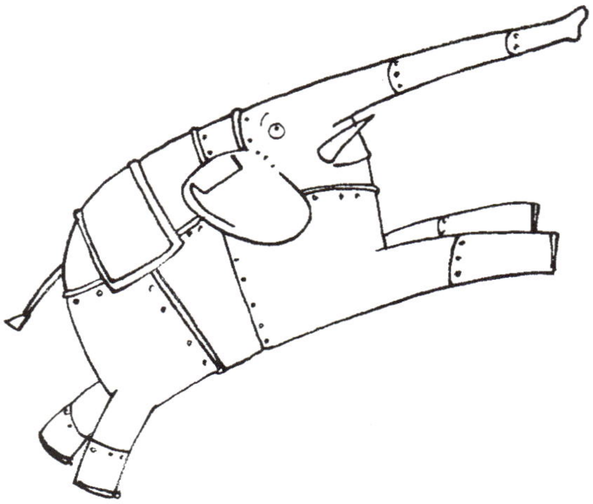

Het the Vet

Skill: Making and writing words ending in -et

Instructions: Use the letters at the top of the sheet to make and write words ending in -et on the lines.

Name ______________________________

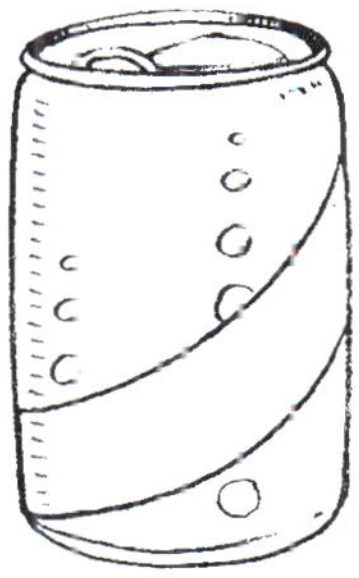

Billy Bop	a can of pop	a magic mop
Billy's shop	a floppy mop	

Billy Bop's Magic Mop

Skill: Matching captions and pictures

Instructions: Cut out the captions and paste them below the matching picture.

RHYME WORLD

Name ______________________________

PCM 4
Stage 2

m p t sh dr fl st

mop

op

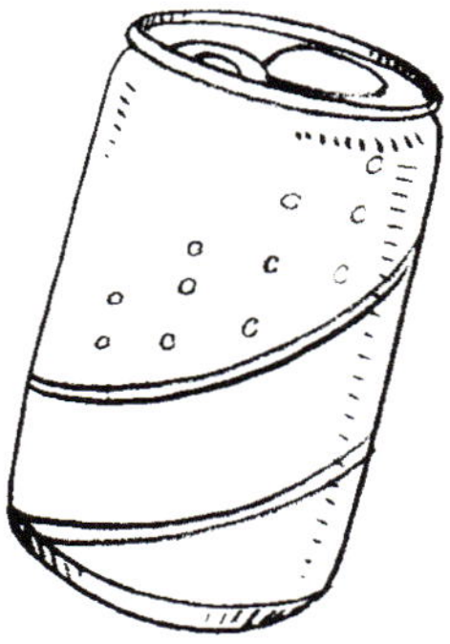

Billy Bop's Magic Mop

Skill: Making and writing words ending in -op

Instructions: Use the letters at the top of the sheet to make and write words ending in -op on the lines.

Name ______________________________

shop wet jet net top
hop drop met stop yet

Composite sheet 1: **Het the Vet / Billy Bop's Magic Mop**

Skill: Recognizing and writing -et and -op words

Instructions: Write the -et words in the jumbo jet. Write the -op words in the shop.

RHYME WORLD

Name ______________________________

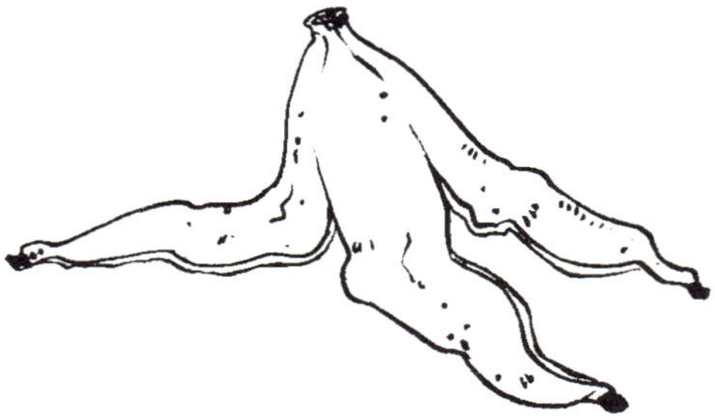

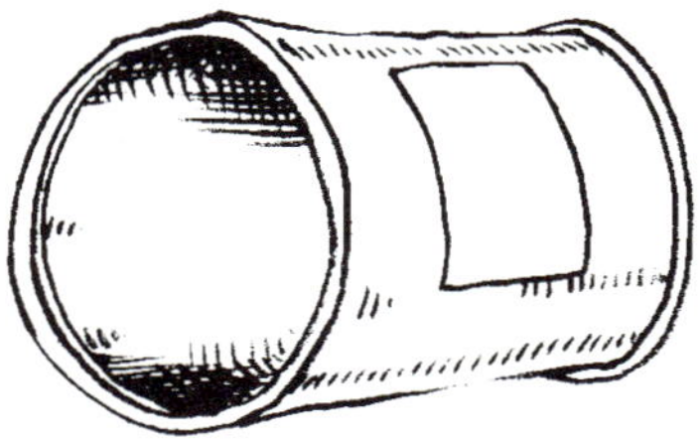

Min and Nin	an empty tin	Min in the bin
Nin on a tin	a banana skin	

The Bin Twins

Skill: Matching captions and pictures

Instructions: Cut out the captions and paste them below the matching picture.

PCM 7
Stage 2

Name ______________________________

M b t d sk th tw

Min

in

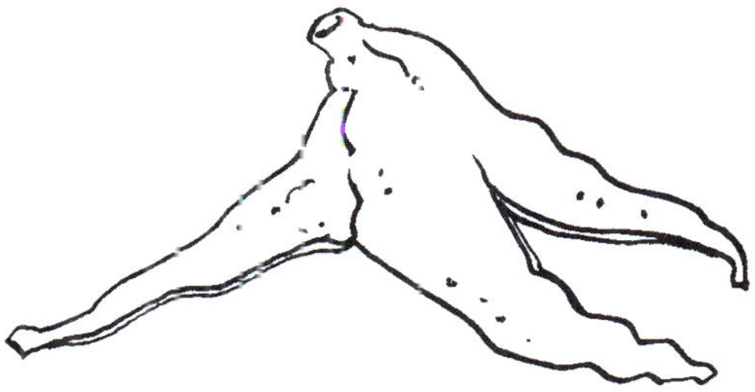

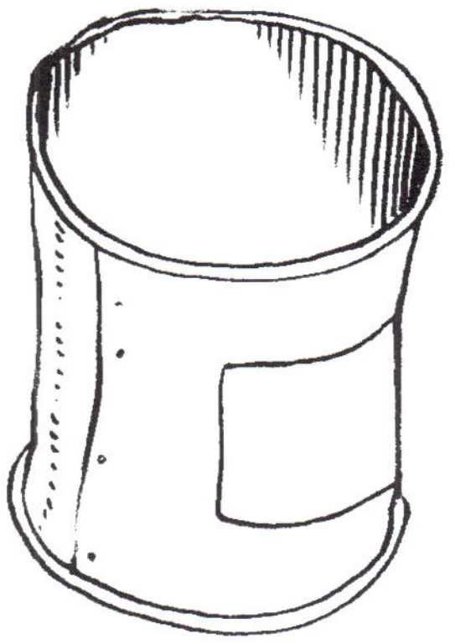

The Bin Twins

Skill: Making and writing words ending in -in

Instructions: Use the letters at the top of the sheet to make and write words ending in -in on the lines.

RHYME WORLD

Name ______________________________

PCM 8
Stage 2

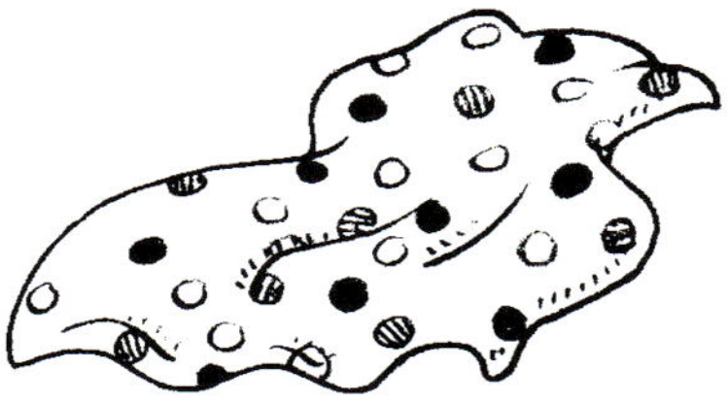

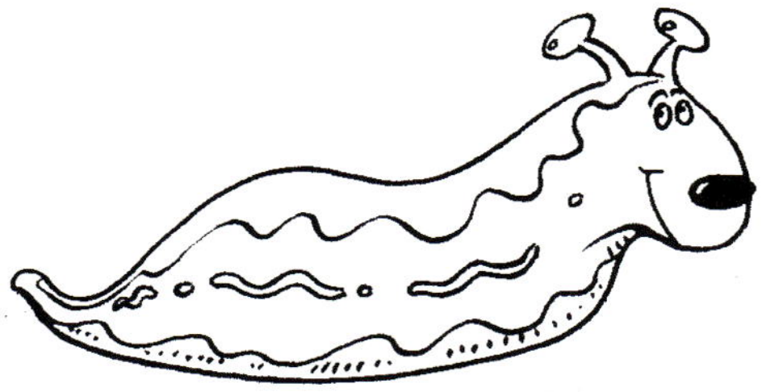

Leggy Lug	Leggy on a coffee mug	a water jug
a slimy slug		Leggy's rug

Leggy Lug

Skill: Matching captions and pictures

Instructions: Cut out the captions and paste them below the matching picture.

PCM 9
Stage 2

RHYME WORLD

Name ______________________________

b m j r sl h sn

bug

ug

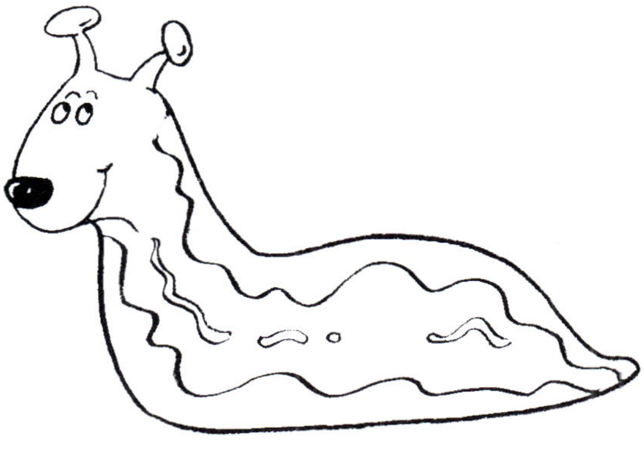

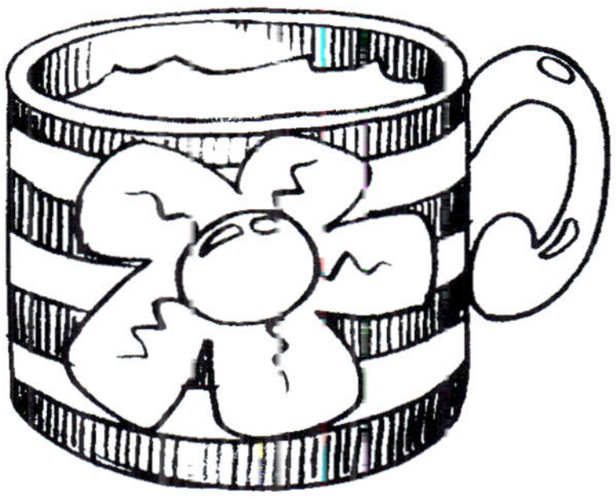

Leggy Lug

Skill: Making and writing words ending in -ug

Instructions: Use the letters at the top of the sheet to make and write words ending in -ug on the lines.

RHYME WORLD

Name ______________________________

bin bug tin hug din tug
twin rug thin slug

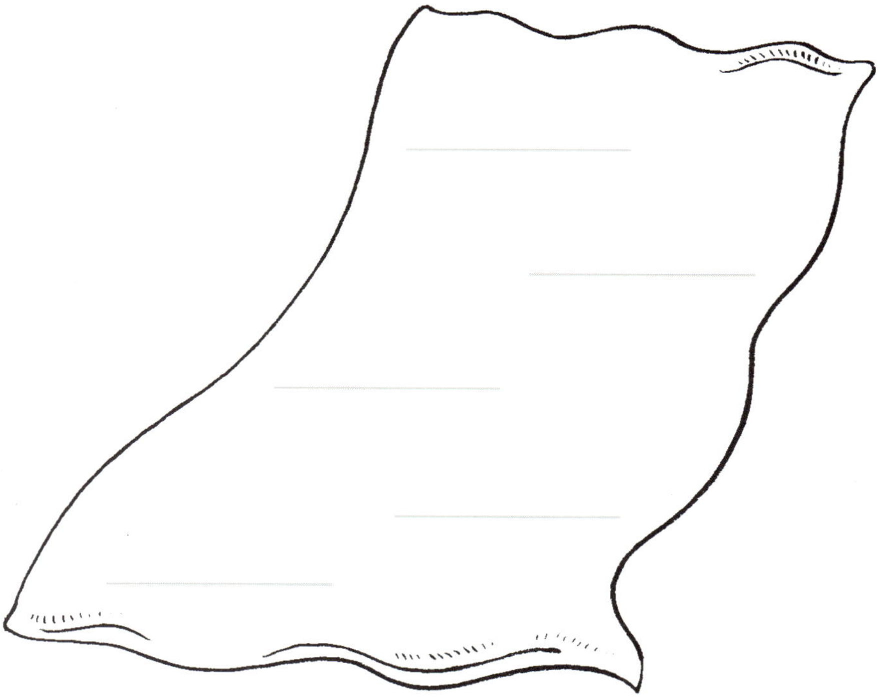

Composite sheet 2: **The Bin Twins / Leggy Lug**

Skill: Recognizing and writing -in and -ug words

Instructions: Write the -in words in the bin. Write the -ug words on the rug.

PCM 11
Stage 2

RHYME WORLD

Name ______________________

Ben	a golden hen	a fox's den
Ben and his hen	a crowd of men	

Ben and the Hen

Skill: Matching captions and pictures
Instructions: Cut out the captions and paste them below the matching picture.

RHYME WORLD

Name ______________________

PCM 12
Stage 2

B h p th m d t

Ben

en

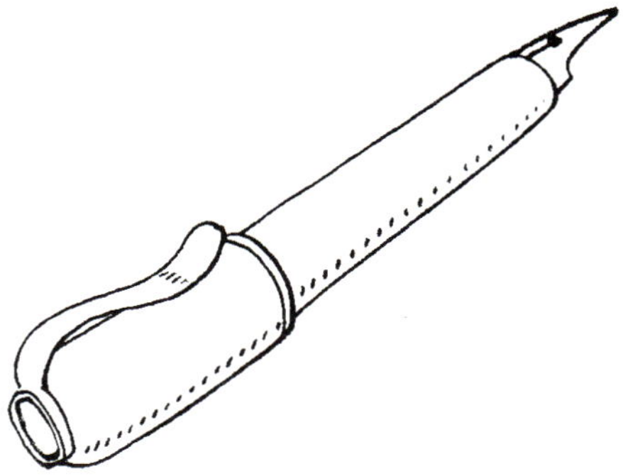

Ben and the Hen

Skill: Making and writing words ending in -en

Instructions: Use the letters at the top of the sheet to make and write words ending in -en on the lines.

PCM 13
Stage 2

Name ______________________________

Mr Clog	a dog in the fog

Mr Clog can jog	a frog on a log	Mr Clog and his dog

Mr Clog and the Log

Skill: Matching captions and pictures

Instructions: Cut out the captions and paste them below the matching picture.

PCM 14
Stage 2

Name ______________________________

Clog

og

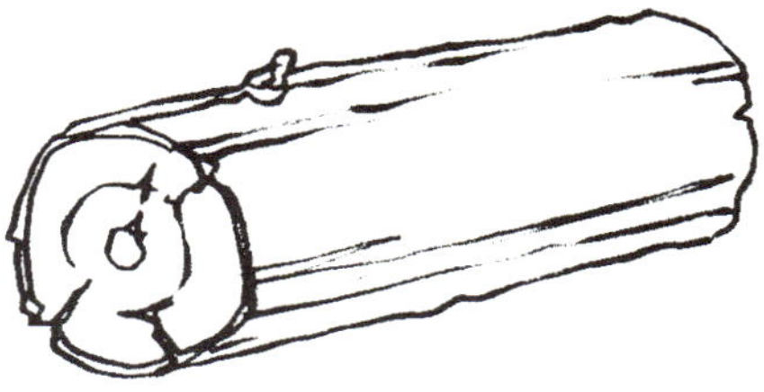

____

____

____

____

____

Mr Clog and the Log

Skill: Making and writing words ending in -og

Instructions: Use the letters at the top of the sheet to make and write words ending in -og on the lines.

Name ______________________________

PCM 15
Stage 2

log Ben pen jog fog men frog ten dog hen

Composite sheet 3: **Ben and the Hen / Mr Clog and the Log**

Skill: Recognizing and writing -en and -og words

Instructions: Write the -en words in the hen. Write the -og words in the dog.

RHYME WORLD

Name ______________________________

✂ -

a man with a cat	a tap	a dog on a lap
a man with a map	a cat in the flap	

Zap!

Skill: Matching captions and pictures

Instructions: Cut out the captions and paste them below the matching picture.

RHYME WORLD

Name ______________________

PCM 17
Stage 2

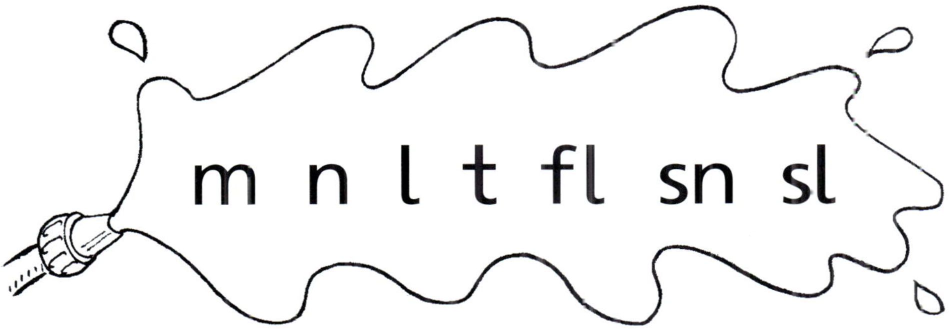

map

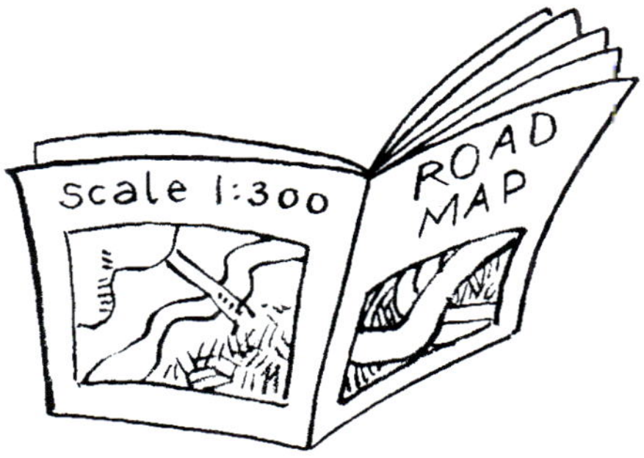

ap

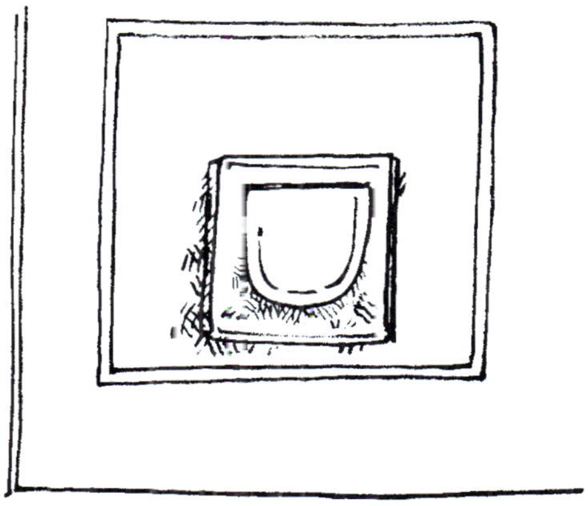

____

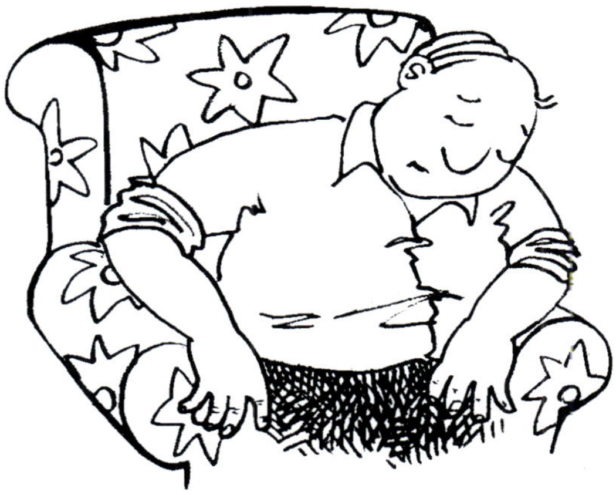

____

____

____

____

Zap!

Skill: Making and writing words ending in -ap
Instructions: Use the letters at the top of the sheet to make and write words ending in -ap on the lines.

Name ______________________

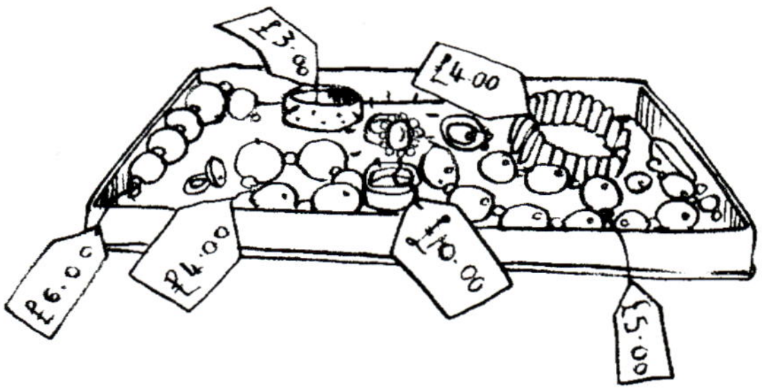

Minnie May	a rainy day	a jay
a jay on a tray		jewels on a tray

Minnie May and the Jay

Skill: Matching captions and pictures

Instructions: Cut out the captions and paste them below the matching picture.

Name ______________________________

M j d p w tr pl

May

ay

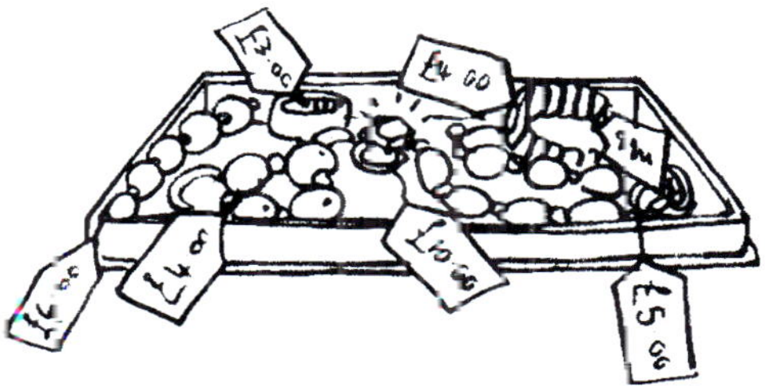

Minne May and the Jay

Skill: Making and writing words ending in -ay

Instructions: Use the letters at the top of the sheet to make and write words ending in -ay on the lines.

RHYME WORLD

Name ______________________________

may map tap play
jay lap day nap say snap

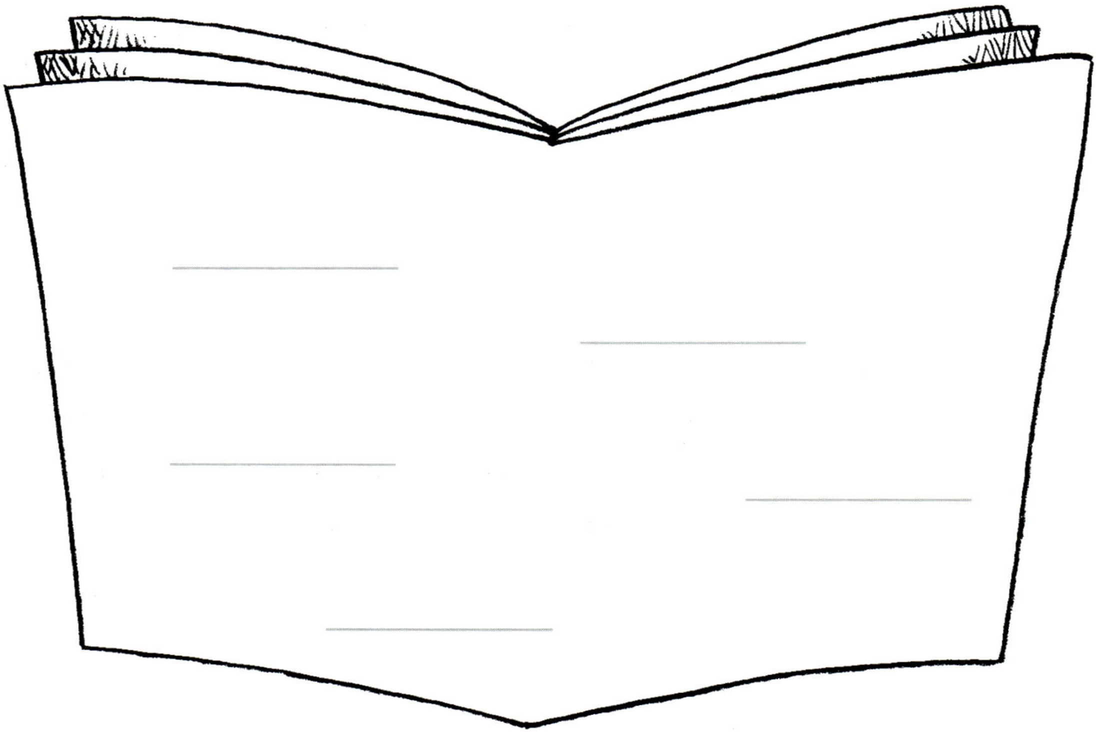

Composite sheet 4: **Zap! / Minnie May and the Jay**

Skill: Recognizing and writing -ap and -ay words

Instructions: Write the -ap words on the map. Write the -ay words in the hay.

RHYME WORLD

Dear Parent/Carer

The books in Stage 2 of Rhyme World help children to learn to read regular words by dividing them into two components: the initial sound of the word and the part that makes it rhyme with others. For example:

d - og

f - og

l - og

fr - og

As you can see from the book that your child has brought home, the rhyming stories are presented in a split-page format. This enables children to combine different initial sounds with a common ending each time they turn a page.

Below is a suggested sequence of activities that you can follow when reading the book with your child.

1 Talk about the illustrations and characters.

2 Read the book to your child. Ask your child to follow the line with a finger.

3 Read the book in chorus together. Your child follows each line with a finger.

4 Now let your child turn the pages in order to read the last rhyming word on each line. We don't expect your child to read the rest of the text independently.

5 You might like to finish by re-reading the story once more together.

RHYME WORLD

PCM 22
Stage 2

Class Record Sheet

To complete the record, see the Stage 2 Assessment Sheets (Photocopy Masters 23–30)

Reading

Spelling

Name	*Het the Vet* (–et)	*Billy Bop's Magic Mop* (–op)	*The Bin Twins* (–in)	*Leggy Lug* (–ug)	*Ben and the Hen* (–en)	*Mr Clog and the Log* (–og)	*Zap!* (–ap)	*Minnie May and the Jay* (–ay)

Assessment Sheet

Het the Vet

READING Ask the child/children to read the words listed below.
SPELLING This can be done on a class, group or individual basis.
Dictate each word listed below to the child/children.

If the child scores 8 or more for reading, spelling, or both, record this on the Class Record Sheet (Photocopy Master 22) by colouring in the appropriate box

Het vet

met

jet pet

wet

net get

yet

set let

RHYME WORLD

Assessment Sheet

Billy Bop's Magic Mop

READING Ask the child/children to read the words listed below.
SPELLING This can be done on a class, group or individual basis.
Dictate each word listed below to the child/children.

If the child scores 8 or more for reading, spelling, or both, record this on the Class Record Sheet (Photocopy Master 22) by colouring in the appropriate box.

Bop

mop shop

pop

drop slop

flop

stop top

hop

Assessment Sheet

The Bin Twins

READING Ask the child/children to read the words listed below.
SPELLING This can be done on a class, group or individual basis.
Dictate each word listed below to the child/children.

If the child scores 8 or more for reading, spelling, or both, record this on the Class Record Sheet (Photocopy Master 22) by colouring in the appropriate box

bin twin

thin

tin din

in

skin Min

Nin

pin win

Assessment Sheet

Leggy Lug

READING Ask the child/children to read the words listed below.
SPELLING This can be done on a class, group or individual basis.
Dictate each word listed below to the child/children.

If the child scores 8 or more for reading, spelling, or both, record this on the Class Record Sheet (Photocopy Master 22) by colouring in the appropriate box.

Lug

bug jug

slug

mug rug

hug

snug tug

plug

RHYME WORLD

Assessment Sheet

Ben and the Hen

READING Ask the child/children to read the words listed below.
SPELLING This can be done on a class, group or individual basis.
Dictate each word listed below to the child/children.

If the child scores 6 or more for reading, spelling, or both, record this on the Class Record Sheet (Photocopy Master 22) by colouring in the appropriate box.

Ben

hen

pen

then

men

den

ten

Assessment Sheet

Mr Clog and the Log

READING Ask the child/children to read the words listed below.
SPELLING This can be done on a class, group or individual basis.
Dictate each word listed below to the child/children.

If the child scores 6 or more for reading, spelling, or both, record this on the Class Record Sheet (Photocopy Master 22) by colouring in the appropriate box.

Clog

log dog

cog

jog fog

frog

Assessment Sheet

Zap!

READING Ask the child/children to read the words listed below.
SPELLING This can be done on a class, group or individual basis.
Dictate each word listed below to the child/children.

If the child scores 8 or more for reading, spelling, or both, record this on the Class Record Sheet (Photocopy Master 22) by colouring in the appropriate box.

zap map

nap

lap flap

yap

snap tap

slap

trap cap

RHYME WORLD

Assessment Sheet

Minnie May and the Jay

READING Ask the child/children to read the words listed below.
SPELLING This can be done on a class, group or individual basis. Dictate each word listed below to the child/children.

If the child scores 7 or more for reading, spelling, or both, record this on the Class Record Sheet (Photocopy Master 22) by colouring in the appropriate box.

May jay

tray

day play

away

pay say

Name ______________________________

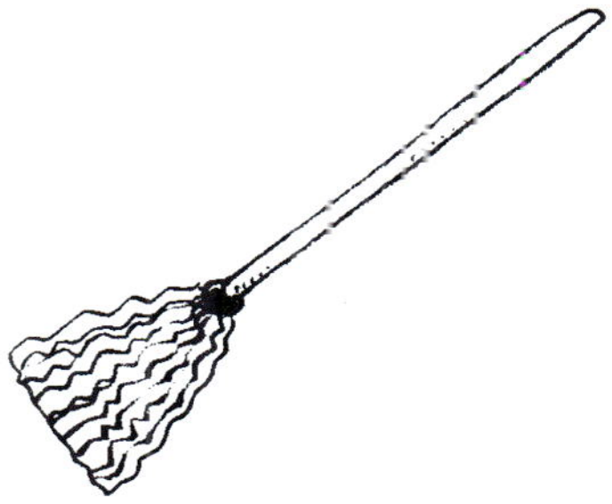

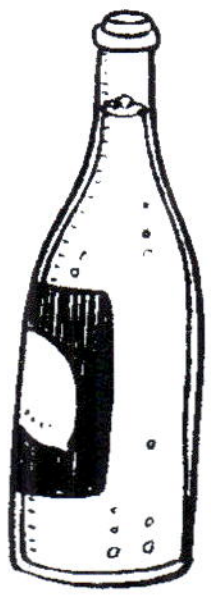

a bottle of pop | hopscotch | a mop

hop to the shop | hop to the top

Hopscotch

Skill: Matching captions and pictures

Instructions: Cut out the captions and paste them below the matching picture.

RHYME WORLD

Name ____________________

PCM 32
Stage 3

h m p r t dr sh st f

hop

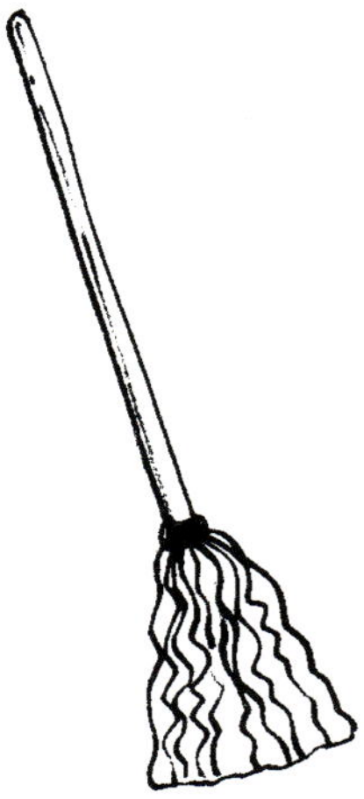

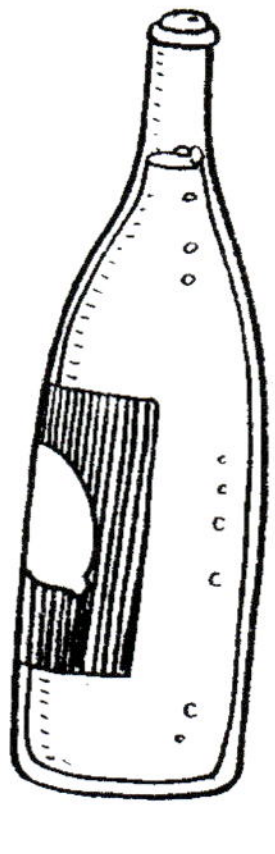

Hopscotch

Skill: Making and writing words ending in -op

Instructions: Use some of the letters at the top of the sheet to make and write words ending in -op on the lines.

Name ______________________________

a clump of reeds	Duck has a rest

Duck on the pond	Duck eating bread	Duck's head under her wing

On the Pond

Skill: Matching captions and pictures

Instructions: Cut out the captions and paste them below the matching picture.

PCM 34
Stage 3

RHYME WORLD

Name ______________________________

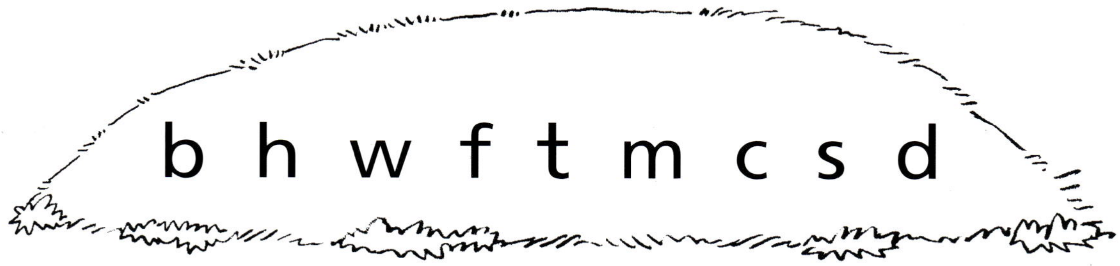

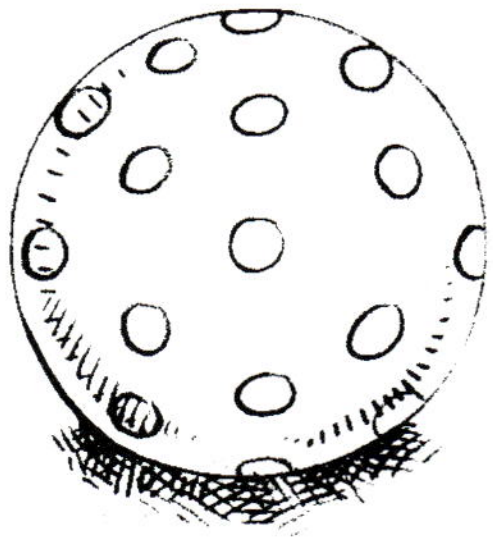

fall ______ hill ______

______ ______

______ ______

______ ______

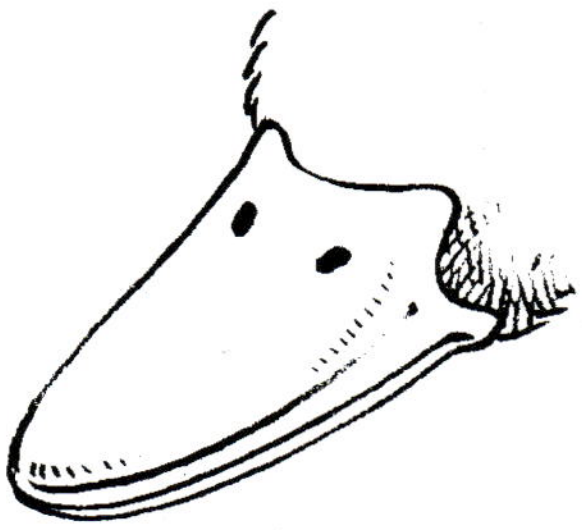

______ ______

______ ______

On the Pond

Skill: Making and writing words ending in -all and -ill
Instructions: Use some of the letters at the top of the sheet to make and write words ending in -all and -ill on the lines.

RHYME WORLD

PCM 35
Stage 3

Name ______________________________

b f h m n p t dr sh st

Composite sheet 1: **Hopscotch / On the Pond**

Skill: Word building

Instructions: Choose some of the letters at the top of the sheet and write rhyming words in each duck. Read your words to your partner.

RHYME WORLD

PCM 36
Stage 3

Name ______________________________

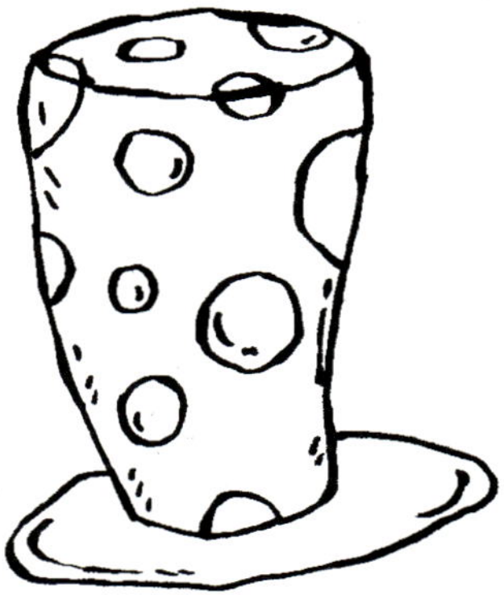

a top hat	a flat hat	a nest for a hen
a fishing net	a bed for a pet	

Mr Bell's Top Hat

Skill: Matching captions and pictures

Instructions: Cut out the captions and paste them below the matching picture.

PCM 37
Stage 3

RHYME WORLD

Name ________________________________

s f b w fl c p t sp

bat ____________ well ____________

____________ ____________

____________ ____________

____________ ____________

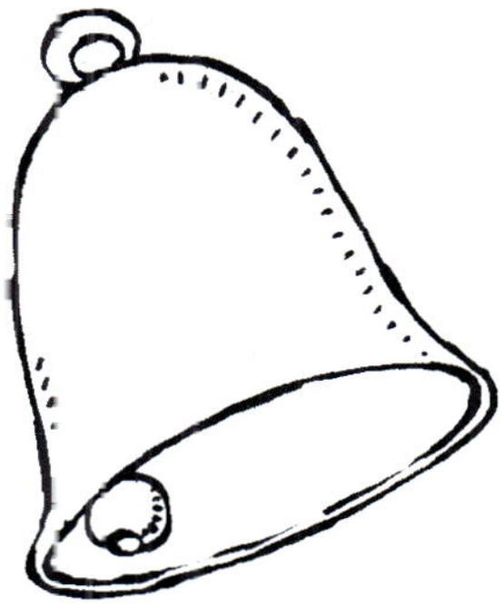

____________ ____________

____________ ____________

Mr Bell's Top Hat

Skill: Making and writing words ending in -at and -ell

Instructions: Use some of the letters at the top of the sheet to make and write words ending in -at and -ell on the lines.

PCM 38
Stage 3

RHYME WORLD

Name ______________________________

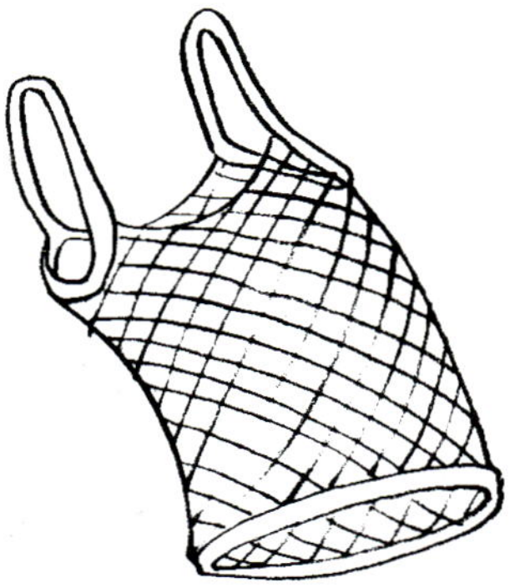

✂ -

| a slug in a mug | a frog | Grandpa's vest |
| Molly Best | a hamster's nest | |

Molly Best

Skill: Matching pictures and captions

Instructions: Cut out the captions and paste them below the matching picture.

RHYME WORLD

Name ____________________

d t p r cr b n cl v f w br

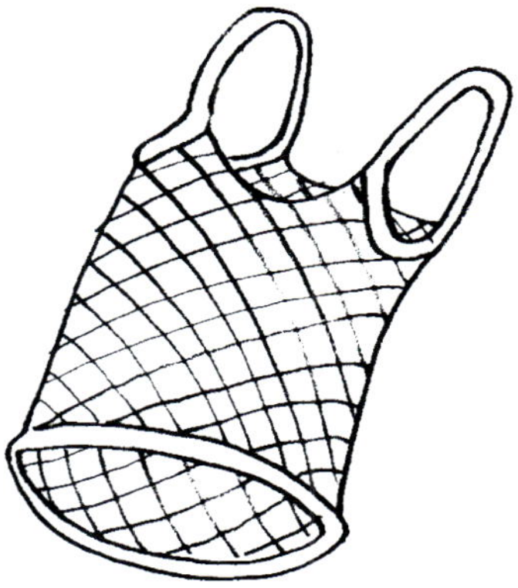

west ______ town ______

______ ______

______ ______

______ ______

______ ______

Molly Best

Skill: Making and writing words ending in -est and -own

Instructions: Use some of the letters at the top of the sheet to make and write words ending in -est and -own on the lines.

RHYME WORLD

Name ______________________

PCM 40
Stage 3

b g n j l m p r s v w
cl fl fr sl th

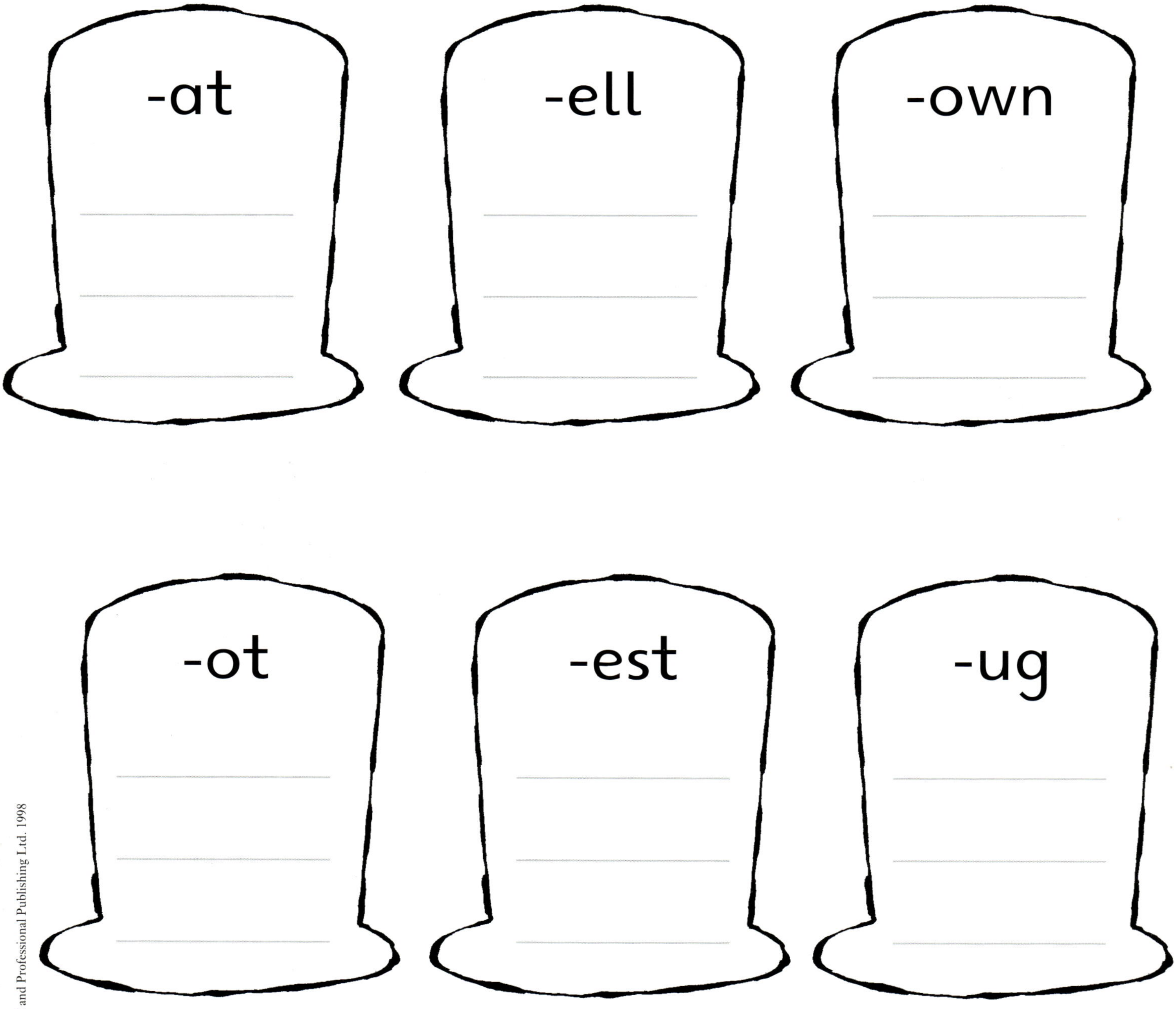

Composite sheet 2: **Mr Bell's Top Hat / Molly Best**

Skill: Word building

Instructions: Choose some of the letters at the top of the sheet and write rhyming words in each top hat. Read your words to your partner.

RHYME WORLD

Name ______________________________

Jill	a beanstalk

Giant	a harp	a hen

Jill and the Beanstalk

Skill: Matching captions and pictures

Instructions: Cut out the captions and paste them below the matching picture.

Name ______________________________

k tr sk sl sh cr fl m d st

sky creep

Jill and the Beanstalk

Skill: Making and writing words ending in -y and -eep

Instructions: Use some of the letters at the top of the sheet to make and write words ending in -y and -eep on the lines.

Name ______________________________

Jack with a sack	a tumbledown shack	a great big sack
Fat-Cat Charlie	Mean-Eyed Jack	

Jack's Sack

Skill: Matching captions and pictures

Instructions: Cut out the captions and paste them below the matching picture.

Name ______________________

PCM 44
Stage 3

b s bl cr sh wh d J

Jack

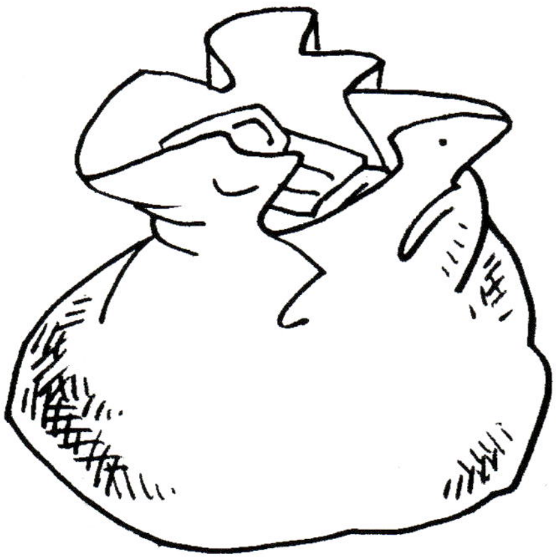

____

____

____

____

____

Jack's Sack

Skill: Making and writing words ending in -ack
Instructions: Use some of the letters at the top of the sheet to make and write words ending in -ack on the lines.

RHYME WORLD

Name ______________________________

b j s t bl ch cr sh sk sl st tr wh

Composite sheet 3: **Jill and the Beanstalk / Jack's Sack**

Skill: Word building

Instructions: Choose some of the letters at the top of the sheet and write rhyming words in each sack. Read your words to your partner.

Name ______________________________

a bell	fruit to fling

the monkey king	a monkey can swing	the monkey with a bell

The Monkey King

Skill: Matching captions and pictures

Instructions: Cut out the captions and paste them below the matching picture.

Name ______________________

b t k s th r w fl sw f sp

sing

bell

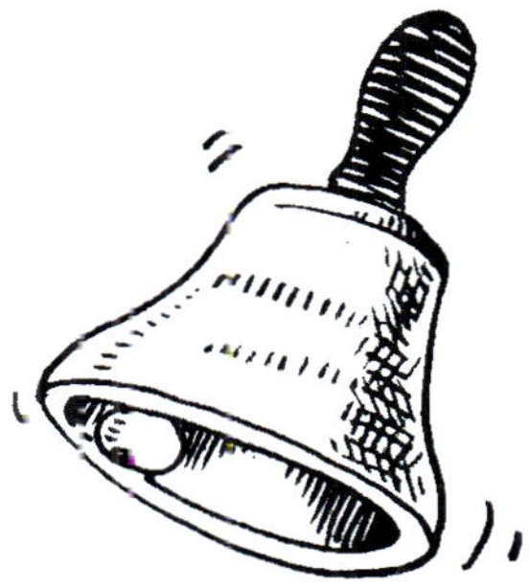

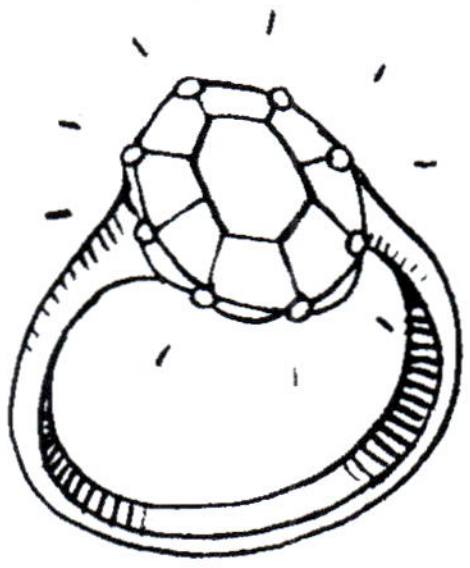

The Monkey King

Skill: Making and writing words ending in -ing and -ell

Instructions: Use some of the letters at the top of the sheet to make and write words ending in -ing and -ell on the lines.

RHYME WORLD

PCM 48
Stage 3

Name ______________________________

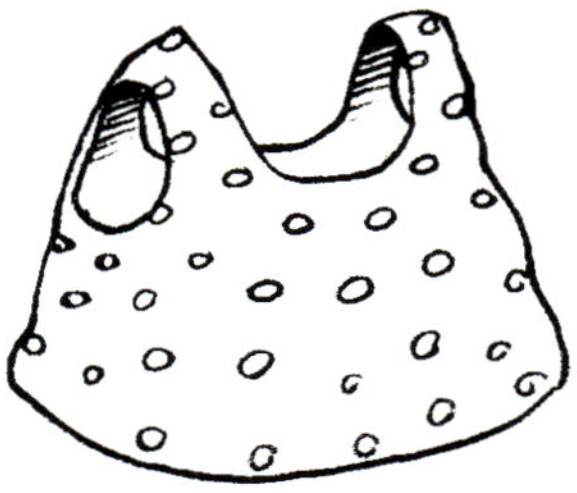

a dragon	a man with a net	a frog on a log
a dragon's nest		a dragon's vest

Little Red Dragon

Skill: Matching captions and pictures

Instructions: Cut out the captions and paste them below the matching picture.

PCM 49
Stage 3

RHYME WORLD

Name ______________________

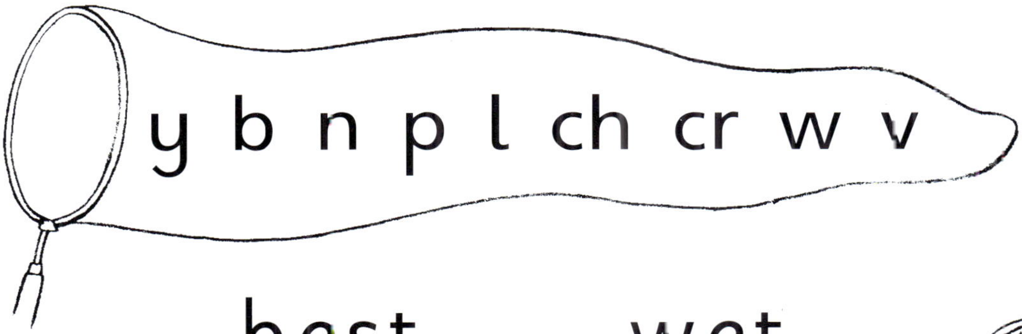

best

wet

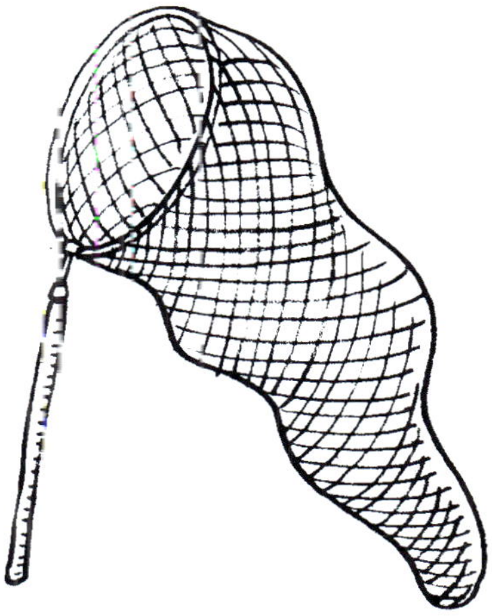

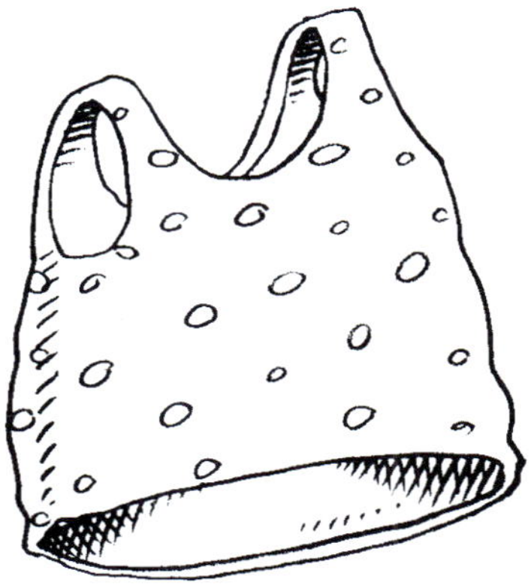

Little Red Dragon

Skill: Making and writing words ending in -est and -et

Instructions: Use some of the letters at the top of the sheet to make and write words ending in -est and -et on the lines.

RHYME WORLD

Name ______________________________

PCM 50
Stage 3

b d k l n p r s t v
ch fl fr pl st sw

Composite sheet 4: **The Monkey King / Little Red Dragon**

Skill: Word building

Instructions: Choose some of the letters at the top of the sheet and write rhyming words in each bell. Read your words to your partner.

Name ____________________

mice in rice

see the band play

slimy slugs

beetles and bugs

snake in a cake

Monster Café

Skill: Matching captions and pictures

Instructions: Cut out the captions and paste them below the matching picture.

RHYME WORLD

Name ______________________________

b c d m r t sn sp fl tw

rice | bake

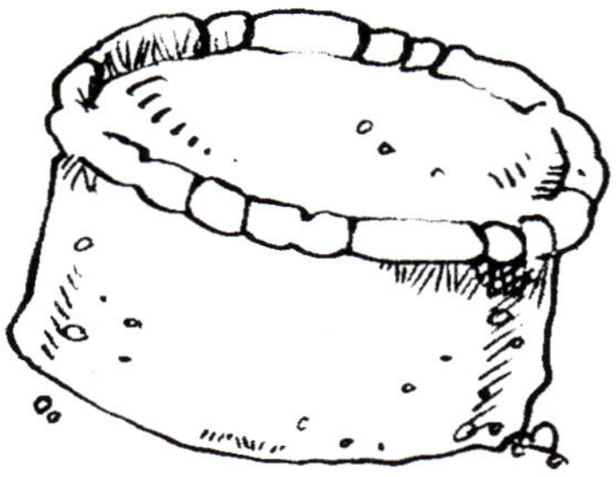

Monster Café

Skill: Making and writing words ending in -ice and -ake
Instructions: Use some of the letters at the top of the sheet to make and write words ending in -ice and -ake on the lines.

Name ______________________________

Skid and Skip	a treasure ship	a hungry shark
the skeletons find treasure	the shark looks ill	

The Shark and the Shipwreck

Skill: Matching captions and pictures

Instructions: Cut out the captions and paste them below the matching picture.

PCM 54
Stage 3

Name ______________________

latch cold

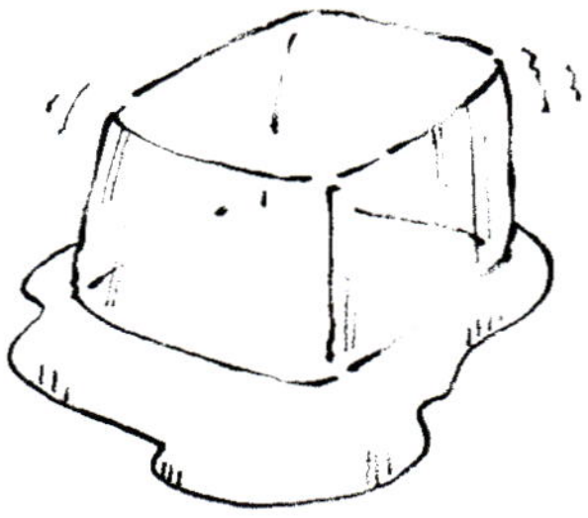

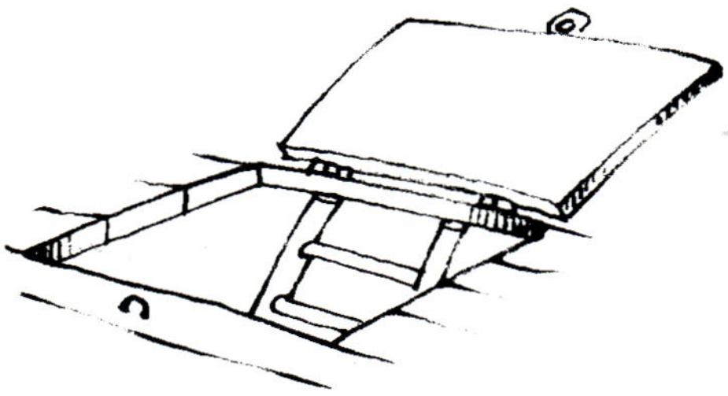

The Shark and the Shipwreck

Skill: Making and writing words ending in -atch and -old
Instructions: Use some of the letters at the top of the sheet to make and write words ending in -atch and -old on the lines.

RHYME WORLD

Name ________________________________

c g h j l m n p r fr sl sn sp

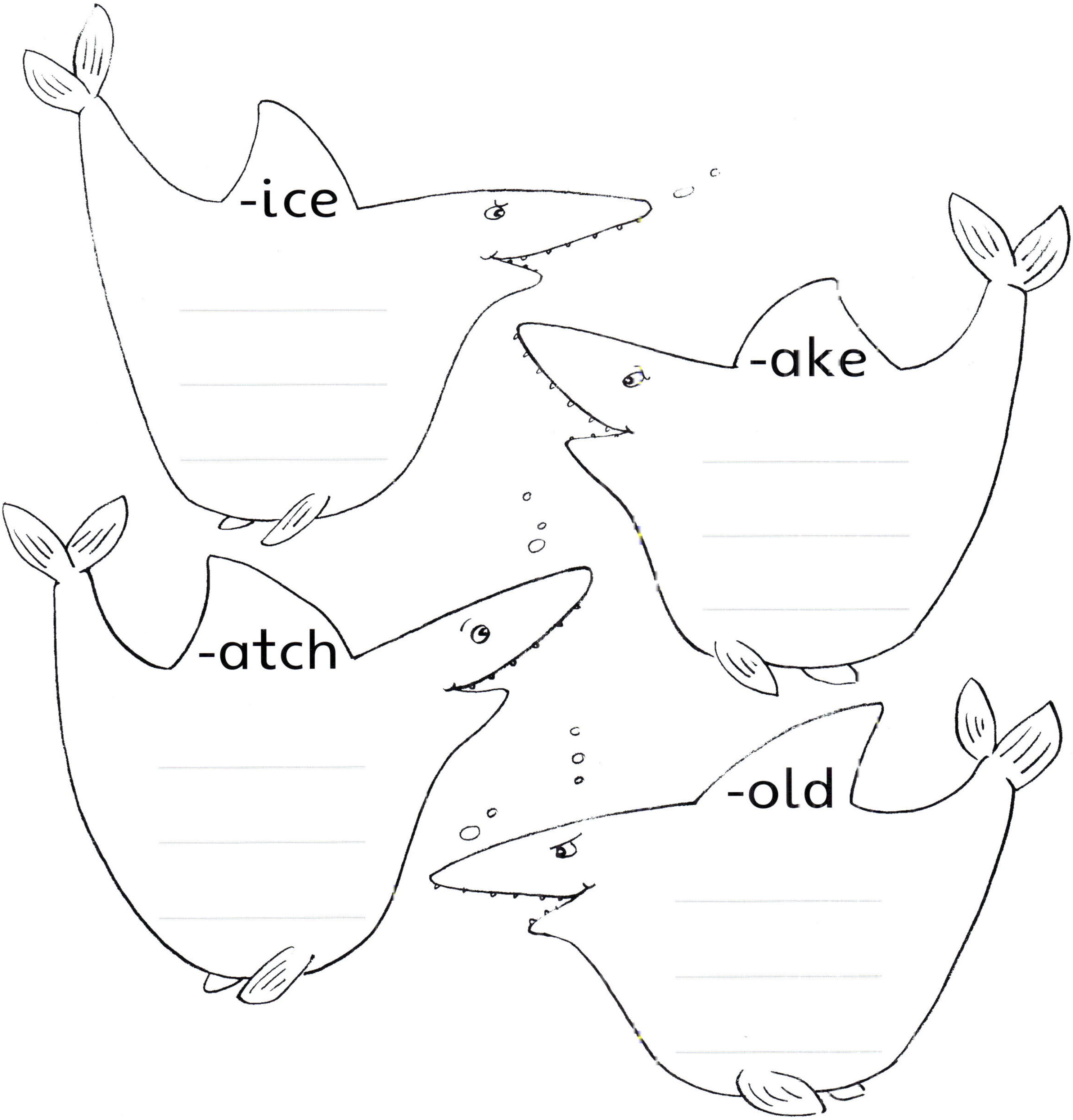

Composite sheet 5: **Monster Café / The Shark and the Shipwreck**

Skill: Word building

Instructions: Choose some of the letters at the top of the sheet and write rhyming words in each shark. Read your words to your partner.

Dear Parent/Carer

The books in Stage 3 of Rhyme World are written so that children can see rhyming words underneath one another and so notice the similarity between sound and spelling patterns.

Below is a suggested sequence of activities that you can follow when reading the book with your child.

1 Look through the book page by page and discuss the events in the story as shown in the illustrations.

2 Read the whole book to your child. Read at a fairly brisk pace so that your child can notice the rhythm and rhyme of the story.

3 Start from the beginning again and read each page more slowly, running your finger along the lines of print. Pause before saying the final rhyming word to give your child a chance to say it first.

4 Read the whole story once more, this time in chorus with your child. Ask your child to point along the line of print as you read together. Your child should be able to read the rhyming words. At this stage we don't expect your child to read the rest of the text independently.

Class Record Sheet

To complete the record, see the Stage 3 Assessment Sheets (Photocopy Masters 58–62).

Reading

Spelling

Name	Hopscotch	On the Pond	Mr Bell's Top Hat	Molly Best	Jill and the Beanstalk	Jack's Sack	The Monkey King	Little Red Dragon	Monster Café	The Shark and the Shipwreck

Assessment Sheet

Hopscotch

On the Pond

READING For each word list, ask the child/children to read the words listed below.
SPELLING This can be done on a class, group or individual basis. For each word list, dictate each word listed below to the child/children.

If the child scores 8 or more for reading, spelling, or both for a word list, record this on the Class Record Sheet (Photocopy Master 57) by colouring in the appropriate box.

Hopscotch

hop pop shop

drop flop stop

mop top slop

bop

On the Pond

bill need fall

best will hill

reed nest seed

all

RHYME WORLD

Assessment Sheet

Mr Bell's Top Hat

Molly Best

READING For each word list, ask the child/children to read the words listed below.
SPELLING This can be done on a class, group or individual basis. For each word list, dictate each word listed below to the child/children.

If the child scores 8 or more for reading, spelling, or both for a word list, record this on the Class Record Sheet (Photocopy Master 57) by colouring in the appropriate box.

Mr Bell's Top Hat

hat	fit	town
well	bell	sit
lot	flat	hot
clown		

Molly Best

mug	vest	frown
pest	gown	west
town	nest	slug
rug		

Assessment Sheet

Jill and the Beanstalk

Jack's Sack

READING For each word list, ask the child/children to read the words listed below.
SPELLING This can be done on a class, group or individual basis. For each word list, dictate each word listed below to the child/children.

If the child scores 8 or more for reading, spelling, or both for a word list, record this on the Class Record Sheet (Photocopy Master 57) by colouring in the appropriate box.

Jill and the Beanstalk

peep top cry

try sky asleep

shop creep stop

fly

Jack's Sack

back black shack

whack pack sack

Jack crack stack

attack

Assessment Sheet

The Monkey King
Little Red Dragon

READING For each word list, ask the child/children to read the words listed below.
SPELLING This can be done on a class, group or individual basis. For each word list, dictate each word listed below to the child/children.

If the child scores 8 or more for reading, spelling, or both for a word list, record this on the Class Record Sheet (Photocopy Master 57) by colouring in the appropriate box.

The Monkey King

yell	swing	well
king	bell	sing
sell	thing	tell
sting		

Little Red Dragon

frog	crest	plop
chest	hop	net
pet	test	log
stop		

Assessment Sheet

Monster Café

The Shark and the Shipwreck

READING For each word list, ask the child/children to read the words listed below.
SPELLING This can be done on a class, group or individual basis. For each word list, dictate each word listed below to the child/children.

If the child scores 8 or more for reading, spelling, or both for a word list, record this on the Class Record Sheet (Photocopy Master 57) by colouring in the appropriate box.

Monster Café

day hush cake

nice spine wine

snake mice play

mush

The Shark and the Shipwreck

catch jump scratch

hold patch thump

fright gold night

snatch

See page 20 (Stage 2) and page 30 (Stage 3) for instructions on how to play this track game.

RHYME WORLD

See page 20 (Stage 2) and page 30 (Stage 3) for instructions on how to play this track game.